THE SEARCH FOR A
WOMAN-CENTERED SPIRITUALITY

Editorial Board

The Cutting Edge:
Lesbian Life and Literature
Series Editor: Karla Jay

Ladies Almanack
BY DJUNA BARNES
WITH AN INTRODUCTION BY SUSAN SNIADER LANSER

Adventures of the Mind:
The Memoirs of Natalie Clifford Barney
TRANSLATED BY JOHN SPALDING GATTON
WITH AN INTRODUCTION BY KARLA JAY

Paint It Today
BY H.D. (HILDA DOOLITTLE)
EDITED AND WITH AN INTRODUCTION BY
CASSANDRA LAITY

I Know My Own Heart: The Diaries of Anne Lister, 1791–1840
EDITED BY HELENA WHITBREAD

(Sem)*Erotics : Theorizing Lesbian Writing*
BY ELIZABETH MEESE

The Search for a Woman-Centered Spirituality
BY ANNETTE J. VAN DYKE

the search for a woman-centered

SPIRITUALITY

ANNETTE VAN DYKE

NEW YORK UNIVERSITY PRESS
New York and London

NEW YORK UNIVERSITY PRESS
New York and London

Library of Congress Cataloging-in-Publication Data
Van Dyke, Annette J.
The search for a woman-centered spirituality / Annette J. Van Dyke.
p. cm.—(The cutting edge : lesbian life and literature)
Includes bibliographical references and index.
ISBN 0-8147-8769-X (alk. paper)—ISBN 0-8147-8770-3
(pbk. : alk. paper)
1. Literature—Women authors—History and criticism. 2. Feminism and literature. 3. Women and literature. 4. Lesbian writings—History and criticism. 5. Lesbianism in literature. 6. Femininity (Psychology) in literature. I. Title II. Series: Cutting edge (New York, N.Y.)
PN3437.V36 1992
809'.89287—dc20 92-70515
CIP

New York University Press books are printed on acid-free paper, and their binding materials are chosen for strength and durability.

Manufactured in the United States of America

p 10 9 8 7 6 5 4 3 2

Contents

Foreword

DESPITE the efforts of lesbian and feminist publishing houses and a few university presses, the bulk of the most important lesbian works has traditionally been available only from rare-book dealers, in a few university libraries, or in gay and lesbian archives. This series intends, in the first place, to make representative examples of this neglected and insufficiently known literature available to a broader audience by reissuing selected classics and by putting into print for the first time lesbian novels, diaries, letters, and memoirs that are of special interest and significance, but which have mouldered in libraries and private collections for decades or even for centuries, known only to the few scholars who had the courage and financial wherewithal to track them down.

Their names have been known for a long time—Sappho, the Amazons of North Africa, the Beguines, Aphra Behn, Queen Christina, Emily Dickinson, the Ladies of Llangollen, Radclyffe Hall, Natalie Clifford Barney, H.D., and so many others from every nation, race, and era. But government and religious officials burned their writings, historians and literary scholars denied they were lesbians, powerful men kept their books out of print, and influential archivists locked up their ideas far from sympathetic eyes. Yet some dedicated scholars and readers still knew who they were, made pilgrimages to the cities and villages where they had lived and to the graveyards where they rested. They passed around tattered volumes of letters, diaries, and biographies, in which they had underlined what seemed to be telltale hints of a secret or different kind of life. Where no hard facts existed, legends were invented. The few precious and often available pre-Stonewall lesbian classics, such as *The Well of Loneliness* by Radclyffe Hall, *The Price of Salt* by Claire Morgan [Patricia Highsmith], and *Desert of the Heart* by Jane Rule, were cherished. Lesbian pulp was devoured. One of the primary goals of this series is to give the more neglected works, which constitute the vast majority of lesbian writing, the attention they deserve.

A second but no less important aim of this series is to present the "cutting edge" of contemporary lesbian scholarship and theory across a wide range of disciplines. Practitioners of lesbian studies have not adopted a uniform approach to literary theory, history, sociology, or any other discipline, nor should they. This series intends to present an array of voices that truly reflect the diversity of the lesbian community. To help me in this task, I am lucky enough to be assisted by a distinguished editorial board that reflects various professional, class, racial, ethnic, and religious backgrounds as well as a spectrum of interests and sexual preferences.

At present the field of lesbian studies occupies a small, precarious, and somewhat contested pied-à-terre between gay studies and women's studies. The former is still in its infancy, especially if one compares it to other disciplines that have been part of the core curriculum of every child and adolescent for several decades or even centuries. However, although it is one of the newest disciplines, gay studies may also be the fastest-growing one—at least in North America. Lesbian, gay, and bisexual studies conferences are doubling or tripling their attendance. Although only a handful of degree-granting programs currently exist, that number is also apt to multiply quickly during the next decade.

In comparison, women's studies is a well-established and burgeoning discipline with hundreds of minors, majors, and graduate programs throughout the United States. Lesbian studies occupies a peripheral place in the discourse in such programs, characteristically restricted to one lesbian-centered course, usually literary or historical in nature. In the many women's studies series that are now offered by university presses, generally only one or two books on a lesbian subject or issue are included, and lesbian voices are restricted to writing on those topics considered of special interest to gay people. We are not called upon to offer opinions on motherhood, war, education, or on the lives of women not publicly identified as lesbians. As a result, lesbian experience is too often marginalized and restricted.

In contrast, this series will prioritize, centralize, and celebrate lesbian visions of literature, art, philosophy, love, religion, ethics, history, and a myriad of other topics. In "The Cutting Edge," readers can find authoritative versions of important lesbian texts that have been carefully prepared and introduced by scholars. Readers can also find the work of academics and independent scholars who write about other aspects of life from a distinctly lesbian viewpoint. These visions are not only various but intentionally contradictory, for lesbians speak from differing class, racial, ethnic, and religious perspectives. Each author also speaks from and about a certain moment of time, and few would argue that being a lesbian today is the same as it was for Sappho or Anne Lister. Thus no attempt has been made to homogenize that diversity, and no agenda exists to attempt to carve out a "politically correct" lesbian studies perspective at this juncture in history or to pinpoint the "real" lesbians in history. It seems more important for all the voices to be heard before those with the blessings of aftersight lay the mantle of authenticity on any one vision of the world, or on any particular set of women.

What each work in this series does share, however, is a common realization that gay women are the "Other" and that one's perception of culture and literature is filtered by sexual behaviors and preferences. Those perceptions are not the same as those of gay men or of nongay women, whether the writers speak of gay or feminist issues or whether the writers choose to look at nongay figures from a lesbian perspective. The role of this series is to create space and give a voice to those interested in lesbian studies. This series speaks to any person who is interested in gender studies, literary criticism, biography, or important literary works, whether she or he is a student, professor, or serious reader, for the series is neither for lesbians only nor even by lesbians only. Instead, "The Cutting Edge" attempts to share some of the best of lesbian literature and lesbian studies with anyone willing to look at the world through lesbians' eyes. The series is proactive in that it will help to formulate and foreground the very discipline on which it focuses. Finally, this series has answered the call to make lesbian theory, lesbian experience, lesbian lives, lesbian literature, and lesbian visions the heart and nucleus, the weighty planet around which for once other viewpoints will swirl as moons to our earth. We invite readers of all persuasions to join us by venturing into this and other books in the series.

The Search for a Woman-Centered Spirituality by Annette Van Dyke focuses on one of the salient developments of contemporary feminism. Instead of abandoning religious practice altogether as relics of a patriarchal past, large numbers of women have sought to incorporate healing and positive aspects of their spiritual heritage into their lives. Women have also resurrected non-Western traditions and have created alternative rituals, beliefs, and stories to enhance and enlighten our day-to-day existence. This work is a tribute to that creative energy and to the way in which it has enriched feminism for many.

Pace University KARLA JAY

Acknowledgments

MY tireless partner, Cheryl Howard, deserves the highest praise for seeing me through this process from beginning to end. Well remembered are the quarrels over why I said this or that over pie at our favorite restaurant after I completed each chapter. Who knows what the people around us thought. Special thanks goes to Gayle Graham Yates, who served as mentor and friend. Clarke Chambers, Art Geffen, Lillian Bowles, and Shirley Garner read and commented on the manuscript in its early stages. I am indebted to scholars such as Rosemary Ruether and activists such as Antiga (Mary Lee George) who established this field of inquiry and made this book possible. Karla Jay, series editor, and Niko Pfund of New York University Press have been a joy to work with. Thanks goes to Clare Green for what seemed like her endless pursuit of permissions to quote various materials.

This book was partially funded by a Denison University Research Foundation grant.

Grateful acknowledgment is made to Wildfire Books and to Sonia Johnson for permission to quote from *From Housewife to Heretic*, copyright © 1981 by Sonia Johnson.

Grateful acknowledgment is made to Beacon Press and to Mary Daly for permission to quote from *GYN/ECOLOGY*, copyright © 1978 by Mary Daly.

Grateful acknowledgment is made to Harcourt Brace Jovanovich, Inc., and to Alice Walker for permission to quote from *The Color Purple*, copyright © 1982 by Alice Walker.

Grateful acknowledgment is made to Aunt Lute Books and to Paula Gunn Allen for permission to quote from *The Woman Who Owned the Shadows*, copyright © 1983 by Paula Gunn Allen.

Grateful acknowledgment is made to The Charlotte Sheedy Literary Agency, Inc., and to Audre Lorde for permission to quote from *Zami: A New Spelling of My Name*, The Crossing Press Edition, copyright © 1982 by Audre Lorde.

Grateful acknowledgment is made to Viking Penguin, a division of Penguin Books USA, Inc., and to Leslie Marmon Silko for permission to quote from *Ceremony*, copyright © 1977 by Leslie Silko.

Grateful acknowledgment is made to Scott Meredith Literary Agency, Inc., 845 Third Avenue, New York, New York 10022, and to Marion Zimmer Bradley, for permission to quote from *The Mists of Avalon*, copyright © 1982 by Marion Zimmer Bradley.

The lines from "Solstice" and "125th Street and Abomey" are reprinted from *The Black Unicorn*, Poems by Audre Lorde, by permission of W. W. Norton and Company, Inc. Copyright © 1978 by Audre Lorde.

The lines from "Outlines," "On My Way Out I Passed Over You and the Verrazano Bridge," and "Call" are reprinted from *Our Dead Behind Us*, Poems by Audre Lorde, by permission of W. W. Norton and Company, Inc. Copyright © 1986 by Audre Lorde.

Abbreviations and Editions Used in the Text

BGF	*Beyond God the Father: Toward a Philosophy of Women's Liberation.* Mary Daly. Boston: Beacon, 1973.
BU	*The Black Unicorn.* Audre Lorde. New York: W. W. Norton, 1978.
C	*Ceremony.* Leslie Marmon Silko. New York: New American Library, 1977.
CP	*The Color Purple.* Alice Walker. New York: Harcourt Brace Jovanovich, 1982.
CSS	*The Church and the Second Sex.* Mary Daly. Boston: Beacon, 1968; reprint 1975 with the *Feminist Postchristian Introduction* and in 1985 with a *New Archaic Afterwards.*
DD	*Dreaming the Dark: Magic, Sex and Politics.* Starhawk. Boston: Beacon, 1982.
GE	*Gyn/Ecology: The Metaethics of Radical Feminism.* Mary Daly. Boston: Beacon, 1978.
GOM	*Going Out of Our Minds: The Metaphysics of Liberation.* Sonia Johnson. Freedom, Calif.: The Crossing Press, 1987.

HH	*From Housewife to Heretic.* Sonia Johnson. Garden City, N.Y.: Doubleday, 1981.
MA	*The Mists of Avalon.* Marion Zimmer Bradley. New York: Ballantine, 1984.
ODBU	*Our Dead Behind Us.* Audre Lorde. New York: W. W. Norton, 1986.
PL	*Pure Lust: Elemental Feminist Philosophy.* Mary Daly. Boston: Beacon, 1984.
SD	*The Spiral Dance: A Rebirth of the Ancient Religion of the Great Goddess.* Starhawk. San Francisco: Harper and Row, 1979.
TD	*Truth or Dare, Encounters with Power, Authority, and Mystery.* Starhawk. San Francisco: Harper and Row, 1987.
TF	*The Temple of My Familiar.* Alice Walker. San Diego: Harcourt Brace Jovanovich, 1989.
WIS	*Wildfire: Igniting the She/Volution.* Sonia Johnson. Albuquerque, N.M.: Wildfire Books, 1989.
WOS	*The Woman Who Owned the Shadows.* Paula Gunn Allen. San Francisco: Spinsters, Ink, 1983.
Z	*Zami: A New Spelling of My Name.* Audre Lorde. Watertown, Mass.: Persephone Press, 1982.

ONE

Introduction: Wild Women and Lesbian Sensibilities

THE lesbian-feminist movement has matured. For years, we have had businesses such as bookstores, cultural events such as the Michigan Women's Music Festival, and even cartoons promoting and chronicling lesbian-feminist culture. Lesbian scholarship and lesbian studies are expanding, and women-centered spiritual traditions can be a vital link in this evolving lesbian-feminist culture, giving women from different cultural traditions and ethnic backgrounds strong, powerful models to counter the traditional Euro-American perspective of women as weak and submissive. Although they arise from different traditions, women-centered spiritualities offer many commonalities, allowing women a base from which to appreciate difference as strength and to value connectedness.

Women-centered spiritual traditions also offer a bridge between heterosexual women and lesbians because they arise out of the woman: she is the center, whatever her sexuality. Models for this lie particularly in women-centered Native American cultures in which gender and sexuality traditionally are two different things. Since the Euro-American culture does not separate these concepts, any woman seen as being in control of herself, not under the control of a man, is called a wild woman, a lesbian, or a witch, among other things. For the purposes of this book, then, "lesbian" is used metaphorically for a woman not under the control of men—the old definition of virgin—the woman-centered woman. Therefore, although not all of the work or figures in this study fit the designation "lesbian" in the sense that they bond with other women sexually, all of them are woman-centered.

In her plenary address to the 1990 National Women's Studies Association Conference, noted lesbian philosopher Marilyn Frye urged the audience not necessarily to bond with women sexually, but to bond with women emotionally and politically—to be "wild women," withdrawing their allegiance to a patriarchal, heterosexist culture. Such women would be acting with lesbian sensibilities and critiquing Euro-American culture from a lesbian stance.

This study begins with and uses as its core a woman-centered spiritual tradition as seen through the works of two contemporary writers, Leslie Marmon Silko and Paula Gunn Allen, both of whom come with a Native American perspective, specifically Laguna Pueblo. While Allen identifies herself as lesbian, Silko does not, but both share the same cultural perspective that places women in the center and critiques patriarchal cultural constructs. In 1982 Silko visited the University of Minnesota's Twin Cities campus to read and talk about her work. She read a poem about Coyote, a familiar trickster figure in the oral traditions of the Southwest and Plains Indians, but one almost always recorded as male by ethnographers.[1] Listening to Silko, I began to wonder about the Euro-American biases in which much of anthropology is steeped—biases that seldom allowed the activities and perspectives of women even to be recorded. Silko used the pronoun "she" when referring to Coyote. As I listened to Silko, it became apparent that her language was appropriate to her culture and that it indicated the importance of the female among her people. I came away convinced that an integral part of her traditional culture was what Euro-American culture would call feminism—and more than that, it pointed to a culture in which the traditional Euro-American biases were turned upside down. Instead of the male being the measure of the universe, the female was central. In this context, the traditional society would not have needed the concept of feminism because, as I discovered, what I came to call "the female principle" was always an integral part of that society.

I had heard comments such as Silko's elsewhere, particularly in the work of some African-American women writers and white, feminist activists. This study thus evolved from my personal desire to trace the connections between these strands of women's spirituality, using my lesbian sensibilities, and in so doing, trying to address some contemporary lesbian-feminist dilemmas such as how lesbians from different cultures might work together. What are our commonalities? Around which issues can we bond? How can we work together and still honor each other's differences? And what are we working for?

The figures chosen for this study illustrate how one can put mind and spirit back together again, and how to make what has been designated as female important and not inferior. Each delineates a kind of journey to wholeness—a "curing ceremony or ceremonies" to heal the split between mind/body and the split that results from one's access to a worldview different than that promoted by white, male Euro-Americans. For women of color, a feature of the journey is to use cultural roots that lie outside the mainstream to create new visions and new possibilities, and largely to reject the Christianity that attempted to exert primal influence as part of colonization. Important to this study is the attempt to place each figure in her cultural context and to try to avoid imposing Euro-American values on that culture.

Because most established Euro-American religions also contribute to the mind/body split, they are also part of the problem.

While there are many feminists who work to bring women into full partnership with men in institutionalized religion, believing that women can make a change from within, others such as Audre Lorde believe that "the master's tools will never dismantle the master's house."[2] The figures in this study who identify themselves as feminists are prominent members of contemporary American spiritual groups or movements outside the Judeo-Christian mainstream. Several have attempted to find feminism in their cultural heritage but, failing that, have invented their own traditions. Most of the threads that we will examine here have as a focal point the Goddess, who is called by various names. However, even when the Goddess is not a point of reference, there is still something I have named "the female principle," in which the spiritual center is that force which creates, nourishes, and transmutes everything on earth and in the universe. For instance, Alice Walker calls herself a "womanist." She says, "Womanist is to feminist as purple is to lavender."[3] This term, like "woman-centered," suggests woman, Goddess, spiritual force, which acts in the best interest of women and thereby of humanity, perhaps despite the wishes of men. As a friend told me, "If the Goddess cooked it, She can uncook it." The female principle, then, is a force in which everything is connected—life and death—and can be better understood through reading poetry and fiction than by a simple definition. Poetry and fiction become women's "bibles" because they are among the few places one can find the traditions recorded. Since many of these traditions have evolved from the oral tradition—storytelling—they are appropriate texts.

Carol Christ has suggested in *Diving Deep and Surfacing: Women Writers on a Spiritual Quest* that women often use literature, particularly fiction and poetry, as a "sacred text" to replace other forms of sacred texts such as the Bible when they are searching for new ways to understand spirituality. Accordingly, some women writers create text, which then serves for their women readers as literature from which to glean spiritual insights and a vision of possibility. In *The Land Before Her: Fantasy and Experience of the American Frontiers, 1630–1860*, Annette Kolodny elaborates on the connection between text and life, pointing out, however, that "the danger in examining the projections of fantasy is the temptation to construe them as unmediated models of behavior."[4] She continues:

> In fact, what we are examining here are not blueprints for conduct, but contexts of imaginative possibility. Fantasy, in other words, does not necessarily coincide with how we act or wish to act in the world. It does, however, represent symbolic forms (often repressed or unconscious) that clarify, codify, organize, explain, or even lead us to anticipate the raw data of experience. In that sense, fantasy may be mediating or integrative, forging imaginative (and imaginable) links between our deepest psychic needs and the world in which we find ourselves.[5]

In spite of these cautions, Kolodny points out that imaginative thought or fantasy expressed in fiction, poetry, and language, as we are using the concept here, can influence behavior if the opportunity occurs within the cultural constraints of the historical time period—in other words, if society allows that behavior. It is clear that with the pressure exerted by the reawakening of the feminist movement in the late 1960s and early 1970s, we are living in a time ripe for exploration of women's spirituality outside traditional religious institutions. One of the major figures in this exploration has been Mary Daly, who has been a foremother in attempting to revision the possibilities of daily life by her philosophical reconstructions of language and her insistence that patriarchal concepts of God are no longer usable for women.

In 1973 Daly argued in *Beyond God the Father (BGF)* "that the women's revolution . . . is a spiritual revolution, pointing beyond the idolatries of sexist society and sparking creative action in and toward transcendence. The becoming of women implies universal human becoming. It has everything to do with the search for ultimate meaning and reality, which some would call God" (p. 6). Indeed, the plan she lays out for "transcendence" is the path other feminists have also seen. Daly says, "What is required of women at this point in history is a firm and deep refusal to limit our perspectives, questioning, and creativity to any of the preconceived patterns of male-dominated culture" (p. 7). Because Daly saw "the entire conceptual systems of theology and ethics developed under the condition of patriarchy" as serving "the interests of sexist society" (p. 4), she urged women to withdraw their support and step outside these systems and bond together to foster "the becoming of women and men" (p. 71).

Further, Daly pointed to Mary, Mother of God, particularly the Catholic church's doctrine of the Immaculate Conception of Mary, as a symbol that "can be recognized as having been an infiltrator into sexist territory, an unrecognized harbinger of New Being." She says this doctrine "can be read as . . . reflecting the power and influence of the Mother Goddess symbol which Christianity was never able to wipe out entirely," and that it says that "the female does not need to be 'saved' by the male" (*BGF*, 87). According to Daly, "[T]he prophetic dimension in the symbol of the Great Goddess . . . is the key to salvation from servitude to structures that obstruct human becoming. . . . [I]t is women who must make the breakthrough that can alter the seemingly doomed course of human evolution" (pp. 96–97).

Daly did not envision in 1973 all the ways in which contemporary feminists would reclaim this symbol. Today some Native American and African-American women are reclaiming traditional spiritual concepts in which the divine was conceived of as female; an activist such as Sonia Johnson has found the Goddess within her own Mormon religion and used it to transcend that religion; and those such as Starhawk practice what they call the Old Religion, or the worship of the Great Goddess. All of these feminists see themselves as reclaiming their spirituality—rescuing it, if you will, from the deadening influence of a patriarchal religion that creates and perpetuates attitudes and actions that, they feel, are destroying the planet.

To change the attitudes and actions stemming from patriarchal systems has thus become a matter of priority to these and other feminists. The dominant culture needs to be "cured" or changed if the destruction is to end and well-being is to be restored. All of these feminists take this goal very seriously, offering varying kinds of "ceremonies" to bring those who choose to participate closer to the female principle—to discovering it within themselves and acting upon it. As with other spiritual groups, there is at base a faith that individuals and the world can be changed, and that many people will be receptive to change. The concept of "ceremony" in this context goes beyond a traditional Euro-American meaning of a specific ritual conducted in some special place set aside for the purpose of healing. While these elements may be present in a ceremony in the sense in which I am using the word, a piece of literature could also be a ceremony in that the author saw the writing of it as a spiritual act, serving the deity, and that, if it is approached in this way by a reader, a bonding with a spiritual force could take place. This concept also applies to storytelling—the oral tradition now written into Silko's and Allen's texts, for instance. The storytelling mode is important as both a means of transmitting the sacred in the texts studied and as part of the method of this study.

Furthermore, the idea of ceremony as a repeated, formal ritual becomes a way of life—a process—carried on with deliberate intention to participate in the reality of the Goddess. For instance, Leslie Silko calls attention to the responsibility of every human to choose words and actions very carefully because we are all connected.[6] The concept of curing moves from the healing of a specific illness toward connection with the female principle, which implies the physical and spiritual healing of the self as well as the healing of the planet—a continuous process.

This, then, is the story of the journeys of some prominent

members of these groups and how some of their woman-centered literature, language, and thoughts have contributed to the current search for spiritual alternatives outside mainstream religious institutions by offering a personal experience of the female principle to those who choose to participate. There are others, of course, whose works could be studied in this way, and it is my hope that this book might serve as a model. Since I began this study, glimpses of woman-centered Jewish-American spiritual traditions have begun to appear in the works of Alice Boch, E. M. Broner, and Kim Cherin, for instance, but it remains for someone else to separate this particular thread from patriarchal Jewish traditions and place it into a cultural context. The question of lesbian theologian Carter Heyward's independence from mainstream Episcopal tradition is ripe for exploration and might produce another story. In addition, in explorations of woman-centered threads outside mainstream religions, Gloria Anzaldua comes to mind for a Chicana tradition, and surely there is also an Asian-American woman-centered thread. All of these—and others—might be fruitful subjects of study but are beyond the scope of this book.

Nevertheless, the subjects of this study are representative of the great variety of current approaches to the female principle—what I have called "threads," which emanate from the female principle and have been highly important in articulating it. Not only does the work of these writers and activists contribute to a vision of a world based on a female principle, but taken together it also delineates and exemplifies a lesbian-feminist ethics.

Of the figures selected for this study, I have chosen to look only at those works and events connected with them which can aid in understanding the female principle. By works I mean spiritual "events" as well as literature. To do this study justice, one must cross many artificial boundaries—boundaries between history, fiction, anthropology, literary criticism, religion, and philosophy—and bring them together. I attempt to look at each figure in this study in the context of her culture, and I have paired the women whose work seems to flesh out the search for the Goddess or the female principle in that particular context.

Various difficulties arise when one attempts to look at figures in context; some are easier to resolve than others. For instance, quite a bit of material can be found concerning a Native American spiritual thread in the novels of Leslie Marmon Silko and Paula Gunn Allen. Since Allen is also a scholar and teacher and writes eloquently about Silko's work, her fiction serves to document a Laguna Pueblo view and her essays are interpretations from a Laguna perspective. Important to the theory of my study is Allen's observation that all Keres-speaking peoples (the language family to which many Pueblo groups belong) have a feminist base, which she calls "gynocratic."[7]

Looking at a thread of African-American spirituality that has roots in West African culture is more difficult, however. A great deal of time has passed since the African-American ancestors were taken from their homelands and the conditions of slavery resulted in a melding of African traditions. Luisah Teish refers to the culture that resulted from the mass dispersion of African peoples as "Afro-diasporic."[8] She claims that the African peoples who made up the main part of the slave trade "spoke the dialects of the *Kwa* and *Bantu* languages" and that they also "shared a belief in nature worship and ancestor reverence and performed similar magical practices,"[9] which today can be seen in the practice of voodoo. Therefore, although the names of specific gods and goddesses and specific religious practices might be different today, they were once at base similar. Which specific religious practices evolved in which place depended on which group predominated, but because of these commonalities, scholars speak of a West African or diasporic tradition. Therefore, even though Lorde comes from a Caribbean and African-American tradition, they can still be considered as related to the West African tradition.

Another problem with the West African or diasporic tradition is that the melding of traditions to create new traditions when the slaves left Africa makes the tracing of actual gods and goddesses to a particular African culture more difficult.[10] Therefore, I have not tried to tie the goddess names that Lorde or Walker uses to a particular African culture, but have instead relied on their identifications. Lorde uses the Black mother as a general designation for the Goddess, though she could have represented her by at least half a dozen African names, as Walker shows in her novel, *The Temple of My Familiar*.

Their African heritage has been such a strong component in black American writers' lives that they have had to confront it even when the confrontation resulted in a disavowal of much of it.[11] Lorde and Walker respond to that heritage in their work differently. Although they do not have the same perspective on their African heritage, their works both illustrate and promote the female principle.

This book also explores the female principle as manifested in a Celtic pagan tradition that survives in American culture through the writings and rituals of Starhawk, a priestess of the Old Religion and a witch, and through Marion Zimmer Bradley's novel, *The Mists of Avalon*. The Celtic pagan tradition is perhaps the most difficult to view with any kind of objectivity because in Euro-American culture, the idea of "witch" has been generally equated with the devil or evil, as has any religious belief not associated with Christianity. Ancient traditions outside Christianity have often been dismissed by church officials as primitive or as superstitious or, as scholars have shown, they have been absorbed into and blended with Christianity.[12] This blending has, of course, gone two ways: Christianity absorbed many attributes of "pagan" religions, including festivals and rites, and many religions that have come in contact with Christianity also adopted some of the newer practices. Thus it is difficult to claim or reclaim that which society at large condemns or laughs at and actually to separate pagan traditions from Christian. Such is the case with witchcraft, with voodoo (a prominent black tradition), and with many Native American spiritual traditions. I have attempted to take Starhawk at her word and to connect her to traditions that arose out of the British Isles, and to see her spirituality in that context. Here again, as with African traditions, so much time has elapsed that reconstruction is exceedingly difficult, and little evidence is available on which to base assumptions. Nevertheless, Starhawk's spirituality and the portrayal in *The Mists of Avalon* must be seen as arising out of a "creative" tradition.

The female principle is also exhibited in the mainstream-culture areas of politics and religion by white feminists Sonia Johnson, who ran for president of the United States in 1984, and Mary Daly, a prominent theologian. These activists illustrate the current feminist perspective that spirituality is not separate from life but permeates all parts of it, and that spirituality is also political. Johnson and Daly show the female principle in operation in politics and in religion, both of which have traditionally been Euro-American, male fields. They are incorporating spirituality into mainstream traditions in which it is not usually recognized.

There has been a huge expansion of literature on women and spirituality in the last few years. Much of it is on women's roles within the more accepted religions such as Christianity. However, none of these studies attempts to link the threads of women's spirituality that remain outside the dominant Euro-American culture's ideas of religion and that focus on the female principle incorporating the lesbian, the wild woman, the womanist, the medicine woman. This is what I seek to do in this work.

TWO

Curing Ceremonies: The Novels of Leslie Marmon Silko and Paula Gunn Allen

LESLIE Marmon Silko and Paula Gunn Allen, both part Native American and from Laguna Pueblo in New Mexico, continue their cultural tradition in their novels by using them in the same way in which the traditional arts have always functioned for the people of Laguna Pueblo. They have extended traditional storytelling into the modern form of the novel by weaving in tribal history, cultural traditions, and mythology[1] of the Lagunas to create a form of curing ceremony for their readers. Although Silko does not identify herself as lesbian, as does Allen, nor does she have overtly lesbian material in her novel, as does Allen, she is important to this book because she delineates a culture in which such identification would have been natural—an accepted part of the culture—and based on a person's function in the group. "Feminist" would not have been a concept that was needed by her culture, and neither would "lesbian." Together with Allen's *The Woman Who Owned the Shadows (WOS)* Silko's book *Ceremony (C)* gives the reader a rich picture of a culture in which women were central to everything and were, indeed, the gods. It also gives us an understanding of the balanced roles of male and female in this culture. In this context, a curing ceremony will not only dispel Euro-Americans of the perspective that everything around them is for their own gratification, but also allows for a revision of women's place in society and specifically of the role of the lesbian as a sacred calling.

Ceremony was first published in 1977, and Silko has won wide acclaim from reviewers and scholars alike.[2] *The American Indian Quarterly* devoted an entire issue to Silko.[3] Allen's novel, *The Woman Who Owned the Shadows*, was published more recently, in 1983. Allen has written many scholarly articles and chapbooks of poetry, and she edited *Studies in American Indian Literature* (1983). In 1982 her major book of poetry, *Shadow Country*, was published. Her newest book of poetry is entitled *Wyrds* (1987), and a novel, *Raven's Road*, has been excerpted in various anthologies and journals.

Underlying Native American literature are cultural assumptions and a worldview that contrast sharply with most non-Indian literature.[4] To better understand how Silko and Allen use their cultural tradition in their novels, we must know something about the culture from which they come. The Pueblo worldview, like that of other tribal cultures, is based on the concept that all things inanimate and animate are related and are part of the whole. Plants, animals, rocks, and people exist in a reciprocal relationship, and people must perform rituals, say prayers, and make offerings to keep things in balance in that relationship. To the Pueblo, who have kept their worldview essentially intact, life is sacred, and everything, including the arts, contributes to "light, life, well-being."[5] The task of the individual is to contribute to the well-being of the group. As the Navajo medicine man in *Ceremony* says: "Accidents happen, and there's little we can do. But don't be so quick to call something good or bad. There are balances and harmonies always shifting, always necessary to maintain" (p. 137).

Since the invasion of Europeans who brought with them a

worldview that separates spirit and body, the inanimate and the animate, ceremonies have become even more important in keeping the relationships among all things in balance. The ultimate expression of a lack of balance is the development and use of the atomic bomb, to which Silko refers in her novel. In this sense, lack of balance effects not only the individual but the universe. A worldview that separates spirit and body, inanimate from animate, lacks respect for other parts of creation and fails to see the interrelatedness of all things—one's place in the web of being. The Euro-American worldview elevates one part of creation above others: men over women; humans over plants, animals, and earth; and mind/spirit over the physical. This perspective leads ultimately to a lack of balance.

For the Lagunas, geographic place is intricately tied into understanding one's place in the web of being, in a special tie to the land. Balance cannot be achieved without a "knowing" related to continuity in a certain area or locale. The importance of place in Laguna culture is not surprising; after all, the Pueblo are descendants of the people who have inhabited the area from southern Utah and Colorado to northern Mexico since 10,000 B.C. The immediate ancestors of the Pueblo occupied the Four Corners area, the spot where the states of Colorado, Utah, Arizona, and New Mexico intersect, and Allen and Silko's people have occupied their present area since about the thirteenth century.[6]

In contrast to the Lagunas' sense of harmony with the environment, critic Reyes Garcia points out in a discussion of the novel *Ceremony* that the Euro-American way of shaping and controlling the environment "deprive[s] all lives, most of all their own, of substance." He feels that without our being able to "respond to the fertile meaning places hold, . . . our pulsing lives here will stop and Earth will come to an end, its radioactive memory locked in 'witchery's final ceremonial sand painting.' "[7] Allen explores this theme in part of her novel *Raven's Road*, when she suggests that Sun Woman might be reborn as part of the atomic bomb testing taking place in the desert. As the main character watches the rising mushroom cloud, she sees "the old woman or great white bear or sun maiden or sun shield. . . . In her memory's eye she could see that the visual was of an old woman's face huge as the sky."[8] Allen points out that Euro-Americans have no respect for the forces of the environment with which they tamper because they believe that they can control everything. The delicate balances have been disrupted, and we must work to recover them. One way to right the balance is through storytelling.

For the Pueblos, storytelling often functions as a ceremony for curing. Both Silko and Allen continue in this tradition; their novels are offerings to balance the world and to enact healing rituals for themselves and others. For the Pueblos, story is a connecting medium and, according to Simon J. Ortiz, poet from nearby Acoma Pueblo, ensures the very life of the people: "Story is to engender life, and *Ceremony* speaks upon the very process by which story, whether in oral or written form, substantiates life, continues it, and creates it. . . . Because of the insistence to keep telling and creating stories, Indian life continues, and it is this resistance against loss that has made that life possible."[9] Silko's novel had even a more personal "curing" function for her. When asked why she wrote *Ceremony,* Silko said that it was "a ceremony for her to stay sane."[10] As she worked with her character Tayo and he recovered, so did she.

In an essay Allen writes that "at base, every story, every song, every ceremony, tells the Indian he *[sic]* is part of a living whole, and that all parts of the whole are related to one another by virtue of their participation in the whole of being."[11] Since the Europeans first came in the fifteenth century, "the fragile web of identity that long held tribal people secure has gradually been weakened and torn. But the oral tradition has prevented the complete destruction of the web, the ultimate disruption of tribal ways."[12] Through "the women who speak and work and write," the oral tradition continues now in English and helps to mend the web.[13] In an interview, Allen has said that her novel is a "medicine novel" or a "ritual handbook" meant to "get inside" the reader's head.[14]

Silko and Allen's novels, then, can be seen as curing ceremonies—ceremonies to ensure survival and, as Ortiz points out, to create new life. To link these new ceremonies with the old, they use traditional Laguna mythology. Some of this mythology was recorded by ethnologists during the first half of the twentieth century, and by looking at both the recordings and the novels, one can see a continuum of storytelling. However, caution must be observed in this process. It is enormously difficult for outsiders to appreciate the nuances of another culture, and while recordings by ethnologists and anthropologists give readers access to a possible outline of mythology, the recordings have been filtered through the writers' own cultural assumptions. They, of course, also get filtered through the readers' cultural biases. There must also be a recognition that the oral tradition has always accommodated itself to the needs of the community; it has always been a changing and growing process rather than a static one.[15] Therefore, it is a mistake to say that a literature is authentic because it agrees with what ethnographers have recorded, because oral tradition has a changing nature and because the recorders have their own biases. My objective is not to verify the authenticity of either Silko's or Allen's work, but to see how they are using the mythology—how as storytellers they have taken the ancient beliefs and adapted them to a modern setting.

On the matter of ethnographers, Silko says that there was a prevalent opinion "that to be a worthy human being if you were coming from a pueblo, you should know the stories just the way the anthropologists reported them." She continues:

> [I] never sat down with them and said I'm going to make a poem or a story out of this. The more I think about it, I realize I don't have to because from the time I was little I heard quite a bit. I heard it in what would be passed off now as rumor or gossip. I could hear through all

that. I could hear something else, that there was a kind of continuum that was really there despite Elsie Clews Parsons. In 1930, you know, she wrote off Laguna as a lost cause. She said it had no kiva, that it was dead. I think she wrote that somewhere. And the same went for the "oral tradition."[16]

Here Silko affirms the continuing importance of the oral tradition to the Lagunas. Indeed, if one checks the ethnographies, some of the similarities are so close to Silko's renditions that one can conclude that if Silko did not know the ethnographer's versions, but had heard orally all the stories she uses in her poetry and fiction, then the tradition is very much alive and well.[17]

Laguna storytelling, Silko points out, is comprised of many types, including those of creation, clan identity, family identity, and personal experience.[18] The creation stories or sacred accounts serve to place the tribe in the web of being by reminding members that they are the descendants of those who emerged from the four layers of the underworld at Shipap. The mythic tellings about clan identity serve to remind listeners where they fit into the matrilineal organization and about those in the tribe to whom they have special connections and obligations for ritual purposes such as curing, and for economic aid such as work in the fields.[19] The tales about family identity can be a personal reminder that each part is important to the whole. Those about personal experiences can remind listeners that they are not alone: even the bad experiences have happened to others, and they will happen again. Others have survived and each member of the tribe can, too: each is part of the whole. Silko says that people usually want to run off by themselves when something terrible has happened, but this behavior threatens not only the survival of the group, but also the individual or the family: "Inherent in this belief is the feeling that one does not recover or get well by one's self, but it is together that we look after each other and take care of each other."[20] However, the Laguna do not see one kind of story as more important than another, unlike the ethnographers who tried to limit important tales to those that told of the mythic background of the tribe—the creation accounts. For the Laguna all tellings are vital, and it is the wholeness to which they contribute that is seen as most important. As Silko comments:

> I . . . do not limit storytelling to simply old stories, but to . . . go back to the original [Laguna] view of creation, which sees that it is all part of a whole; we do not differentiate or fragment stories or experiences. In the beginning, Tse'itsi'nako, Thought Woman, thought of all these things, and all of these things are held together as one holds many things together in a single thought.[21]

In this way there is no beginning and no end to the stories, and "one thought" or story can hold different time periods together. This is precisely the form which both Allen and Silko use in their novels—the ancient stories juxtaposed against the modern stories. The origin stories in the novels establish the characters' tribal identity as Laguna (Allen uses the fictional name Guadalupe[22] for her character's tribal identity); the clan stories establish the respective clans of the main characters. For instance, in *The Woman Who Owned the Shadows*, Allen identifies Oak as her main character's clan:

> She remembered her own clan, descended of Iyatiku, Earth Woman, Corn Woman. There were four corn clans, then her clan. "I am Oak," she said. "The fifth. My uncle, Oak Man, helped Iyatiku in the beginning. He assisted her in laying down the orders, the rules. The way the people would live. How they would be. He was the first War Captain, the first outside chief." (*WOS*, 81)[23]

It is this juxtaposition of ancient and new which can make the novels difficult reading. Both novels are about journeys to healing. The central characters at the beginning of both novels are mixed-breed persons who have lost the sense of who they are; they are isolated and fragmented as human beings, belonging neither to the Pueblo nor the non-Indian community. Silko's Tayo comes back from World War II with a fragmented self. The reader follows Tayo as he meets with the traditional healer of his tribe and as he goes to a Navajo healer, outside his own tribe, with whom he works out a healing that restores not only health to him but also to his tribe by bringing the rain. Tayo battles the forces of "the witchery," as Silko calls it, to restore balance. For Tayo, one of the difficulties of this battle is that not only the whites but also the friends with whom he served in the war, other tribal members, and sometimes even he himself have become pawns of the witchery. The difficulty is within each of us.

Allen's Ephanie has a fragmented self from an inner war. As a part Guadalupe woman, Ephanie is caught in the erosion of the traditional place of honor and respect in which a Guadalupe woman is held by her tribe. In the non-Indian world she must deal with both the patriarchal stereotypes of Indians and of women. She is surrounded by forces that work to destroy whatever link she has to the traditional culture in which women were central figures. The reader follows her struggle to regain her sanity as she sorts out her childhood and her tribal beliefs and connections, marries a second-generation Japanese-American, and deals with the death of one of their twins. She joins a consciousness-raising group, goes to a psychiatrist, studies the old traditions, tries to commit suicide; but it is only when she is able to synthesize what she has learned from all of this and to see its connection to her tribal traditions—and to reaffirm the importance of the female, especially the importance of the "Amazon tradition"[24]—that she is healed.

The Laguna society to which both Allen and Silko's mothers and maternal grandmothers belonged, but which by the time of the novels has shown the effects of contact with non-Indian society, was matrilineal (with descent recognized through the female line) and matrilocal (the ownership of houses was held by women). Women also owned the crops while men did the farming. Allen says her "mother's Laguna people are Keres Indian, reputed to be the last extreme mother-right people on earth."[25] Women controlled and cared for ceremonial objects,[26] and the power to conduct the ceremonies came from both men and women (Allen interview). According to Allen, one of the problems with Christianity is that it attempts to use only "male power." The primary deities were Thought Woman (Ts'its'tsi'nako) and her sisters, Corn Woman (I'tcts'ity'i) and Earth Woman (Nau'ts'ity'i). For Allen, "womanness . . . is preponderant; it is the source of human male and human female, the giver and bestower of life, ritual, afterlife, social power, and all that is sacred."[27] Because the Laguna society in which Silko and Allen place their characters has lost this central importance of the female, both Laguna and Euro-American society need balancing. The old stories are not effective in acting as curing ceremonies because they do not account for the influence of colonial culture.

In Silko's novel *Ceremony* the main character, Tayo, finds no stories to reflect his personal experience in World War II. The war stories of older days no longer work in a ceremonial sense for him because Tayo does not understand their meaning. Even the Laguna medicine man, Ku'oosh, cannot comprehend the scope of the experience which Tayo has been through in order to relate the old stories to Tayo's experience. New stories addressing his experience must be told, but, in this case, only someone who understands both the old and the new can fulfill the role of storyteller or healer for Tayo.

Allen's main character in *The Woman Who Owned the Shadows* illustrates the isolation and fragmentation that occur if individuals pull away or are left out of the community and their experience or "story" cannot be seen as part of the whole. As a person of mixed ancestry who lives apart, Ephanie is unable to fit into the old ways; there are no stories for her experiences. It is only when she makes sense of the old stories by seeing the continuities in them and how she fits into those continuities that she can be healed, for the Lagunas believe that everything that has happened will happen again, only in a different form. Her journey to healing, unlike that of Silko's main character, is primarily an isolated one,[28] an interior journey. She puzzles over the old stories, searching for answers, looking for the patterns until, one day, she understands their continuity—how they fit together:

> She understood the combinations and recombinations that had so puzzled her. . . . First there was Sussinstinaku, Thinking Woman, then there was She and two more: Uretsete and Naotsete. Then Uretsete became known as the father, Utset because Naotsete had become pregnant and a mother, because the Christians would not understand and killed what they did not know. And Iyatiku was the name Uretsete was known by . . . and so the combinations went on, forming, dissolving, doubling, splitting. . . . All of the stories formed those patterns laid down long before time, so far. (*WOS*, 207–8)

An important role of the storyteller, then, is to tell the story according to the requirements of the listeners. Therefore, the story must be adapted to the particular audience. In *Ceremony*, Betonie, the mixed-breed Navajo healer, with his hazel-green eyes from his Mexican grandmother (Tayo's eyes are hazel-green), his shoeboxes of traditional herbs, and his stacks of newspapers and train calendars, is the only one who is able to tell a curing story for Tayo to show him how his experience fits in. With Betonie's help, Tayo is finally able to connect to the old stories and make sense of his life:

> He cried the relief he felt at finally seeing the pattern, the way all the stories fit together—the old stories, the war stories, their stories—to become the story that was still being told. He was not crazy; he had never been crazy. He had only seen and heard the world as it always was: no boundaries, only transitions through all distance and time. (*C*, 258)

As Silko reminds us in an essay, "Storytelling always includes the audience and the listeners, and in fact, a great deal of the story is believed to be inside the listener and the storyteller's role is to draw the story out of the listeners."[29]

Having identified their readers as needing stories to make sense out of today's complicated world and yet connect to the important legends or values of the past, Silko and Allen each tell a modern story calculated to accomplish this. They begin with the Laguna creation myth, which opens with a female creator spirit, Ts'its'tsi'nako or Thought Woman. She is also identified as Spider Woman in some versions of the myth. She creates two sisters, I'tcts'ity'i (Iyatiku) and Nau'ts'ity'i, who, with various animal helpers, bring the people from the four worlds of the underworld. They emerge at Shipap. Iyatiku or Corn Woman becomes the mother of the Indians while Nau'ts'ity'i or Earth Woman becomes the mother of the others.[30] In their function as storytellers in the Laguna tradition, then, Silko and Allen both evoke Thought Woman at the beginning of their novels. In the opening of *Ceremony,* Silko says:

> Ts'its'tsi'nako, Thought-Woman
> is sitting in her room
> and whatever she thinks about
> appears.
>
> She thought of her sisters,
> Nau'ts'ity'i and I'tcts'ity'i
> and together they created the Universe
> this world
> and the four worlds below.
>
> Thought-Woman, the spider,
> named things and
> as she named them
> they appeared.
>
> She is sitting in her room
> thinking of a story now

I'm telling you the story
she is thinking.

(*C*, 1)

Similarly, Allen's prologue recounts the creation story, and she dedicates *The Woman Who Owned the Shadows* to her "great grandmother, Meta Atseye Gunn./ To Naiya Iyatiku./ And to Spider Grandmother, Thought Woman,/ who thinks the stories I write down" (*WOS*, iii).

By dedicating their novels to Thought Woman, from whose intelligence all life comes, Allen and Silko celebrate her as the supreme storyteller. The stories give Thought Woman/Spider Woman the love and respect she deserves, and in turn she will bless them. "After her," as a line in one of Allen's poems goes, the poet "mend[s] the tear with string"—the poet, following the Creator's example, attempts to weave together the stories to affect healing for the people.[31] Allen and Silko place their novels in the context of the Laguna tradition, signifying that they are honoring Spider Grandmother while at the same time taking part in the grandmother's thinking by telling a story for the people that will unify old and new experiences into a coherent whole. In an essay, Allen writes that such activity attempts "to bring the isolated self into harmony and balance" with the reality celebrated in legends, sacred stories, songs, and ceremonies and "to actualize in language, those truths of being and experience that give to humanity its greatest significance and dignity."[32] In Laguna mythology, there is a story about how Thought Woman's sisters, who have been given the task of naming and giving "human form to the spirit which was the people" (*WOS*, 148), quarrel and separate. This seems to be the beginning of much of the evil in the world. The result in the modern stories is that the children of the two sisters (including whites, Asians, Native Americans, and Africans) have forgotten that they are related and have also forgotten that they are related to things inanimate and animate. Most of the two sisters' descendants do not remember that people must carry on rituals to keep things in balance. This forgetting leads to separation from the land, to drought, to war, to division of the self.

Both Silko's Tayo and Allen's Ephanie are caught in the separation and division of self. Tayo is only part Laguna, the result of his mother's liaison with a white man. In the traditional culture, because of the children they bore,[33] women were so important that any sexual involvement with outsiders, either Mexican or white, was frowned upon. Raised by his aunt when his mother abandons him, the aunt makes Tayo feel his mother's shame in leaving the tribe and becoming involved with outsiders. However, this shame is another sign of the loss of traditional values: since this tribe would have been traditionally organized according to a maternal principle, any child and its mother would have taken a place in the house of its mother and grandmother and both would have been valued.[34] Instead Tayo, is raised in shame:

> He sat for a long time and thought about his mother. There had been a picture of her once, and he had carried the tin frame to bed with him at night, and whispered to it. But one evening, when he carried it with him, there were visitors in the kitchen, and she [Auntie] grabbed it away from him. He cried for it and Josiah [his uncle] . . . asked Tayo why he was crying, but just as he was ashamed to tell Josiah about the understanding between him and Auntie, he also could not tell him about the picture; he loved Josiah too much to admit the shame. (*C*, 73)

When he goes off to war and his aunt's son, Rocky, is killed, he curses the jungle rain. He has forgotten the interrelatedness of all things and his place in the web of being. He fails to remember that there are "no boundaries, only transitions through all distances and time" (*C*, 258). He has forgotten that "in the old stories . . . [i]t took only one person to tear away the delicate strands of the web, spilling the rays of sun into the sand, and the fragile world would be injured. Once there had been a man who cursed the rain clouds, a man of monstrous dreams" (p. 40).

Later he remembers these things, and blames himself for the drought, but he is only part of the difficulties of the community, not the whole. The real difficulty for the community is that they have abandoned the values the Mother taught.

Tayo comes back from the war estranged from himself, not a full-blood Laguna, not white, not Mexican, and not Japanese, a race with which he identifies because their skin color is like his. Tayo has a "drought" of the spirit that parallels the drought he finds in the land when he returns. His journey to cure himself and bring back the rain is also juxtaposed with the traditional story Silko weaves into the novel of how Fly and Hummingbird propitiate the Mother, Nau'ts'ity'i, to bring back the rain. Silko parallels the events of war and the people turning away from the values the Mother had taught with the ancient story of how the people followed a false medicine man's Ck'o'yo' (evil) magic[35] and thus "neglected the mother corn altar" of Nautsityi, who subsequently takes the rain from them:

Our Mother
Nau'ts'ity'i
was very angry
over this
over the way
all of them
even Ma'see'wi and Ou'yu'ye'wi
fooled around with this
magic.

"I've had enough of that,"
she said,
"If they like that magic so much
let them live off it."

So she took
the plants and grass from them.
No baby animals were born.

She took the
rainclouds with her.
(*C*, 50)

In the modern story, Tayo's healing is affected particularly by Ts'eh, a spirit person and a representative of Thought Woman and the female principle. Ts'eh seems to be a reincarnation of Yellow Woman or Ko'chinako from the traditional tales and brings "fertility, growth and summer"[36] to both Tayo and his people. Ts'eh and Night Swan, the Mexican dancer and girlfriend of Tayo's Uncle Josiah, who, as Allen points out in an essay, is "associated with Ts'eh," help Tayo regain his love of life; they bring life back to him by sleeping with him. One might say that the beginning of the curing ceremony of Tayo and his people can be traced to Night Swan, who tells Tayo after he sleeps with her: "You don't have to understand what is happening. But remember this day. You will recognize it later. You are part of it now" (*C*, 105). Allen, a careful reader and student of Silko's work, says that the passages in *Ceremony* which tell of Tayo's intercourse with Night Swan and Ts'eh are not about "an ordinary coupling. . . . These passages tell of the ceremonial nature of man and woman; they embody the meaning of the action of the relation between the characters and Thought Woman that is the basis of Laguna life."[37]

Night Swan begins the transmittal of healing love to Tayo: "She moved under him, her rhythm merging into the sound of the wind shaking the rafters and the sound of the rain in the tree. And he was lost somewhere, deep beneath the surface of his own body and consciousness, swimming away from all his life before that hour" (*C*, 104). Night Swan is also the woman not under the control of any man, the woman unto herself. Silko creates Night Swan as a Mexican woman, not from Laguna, allowing for a manifestation of the Goddess in a nontraditional form. When she comes to Laguna, for purposes only she knows, she is seen as a wanton woman by the town's inhabitants. As an illustration of her power, Night Swan tells a story about "an accident" that happens to a man who dishonors her. In the story she dances until "I could feel something breaking under my feet, the heels of my dancing shoes soaking into something crushed dark until the balance and smoothness were restored once again to the dance floor." Later she heard that the man's "horses had trampled him" (p. 90).

Another representation of the Goddess, Ts'eh, continues the transmittal of healing love. After Tayo sleeps with her, his senses come awake and he feels glad to be alive:

> The air felt damp and cold like the ground after the snow has melted into it, making it dense and rich. He stood on the steps and looked into the morning stars in the west. He breathed deeply, and each breath had a distinct smell of snow from the north, of ponderosa pine on the rimrock above; finally he smelled horses from the direction of the corral, and he smiled. Being alive was all right then: he had not breathed like that for a long time. (*C*, 189)

As the sun comes up, past and present become one. He sees "the Ka't'sina approaching the river crossing," and he sings the ancient song for the sunrise (*C*, 189–90). Tayo and Ts'eh separate, but he dreams of her and her love becomes part of him, healing him, nurturing him: "He was dreaming of her arms around him strong, when the rain on the tin roof woke him up. But the feeling he had, the love he felt from her, remained" (pp. 227–28).

Like Night Swan, Ts'eh also demonstrates that she is in control of her being and that she has considerable other powers. After Tayo goes to hunt his cattle and once again returns to Ts'eh's mountain home, he meets the Mountain Lion Man, presumably also a spirit. Tayo assumes that Ts'eh "belongs" to the Mountain Lion Man, and Ts'eh enjoys teasing Tayo about his fears that the Mountain Lion Man will discover that Tayo and Ts'eh have slept together. Further, Ts'eh demonstrates her control of the weather in this encounter; the snowstorm that has helped Tayo elude his captors stops after Ts'eh folds up her "storm-pattern blanket." Tayo performs a reciprocal ceremony by shaking the snow off the tree in her courtyard, "moving around the tree from the east to the south, and from the west to the north" (*C*, 218). Ts'eh also assures him that his pursuers will not follow him to her house, and when he questions her, "She gave him a look that chilled him" (p. 223). Obviously, Tayo does not know with whom he deals. "When he turned to wave at her, she was gone" (p. 223).

Ts'eh returns to Tayo in the spring. She works further healing to connect Tayo firmly to the earth, to the creative forces of the female principle, warning him of future tests and trials, so that he can be strong enough to turn away from the witchery or destructive forces that want to use him:

> Their days together had a gravity emanating from the mesas and arroyos, and it replaced the rhythm that had been interrupted so long ago; now the old memories were less than the constriction of a single throat muscle. She was with him again, a heartbeat unbroken where time subsided into dawn, and the sunset gave way to the stars, wheeling across the night. The breaking and crushing were gone, and the love pushed inside his chest, and when he cried now, it was because she loved him so much. (*C*, 238)

When his denial of the witchery is complete, when he refuses be a pawn to the witchery and to plunge "the screwdriver into Emo's skull" (*C*, 265) after Emo tormented and killed his friend, he understands his relationship and the Lagunas' relationship to Ts'eh, representative of the Mother, the earth, the mountain: "They had always been loved. He thought of her then; she had always loved him, she had never left him; she had always been there" (p. 267).

Silko clearly shows that it is not just Tayo who is sick, but society as well. Many of the Lagunas, particularly the young men back from the war, blame the whites for their problems, but evil, or what Silko calls "the witchery," only works through the whites; it is not the same as the whites. Now, instead of the two sisters's children being united in caring for one another, they do the work of the witchery and are united in the end result of destruction. The ultimate expression of this is the development and use of the atomic bomb, whose light Tayo's grandmother sees even in her semiblindness during bomb testing in New Mexico:

There was no end to it [the witchery]; it knew no boundaries; and he [Tayo] had arrived at the point of convergence where the fate af all living things, and even the earth, had been laid. From the jungles of his dreaming he recognized why the Japanese voices had merged with Laguna voices, with Josiah's voice and Rocky's voice; the lives of cultures and worlds were drawn in flat dark lines on fine light sand, converging in the middle of witchery's final ceremonial sand painting. From that time on, human beings were one clan again, united by the fate the destroyers planned for all of them, for all living things; united by a circle of death that devoured people in cities twelve thousand miles away, victims who had never . . . seen the delicate colors of the rocks which boiled up their slaughter. (*C*, 257–58)

In both novels, the division of the self in the main characters has to do with their separation from the earth, which is seen as the Mother. Allen says in an essay that the essential nature of femininity is associated "with the creative power of thought," thought of the kind that produces "mountains, lakes, creatures and philosophical/sociological systems." She warns, however, that "it is not in the mind of the Pueblo to simply equate in primitive modes earth-bearing-grain with woman-bearing-child."[38] What Tayo experiences is a reunification of himself with this creative power, which at the same time is also a reunification of the world around him. According to Allen, the normal behavior for a Laguna, both male and female, is that which society ordinarily associates with motherhood—that of nurturing and caring. In fact, these characteristics are even more prominent in males than in females.[39]

When the young Laguna men in Silko's novel go to war, they take on the traits of the white men, who do not value nurturing and caring, which the men also come to associate with being feminine. The young Lagunas come back particularly estranged from their native land and community and attempt to separate out those parts of themselves which the whites see as feminine. In doing so they also project the attributes of nurturing and caring exclusively onto women, devaluing both women and themselves. Their attitude toward Native American women is no longer respectful. They seek relationships with white women to enhance their status. As one Laguna veteran puts it: "They took our land, they took everything! So let's get our hands on white women!" (*C*, 57). The veterans invent profane stories of sexual conquest, which they substitute for the old sacred stories of unity. They have gotten caught up in and do the work of the witchery. In this case it further works to destroy the base of the culture, which is centered in the women. As Allen has pointed out, the degrading of the status of Native American women within their own culture was a tactic used by the white colonizers to destroy and conquer.[40]

In *The Woman Who Owned the Shadows* Allen, too, documents the loss of connection to the Mother—and the consequent division of self—with evil:

> The lake had dried up after the war, when so many soldiers came home, uncleansed, changed. . . . Wanting things they'd never had. Hating themselves and their futility they had begun to kill themselves and each other. Wanting to be done with the old ways, the holy things, they had lately begun to hate the Spider, to ask why their God was not a man. (p. 152)

Silko illustrates another way of cutting oneself off from the Mother in her novel. She shows how Tayo's aunt follows a kind of Ck'o'yo' magic, of which the old stories speak, by allowing the Christian concept of the individual soul to take precedence over the good of the group. Silko shows the divisiveness coming from the Christian concepts embedded in her culture: "Christianity separated the people from themselves; it tried to crush the single clan name, encouraging each person to stand alone, because Jesus Christ would save only the individual soul; Jesus Christ was not like the Mother who loved and cared for them as her children, as her family" (*C*, 70).

In Allen's *The Woman Who Owned the Shadows*, the quarrel and subsequent separation of Corn Woman and Sun Woman forms the central mythic antagonism. In the novel, the sisters are called "double women" (*WOS*, 2), and Allen parallels their story to Ephanie's. Ephanie is separated from herself—she is herself a Double Woman comprised of warring parts: "She wished she could tear out the monstrous other in her, reveal or find the one within that matched her, loving, passionate, wild and throbbing" (p. 132).

Ephanie has lost her connection to the Guadalupe community and the traditions that have sustained them. Being only part Guadalupe, she is caught between cultures—accepted neither as Guadalupe nor as white. In her torment to discover who she is, Ephanie says:

> One thing she could not go back to, though she had tried symbolically, in dreams, in books, was the old heathen tradition. She had never been to a masked dance. She had not been allowed. Even her mother had not been there since she was a small child, taken by Grandma Sylvia, Shimanna, across the spaces between one village and the next, around the lake that was no longer there, to the square to see the katsinas, the gods, enter and bowing, stepping, dance, the spruce collars dipping and swaying gravely with their steps.
>
> "I never saw them," she said quiet, wistful, "because they left, and left me out."
>
> When Sylvia left, when Ephanie's mother grew up and married out as well, those doors had closed. (*WOS*, 148)

Besides her difficulties with her Guadalupe heritage, Ephanie also has difficulty meeting the non-Indians' stereotyped expectations of her. They expected her to be an "Indian maiden" who was "noble . . . wise . . . and exotic" (*WOS*, 66) when, in fact, she was just like other women who had gone to college and been involved in political activities. They just made her feel as if she didn't belong.

Ephanie, Allen's main character, experiences her division from self, from the land, the Mother, differently from Tayo. Because she is a woman, from a traditionally female-centered culture, her separation results in her cutting "herself off from the sweet spring of her own being" (*WOS*, 203). Like the creator sisters of the ancient story who complement one another as they go about their tasks, Ephanie has a best friend as she grows up in Guadalupe—a Chicana named Elena. They were so close they were like twins: "Because Elena's gold-tinged hair looked dark in the photograph's light, no one could say which was Elena, which Ephanie. With each other they were each one doubled. They were thus complete" (p. 22).

However, when they are nine, the nuns find out they have been "playing . . . between each other's legs" (*WOS*, 13) and warn them of the seriousness of their offense. After the nuns tell Elena's mother, Elena has to tell Ephanie that they cannot see each other anymore.

> Ephanie sat. Stunned. Mind empty. Stomach a cold cold stone. The hot sun blazed on her head. She felt sick. She felt herself shrinking within. Understood, wordlessly, exactly what Elena was saying. How she could understand what Ephanie had not understood. That they were becoming lovers. That they were in love. That their loving had to stop. To end. That she was falling. Had fallen. Would not recover from the fall, smashing, the rocks. That they were in her, not on the ground. (*WOS*, 30)

Later at the convent school, Ephanie watches as two nuns fall in love and are joyous in each other's presence in an otherwise joyless and somber place. However, when one of the nuns is sent away, the somberness returns and the girls lament the loss of love and happiness. Step by step, Ephanie learns to distrust herself and her love for other women.

When she is twelve, Ephanie falls from a tree when she is challenged by her cousin Stephen to jump from a rope attached to it. She slips and is seriously injured—two broken ribs and a punctured lung, which collapses. She feels she has been tricked and betrayed by Stephen, and like the loss of her relationship with Elena, this "fall" causes her much pain, both psychically and physically: "After she fell the sun went out. . . . [She] [l]earned to prance and priss, and did not notice the change, the fear behind it. The rage. And did not ever say aloud, not even in her own mind, what it was all about" (*WOS*, 203). The tree from which she falls becomes the symbol of her "drought of the spirit." It was "lying, against the ground, split in two"—"dying, all filthy and rotting and dying" (pp. 132–33). This "fall" negates the Christian Garden of Eden story in which woman causes the fall; here it is clearly a male who causes the fall.

Ephanie begins to put all of her energy into becoming a "lady." Here her Catholicism combines with other pressures to force her to be "alien" to herself. Her Catholic-school experience tries to train her to be the Euro-American ideal of womanhood:

> Long, empty, polished corridors. Silent white faces of women whose whole heads and bodies were encased in black heavy fabric. Whose rosaries hanging dark and heavy down their legs clinked with every quiet step they took. Of those white faces, almost always unsmiling. Of those white hands that never touched a child. Of those white faces smiling, tight and stiff, as though that simple expression caused great pain. Who said she must pray. Must ask to be forgiven. . . . Must sit quietly at the table. And never ask for more. Who must eat when told, sleep when told, wake when told, play when told, work when told, study when told, piss when told, shit when told, and must never never use too much paper to wipe her butt. Her tiny child's butt. (*WOS*, 154)

Part of herself is at war with the other, trying to kill that loving part which had transgressed in Euro-American culture: "She felt rise within her words and pictures, understandings and interpretations that were not hers, not her, alien, monstrous, other than her, in her, that wanted her dead, wanted her to kill, to destroy whatever was of meaning or comfort to her" (*WOS*, 132).

Ephanie had learned to doubt herself and her love for other women. She "abandons" herself—she never again believes in herself: "I was going to be a hero, before I got sidetracked, she thought. I was going to be full of life and action. I wasn't going to be the one who lived alone, afraid of the world. Elena and I, we were going to do brave things in our lives. And we were going to do them together" (*WOS*, 204).

Of lesbianism in traditional Indian cultures, Allen says that because young men and women were often separated from the large group for extended periods, same-sex relationships "were probably common."[41] However, besides this opportunity, there were also those women whose orientation toward other women was a matter of "Spirit direction."[42] In the case of the Lakota (Sioux—part of Allen's heritage), such a woman would have dreamed of Double Woman, and from then on she would be a skilled craftsperson, doing both women's and men's work. According to a Lakota account, a "Double Woman dreamer" could act "like a crazy woman"—"deceptively," promiscuously, and such women are known to "cause all the men who stand near them to become possessed."[43] This account points out the power and special burden that was considered to accompany this kind of dream—a power that was highly respected by the Lakota—and it also mentions a ritual that two women who were Double Woman dreamers might carry out to "become united by the power of the Deity."[44] The Lakotas would have considered a woman who dreamed of the moon spirit, Double Woman, to be a sacred person or *wakan*. According to Allen, such a woman would have been a "medicine woman in a special sense. She probably was a participant in the Spirit . . . of an Entity or a Deity who was particularly close to earth during the Goddess period."[45] Allen goes on to say that "essentially a woman's spiritual way is dependent on the kind of power she possesses, the kind of Spirit to whom she is attached, and the tribe to which she belongs. She is required to follow the lead of Spirits and to carry out the tasks they assign her."[46] However, as Walter Williams has noted, "It is common for people to claim reluctance to fulfill their spiritual duty no matter what vision appears to them. Becoming any kind of sacred person involves taking on various social responsibilities and burdens."[47]

It is also true that by "interpreting the result of the vision as being the work of a spirit, the vision quest frees the person from feeling responsibility for his [or her] transformation."[48] Allen describes this belief in a transforming spirit in an excerpt from her novel, *Raven's Road.* The protagonist Allie Hawker recalls her initiation into lesbian sex by her female army captain:

> She stood, drawing Allie to her until their breasts touched, until their breasts fell into the softness of each other. Then slowly, deliberately, the captain kissed Allie, and that was all there was to it, and just like that, swiftly and silently as a deer pauses a moment then vanishes into the bush, Allie was taken by that twilight world, made a citizen of it, an outcast who forever would belong to wilderness, and there would be at home.
>
> They had stories about it, the Indian people. Some of them, not her tribe, but her friends, had told her about Deer Woman, how she would come to a dance, so beautiful, so enchanting. She would choose you to dance with, circling the drum slowly, circling, circling in the light that blazed darkly from the tall fires that ringed the dance ground; she would dance with you, her elbow just touching yours, her shawl spread carefully around her shoulders and arms, held with breathtaking perfect precision over her cocked right arm, torso making just the right sideward bow, tiny steps perfect in their knowing of the drum. She would dance you, dance into you, holding your gaze with her eyes, for if your eyes looked down at her feet you would see her hooves and the spell

would be broken. And after a time she would incline her head, say, perhaps, come, and you would follow. Away from the fire and the dancing, into the brush, into the night. And you would not return, or if you did, it would be as somebody else.[49]

In *The Woman Who Owned the Shadows*, Ephanie has not followed her spiritual way. As a child she had had a strong sense of herself as brave and free, which she had given up as an adolescent. However, the spirits did not give up on her that easily, and later, when she is an adult, her friend Teresa tells her that "the spirits" are trying to tell her "something important." Again, she tries to avoid hearing their message. Finally, they tell her "to investigate some trouble that has been going on for a long time" (*WOS*, 62). It is the vision of herself rejecting the role which the spirits had given her that she finally remembers. However, before she begins to understand what has happened, she listens to her warring self and tries to hang herself. According to Williams, this action is not particularly unusual for one who resisted her spiritual duty. Williams tells a story of a Lakota boy in the 1880s "who tried to resist following his vision from Double Woman."[50] After his rebellion, the boy committed suicide.

Ephanie, however, hanging from a ceiling pipe, is able to cut herself loose, and this subsequent third fall jars her from her death wish into an understanding and an appreciation of life: "After she had begun to weep, quietly, with relief, with sorrow, with comprehension. Of what had driven her. The grief, the unbearable anguish, the loneliness. The rage. She realized how grateful she was. For air. For life. For pain. Even for the throbbing pain in her throat" (*WOS*, 164).

This fall duplicates the fall of Sky Woman (a Seneca origin myth and the title of a section in *The Woman Who Owned the Shadows*), who with the help of some animals turned what should have been a fall to her death into life, populating a new world. In Ephanie's case, the fall begins a process of healing and reclaiming what is hers. She, like Tayo, must separate the truth from the lies—see how her life could be made one again. Ephanie must see how the Catholicism had acted to reinforce the Euro-American values about gender and sexuality. Euro-American society holds that there are only two genders—male and female; many traditional Native American societies offer another alternative for both men and women—a position "with clearly recognized and accepted social status, often based on a secure place in the tribal mythology."[51] In the Laguna tradition, for example, one of the creator sisters was changed to a male so that the Christians could understand how the creators could give birth to the people. Ephanie must see that her traditional culture would have seen her desire to live with and love women as a spiritual calling. They would have urged her to use the special powers she would have been given by her acceptance of her spiritual duty for the good of the tribe and her clan.

The Woman Who Owned the Shadows is patterned into sections in which the contemporary story parallels the mythic accounts at the beginning of each section. Part 2, for instance, begins with a prologue entitled "Rite of Exorcism: (The Spruce Dress)," which promises that Ephanie will recover. In the prologue, the spirits join the patient, aiding her with their power: "She dwells with me." The patient with their help becomes "one who slays alien gods," thereby "sweeping away the sickness" (*WOS*, 51–52) until she can accept the gifts of the gods. In the contemporary story, part of her healing comes when she recovers her own vision of herself and realizes her strong connection to the ancient tribal power of the medicine women:

> And she understood. For those women, so long lost to her, who she had longed and wept for, unknowing, were the double women, the women who never married, who held power like the Clanuncle, like the power of the priests, the medicine men. Who were not mothers, but who were sisters, born of the same mind, the same spirit. They called each other sister. They were called Grandmother by those who called on them for aid, for knowledge, for comfort, for care. (*WOS*, 211)

Like Tayo, she comes to understand how "spirit, creatures and land can occupy a unified whole."[52] According to Williams, the role of the man or woman who took on qualities of the other sex was to act as a mediator not only "between the sexes but between the psychic and the physical—between the spirit and the flesh. . . . They have double vision, with the ability to see more clearly than a single gender perspective can provide."[53] But this gift of the spirits was also a burden, as Ephanie comes to realize. If her understanding is doubled, in times of trouble there is also double pain and the task of healing:

> The curse laid upon her flesh was her gift as well. She knew that with certainty. That she was always, unendingly, aware of the pain. Of the people. Of the air. Of the water. Of the beasts and the birds. She could not escape that knowledge. In every eye, in every mind, the pain lay, blossoming in bewilderment, in blood. They never knew why they suffered. Nor did she. . . . And they also understood the gift, the curse, some of them. . . . They thought she could make them well. (*WOS*, 185)

As her room fills with the spirits of the Grandmothers, she is able to join them in their dance and listen to their message. They tell her: "There are no curses. There are only descriptions of what creations there will be" (*WOS*, 212). A spirit woman shows Ephanie her destiny—how she fits into the Double Woman pattern: "'It is the sign and the order of the power that informs this life and leads back to Shipap. Two face outward, two inward, the sign of doubling, of order and balance, of the two, the twins, the doubleminded world in which you have lived,' she chanted" (p. 207). Ephanie is told to pass the story—the information—on to the Euro-American woman, Teresa, "the one who waits" (p. 210), and presumably on to us, the readers. By accepting her spiritual duty, Ephanie is healed and the story is complete.

By allowing the reader to participate in the curing ceremonies of the novels by following the main characters in their own restoration of balance, both Allen and Silko seek to restore balance to the community-at-large. Through this the reader is reminded of the power of storytelling and the responsibility of each human to the community. As the healer, Ku'oosh, in Silko's novel says: "But you know, grandson, this world is fragile," Silko goes on to explain that the fragility is like "spider webs woven across paths through sand hills," which connects us all and in which we are all entangled. It is our responsibility to choose our actions and words with "great patience and love" because of this entanglement (*C*, 36–37).

Further, if as Judy Grahn says in her comment on the back cover of Allen's *The Woman Who Owned the Shadows*, "you come with an honest heart," the novel enables the non-Indian reader to begin to see from a non-Euro-American perspective. To begin to change the Euro-American vision of disconnectedness to one of connectedness would be a "curing" indeed. As Williams notes, a most important function of a curing is a "healing of the mind."[54] Although the novel ends with Ephanie's understanding of her connection to her heritage, and although the reader does not see how it will affect her life, Allen's novel is also an important offering to Native American lesbians. She has shown a connection that present-day lesbians might make to a special spiritual heritage and role played by such women in Native American cultures. As Allen says, "It all has to do with spirit, with restoring an awareness of our spirituality as gay people."[55]

In both novels, the healing of the main character occurs when they are able to reconnect with the female principle, exemplified in Thought Woman and her sisters and consisting particularly of nurturing and caring, life and strength. Ephanie recovers the ancient qualities of woman who was seen as "strong and powerful," balancing the ancient qualities of man who was seen as having "transient or transitory" qualities.[56] This balancing of qualities where "woman-ness is not of less value than manness"[57] allows both the individual and tribe to continue and prosper. The telling of the stories allows the listeners/readers to visualize how their experiences fit into the great web of being, the patterns of life. The stories and the experiences become one, leading to harmony and healing.[58] By using these journeys as models, we can begin to see how to reclaim our female deities and "the wholistic, pacifistic and spirit-based"[59] principles of our grandmothers in order to bring together mind/spirit and body, inanimate and animate, to ensure continuance of the earth as well as the individual.

THREE

The West African Tradition and the Female Principle: The Writings of Audre Lorde and Alice Walker

ALTHOUGH many scholars have commented on the continuities of West African tradition in African-American lives, they disagree about the extent of that continuity in the lives of current African-Americans. Yet most agree that vestiges of West African cultural traditions have been found in African-American life, particularly in religion, folklore, storytelling, language, music, dance, artwork, in crafts such as basketry, pottery, metalworking, carpentry, and clothmaking, and in patterns of cooperative work.[1] August Meir and Elliott Rudwick point to class and regional differences in the retention of these vestiges but comment that both the black civil rights movement and "the rise of African nations to independence and international influence make larger numbers of blacks genuinely proud of their West African heritage."[2]

Alice Walker and Audre Lorde consciously explore the effects of West African diasporic traditions in much of their writings.

For the purposes of this study, I have used selected pieces to illustrate this exploration. As black women writers, Walker's and Lorde's West African heritage and its intersection with the Euro-American tradition become a major part of their writing, but they respond very differently to this intersection. Walker looks at the traditions of West African culture but rejects much in both African-diasporic tradition and in Euro-American tradition. Instead, she creates a model for a "womanist"[3] tradition in her novels, *The Color Purple (CP)*, and *The Temple of My Familiar (TF)*, while delineating spiritual journeys to healing. Lorde draws from the female African-diasporic tradition in tracing her spiritual journey to healing. The result is similar to the healing journeys that Silko and Allen took via their novels, drawing on Laguna Pueblo traditions. If literature can be said to allow us visions of the possible, then Walker's novels allow just such a vision, and Lorde's essay, "Uses of the Erotic: The Power of the Erotic," shows the theory and poetics of the vision. Taken together and coming from African-American perspectives that take West African traditions into account, they provide us with models for healing similar to the novels of Silko and Allen.

Both Walker and Lorde make specific use of West African elements. Walker uses them in her short stories, in *The Temple of My Familiar*, and in what she calls her "historical"[4] novel, *The Color Purple*, in which she places the sister of the main character in Africa as a missionary. Lorde makes frequent references to West African cultures in her poetry, particularly *The Black Unicorn (BU)* and *Our Dead Behind Us (ODBU)*, and in her autobiographical work *Zami (Z)* and her essays. Both seek to remind their readers of some of the positive aspects of West African culture and of the importance of retaining those aspects. Walker also weighs some of the negative aspects of West African culture and finds it wanting, freeing her to begin to put together womanist traditions. Lorde points out that "there are no new ideas still waiting in the wings to save us as women as human. There are only old and forgotten ones, new combinations, extrapolations and recognitions from within ourselves—along with the renewed courage to try them out."[5]

Both Walker and Lorde can be said to use these "extrapolations and recognitions" to create "new combinations" of African-diasporic, African, and American traditions. Like Silko and Allen, they show that all stories are part of a continuing story. Walker and Lorde also use the African traditions to remind us that there are other alternatives to the Euro-American perspective, particularly the Euro-American perspective on the role of women. While Walker creates a new perspective after exploring the role of women in both patriarchal African and Euro-American traditions, Lorde draws on African goddesses and warrior-women as models of strength both in her poetry and her prose.

Lorde, like Allen and Silko, draws on an ancient, holistic culture in which plants, animals, humans, and inanimate beings are all connected in the Spirit. African-American scholar John Mbiti's description of the underlying world view of African cultures is very close to that given for Laguna culture: "Because traditional [African] religions permeate all departments of life, there is no formal distinction between the sacred and the secular, between the religious and non-religious, between the spiritual and material areas of life."[6] Language and words are important in African tradition just as they are in Laguna tradition: "There is mystical power in words. . . . Formal 'curses' and 'blessings' are extremely potent; and people may travel long distances to receive formal blessings and all are extra careful to avoid formal curses."[7] The difference between Lorde's (and Walker's as well) use of African traditions and between Silko's and Allen's is one of distance and time. The Laguna Pueblo tribe to which Silko and Allen belong and in which they grew up, even as members with a mixed heritage, has occupied its particular place in New Mexico since the thirteenth century. The continuity of the way of knowing and understanding that is connected to that particular place existed even long before that. However, as part of the African-diasporic tradition, Lorde and

Walker have been cut off from their original place and way of knowing for hundreds of years. This and the fact that the different African traditions have melded in the African-diasporic traditions make it difficult both for scholars and for African-American writers to trace specific African-American traditions to African traditions.[8] There are, however, stories that have been handed down orally for generations, changing and blending cultures.

A central concept in African as well as other holistic cultures is the power of the word, which can be used to conjure sickness, health, or any number of other creations. In African culture, according to Janheinz Jahn, the duty of people, living or dead, is to use their "active intelligence" ("knowledge of the nature and relationships of the world")[9] to wake up the sleeping forces in everything through the word, which is "the life force, which produces all life." Since people have "power over the word," they order "the life force."[10] He continues: "No 'medicines', 'talismans', 'magic horns', no, not even poisons are effective without the word. If they are not 'conjured', they are of no use in themselves. They have no activity at all. Only the intelligence of the word frees these forces and makes them effective."[11] People are placed in a "hierarchy . . . according to the force of each one's word. The word itself is force. . . . There is no 'harmless', noncommittal word. Every word has its consequences."[12] It is the responsibility of individuals to use carefully this power of words to activate selectively the power in everything using their understanding of relationships.

Jahn also links this power in the word with the writing of poetry. He notes that when African-Americans were freed and "spoke the first *free* word that they were allowed to speak in their acquired or inherited European languages with that same degree of commitment proper to the word in African culture, . . . [they] transformed the European word into an African word."[13] He maintains that African-Americans continued the tradition of "the central significance of the word."[14] Therefore, "to command things with words is to practice 'magic'. And to practice word magic is to write poetry."[15] Poetry has the power not only to create but to mythically transform. Jahn notes that "the word creates images upon images and transforms them and the poet with them."[16] An example of this idea appears in the epilogue to *Zami,* in which Lorde says of the writing of *Zami:* "We carry our traditions with us. . . . Recreating in words the women who helped give me substance. *Ma-Liz, DeLois . . . and Afrekete, her youngest daughter, the mischievous linguist, trickster, best-beloved, whom we must all become*" (Z, 255). The suggestion here is not only a re-creation of the images of these women in the minds of the readers, but of a transformation of both the women, the readers, and the poet herself toward a becoming of Afrekete.

To make a comparison with the Laguna Pueblo, a passage particularly applicable to this concept of the importance of the word and one's responsibility to it is the one in Silko's *Ceremony,* in which Ku'oosh, the medicine man, explains the importance of the word to the Lagunas:

> "But you know, grandson, this world is fragile." . . . It took a long time to explain the fragility and intricacy because no word exists alone, and the reason for choosing each word had to be explained with a story about why it must be said this certain way. That was the responsibility that went with being human, old Ku'oosh said, the story behind each word must be told so there could be no mistake in the meaning of what had been said; and this demanded great patience and love. (*C*, 36–37)

As in the African tradition, the responsibility of being human is to activate the things or events by using the appropriate words in an appropriate manner in the right context. Tayo failed to use his "active intelligence" when he cursed the rain. He forgot that because he was of the water clan, he was responsible to the tribe for the rain-producing clouds. But Tayo's words do not cause the drought; his words are only a symptom of the disunity of the tribe brought on in part by the contact with white civilization and its wars. The old medicine man asks Tayo to explain what happened, and Tayo illustrates the Laguna belief in the power of words and the grave responsibility that comes with that power. The old medicine man fears that Tayo has come back into the village after killing an enemy without first purifying himself. This might be the cause of Tayo's illness and would also bring harm to the community. Tayo, however, knows that he has not killed an enemy, but believes that his words have brought on the drought: "The effects were everywhere in the cloudless sky, on the dry brown hills, shrinking skin and hide taut over sharp bone" (*C*, 37). His belief, in part, has made him ill.

Like Silko and Allen, Lorde uses story and the "mystical power" in words—power which is lost when those words connect only to reason as is taught in a Euro-American tradition—to create new possibilities, new ceremonies. In this context, Walker's and Lorde's written creations of models of journeys to healing can be seen as conjuring in the African tradition. For Lorde, poetry expresses freedom and change by connecting emotion and reason unified in the Black mother. In an essay entitled "Poetry Is Not a Luxury," she writes:

> The white fathers told us: I think, therefore I am. The Black mother within each of us—the poet—whispers in our dreams: I feel, therefore I can be free. Poetry coins the language to express and charter this revolutionary demand, the implementation of that freedom. . . . In the forefront of our move toward change, there is only poetry to hint at possibility made real. Our poems formulate the implications of themselves, what we feel within and dare make real (or bring action into accordance with), our fears, our hopes, our most cherished terrors.[17]

Here, Lorde is discussing not a disregard for intellect, but an integration of that old mind/body split—speaking from intellect as well as emotion—the "Black mother within each of us"—which corresponds to the creative intelligence of Silko's and Allen's Thought Woman. In this context, the individual responsibility is to connect carefully with that creative intelligence and thereby to create visions for a changed world:

> For there are no new ideas. There are only new ways of making them felt—of examining what those ideas feel like being lived on Sunday morning at 7 a.m., after brunch, during wild love, making war, giving birth, mourning our dead—while we suffer the old longings, battle the old warnings and fears of being silent and impotent and alone, while we taste new possibilities and strengths.[18]

Elsewhere, Lorde calls this "Black mother within us" the power of the erotic. She defines the erotic as a "resource within each of us that lies in a deeply female and spiritual plane, firmly rooted in the power of our unexpressed or unrecognized feeling."[19] It is "an assertion of the lifeforce of women; of that creative energy empowered, the knowledge and use of which we are now reclaiming in our language, our history, our dancing, our loving, our work, our lives."[20]

In her poem "125th Street and Abomey," Lorde marks the coming together of the Euro-American and African-American cultures and the strength she derives from her African roots. Having returned to New York City after an African visit, Lorde recalls the impact that her visit had upon her as she walks through the New York snow. Lorde evokes the goddess of Abomey, Seboulisa, an aspect of MawuLisa who is the creator of all, like the Laguna Thought Woman. She says she carries Seboulisa "printed inside the back of my head" (*BU*, 12). She remembers the offerings she has made to her ("I poured on the red earth in your honor"). As with the Laguna, story and sense of place ("of brown rain in nim trees") are part of Lorde's connection to the Goddess, even though she is "[h]alf earth and time" away (*BU*, 12).

Lorde identifies with the woman warriors of Dahomey ("like my warrior sisters/who rode in defense of your queendom"), needing to be strong like they are in her time of need (her mastectomy). She pledges to continue doing the Mother's work as a poet-warrior although she is "severed"[21] from Africa ("laughing our name into echo/all the world shall remember"; *BU*, 13). Like Allen, who, after the model of the Goddess in the guise of the spider "mend[s] the tear with string,"[22] Lorde also identifies herself with the Goddess Seboulisa to do her bidding. Lorde's "laugh" is the "laugh" of the outlaw woman, for Euro-American culture has no place for a black goddess, nor a black warrior-woman—an Amazon.[23]

The last poem in *The Black Unicorn* is called "Solstice" and is a prayer for renewal. The first two stanzas are a confession which, like the stories in Silko's *Ceremony*, document a turning away from the gods, from spiritual observance:

> We forgot to water the plantain shoots
> when our houses were full of borrowed meat
>
> . . . . .
>
> Our skins are empty.
> They have been vacated by the spirits
> who are angered by our reluctance
> to feed them.
>
> (*BU*, 117)

The third stanza begins the renewal with a reference to a snake being renewed by shedding its skin[24] ("My skin is tightening/soon I shall shed it"), and the fourth reaffirms the cyclical connections to the gods in a litany that is a prayer for remembrance so that the drought of the spirit and the land need not come again:

> May I never remember reasons
> for my spirit's safety
> may I never forget
> the warning of my woman's flesh
> weeping at the new moon

may I never lose
that terror
that keeps me brave
May I owe nothing
that I cannot repay.

(*BU*, 118)

Like Silko and Allen, Lorde connects with a female tradition: she notes that there have been black warrior queens, freedom fighters like Harriet Tubman, and, today, market guilds made up of women in West Africa—all of whom form "a history of the use and sharing of power": "We have a tradition of closeness and mutual care and support, from the all-woman courts of the Queen Mothers of Benin to the present-day Sisterhood of the Good Death, a community of old women in Brazil who, as escaped slaves, provided escape and refuge for other enslaved women, and who now care for each other."[25]

The tradition Lorde cites includes the African-diasporic tradition in America (Harriet Tubman), in Brazil, and in present-day West Africa, showing her belief in a common tradition. However, the tradition of the Black mother she cites is not only for women, nor only for black women. While Lorde believes that "the Black mother exists more in women," she also exists in men. Like Silko and Allen, Lorde believes that the Black mother represents a kind of "humanity" which we all have, but which men often deny. Men "have taken a position against that piece of themselves, and it is a world position, a position throughout time." Because of men's denial of that part of themselves, Lorde says "the human race is evolving through women."[26] For the human race to evolve, reason and emotion must come back together.

As a lesbian poet identifying with the Goddess as muse, Lorde is also demonstrating a different kind of creativity than many women writers seem to display. Such feminist critics as Susan Gubar have noted that women writers of the nineteenth century had to overcome the idea that men were the creators, using the pen (penis) to interact with the female muse to create the female product—the writing on the page. Gubar goes on to say that "like their nineteenth-century foremothers, twentieth-century women often describe the emergence of their talent as an infusion from a male master rather than inspiration from or sexual commerce with a female muse."[27] This seems not to be true of some lesbian or woman-centered writers like Silko, Allen, Walker, and Lorde, and this new model of female creativity may be one of their greatest contributions.

All of these writers see themselves as directly drawing on the female principle, often in the guise of the Goddess. Both Silko and Allen as storytellers become the Goddess in their act of creativity. Both illustrate the importance of "sexual commerce with a female muse"—Silko through the restoration of Tayo to health, partly through his sexual relations with Night Swan and later Ts'eh. Tayo is then able to create/tell his own story, restoring him to normalcy within his group. Allen illustrates what happens to her character when she refuses the inspiration of the Goddess—she is "shut off from her own sweet self," from her own creativity, unable to tell her story. Walker becomes a "medium" for the voices of her characters so that her "readers . . . can recognize their common literary ancestors (gardeners, quilt makers, grandmothers, root workers, and women who wrote autobiographies) and to name each other as a community of inheritors." As Marjorie Pryse says, Walker becomes a "metaphorical conjure woman."[28]

Lorde becomes a character in her own story, always inspired by the female principle, the women, and her sexual encounter with Kitty/Afrekete marks her for life as a devotee of the Goddess, but also as one through whom the Goddess speaks—a becoming of the Goddess. In her later poems, she grows fierce as she again dons the warrior guise of the Goddess to fight for her love, the women, her community, Africa, and the planet with the word. For example, the poem "Outlines" ends with a stanza that compares her battle to live and love as half of an interracial, lesbian couple with the continuity of life on the planet. She brings together issues of race, gender, and the right to live and love as one pleases with the final holocaust:

> I trace the curve of your jaw
> with a lover's finger
> knowing the hardest battle
> is only the first
> how to do what we need for our living
> with honor and in love
> we have chosen each other
> and the edge of each other's battles
> the war is the same
> if we lose
> someday women's blood will congeal
> upon a dead planet
> if we win
> there is no telling.
>
> (*ODBU*, 13)

For Lorde, heterosexism ("a belief in the inherent superiority of one form of loving over all others and thereby the right to dominance") and homophobia ("a terror surrounding feelings of love for members of the same sex and thereby a hatred of those feelings in others") are crucial parts of what is destroying the earth.[29] As Lorde says: "It is not who I sleep with that defines the quality of these acts, not what we do together, but what life-statements I am led to make as the nature and effect of my erotic relationships percolate throughout my life and my being. As a deep lode of our erotic lives and knowledge, how does our sexuality enrich us and empower our actions?"[30]

Furthermore, when she speaks of parenting in an essay called "Turning the Beat Around: Lesbian Parenting 1986," she speaks with a voice outside the usual construct of motherhood, as seen through the gaze of the patriarchy; she speaks "with the urgency born of my consciousness as a Lesbian and a Black African Caribbean american woman staked out in white racist sexist homophobic america" but believing in the possibilities: "And if we can keep this earth spinning and remain upon it long enough, the future belongs to us and to our children because we are fashioning it with a vision rooted in human possibility and growth, a vision that does not shrivel before adversity."[31]

Like Silko and Allen, she documents the destruction of the earth, which is making it inhospitable to human life:

> The broad water drew us, and the space
> growing enough green to feed ourselves over two seasons
> now sulfur fuels burn in New Jersey
> and when I wash my hands at the garden hose
> the earth runs off bright yellow
> the bridge disappears
> only a lowering sky
> in transit.[32]

In all this it is the African Goddess in her many guises who informs her work and to whom she has dedicated her life:

> I have written your names on my cheekbone
> dreamed your eyes   flesh my epiphany
> most ancient goddesses   hear me
> enter
> I have not forgotten your worship
> nor my sisters
> nor the sons of my daughters
> my children watch for your print
> in their labors
> and they say Aido Hwedo is coming.
>
> . . . . .
>
> Rainbow Serpent who must not go
> unspoken

I have offered up the safety of separations
sung the spirals of power
and what fills the spaces
before power unfolds or flounders
in desirable nonessentials
I am a Black woman   stripped down
and praying
my whole life has been an altar
worth its ending
and I say Aido Hwedo is coming.[33]

Walker, too, connects homophobia to the destruction of human life. She says that

perhaps black women writers and nonwriters should say, simply, whenever black lesbians are being put down, held up, messed over, and generally told their lives should not be encouraged, *We are all lesbians.* For surely it is better to be thought a lesbian, and to say and write your life exactly as you experience it, than to be a token "pet" black woman for those whose contempt for our autonomous existence makes them a menace to human life.[34]

Clearly, she sees herself as a woman outside the confines of control by men, and "lesbian" is a word which describes that empowerment. For her, being connected to all things and realizing that connectedness is more important than distinctions made on the basis of sexuality. In fact, it is the connectedness which allows the understanding; in a recent book of essays, Walker describes herself as "homospiritual"—connecting to the spirit in all things.[35]

Like Lorde, Alice Walker also uses the African tradition in her writings. In a way similar to Silko and Allen, she documents the spiritual journey of reclaiming one's heritage or connecting with Lorde's "Black mother within" in *The Color Purple.* Written in the epistolary form, *The Color Purple* consists of the letters of two sisters: Celie, who writes from the South first to

God and then to her sister Nettie in Africa, while Nettie writes to Celie. This novel is in the tradition of Zora Neale Hurston who, as Barbara Christian and others note, is a "spiritual ancestor"[36] of contemporary black women writers. Hurston, who explored her native African-American culture in her anthropological works such as *Of Mules and Men,* was one of the first to write fiction about the black woman's relationship to her own black community rather than about her relationship to the white community.[37] She uses black language and incorporates black folklore and custom into her fiction, particularly *Their Eyes Were Watching God.*

It is this African-American tradition—a tradition of a "deep sense of racial pride"[38] and concern for relationships within the black community—from which Walker writes. Her novel, in the tradition of Hurston, is told entirely in Celie's language without an outside narrator to correct the language of the character according to Euro-American standards. The use of this device allows the reader to immerse herself or himself in the world of the novel, and, like Allen's novel, *The Color Purple* seems to "get inside the reader's head"[39] in tracing Celie's spiritual journey to wholeness. Part of Celie's journey, like that of Silko's and Allen's main characters, is to reclaim what is useful from her traditional heritage—her West African roots—and to rid herself of the influences of the surrounding Euro-American culture, which have split that wholeness. What emerges is not West African, nor African-American, but a new compilation—"womanist," which Walker says "is to feminist as purple is to lavender."[40] Particularly pertinent to our study is Walker's expansion of this definition, in which womanist can also be seen as a synonym for lesbian:

> *Also:* A woman who loves other women, sexually and/or nonsexually. Appreciates and prefers women's culture, women's emotional flexibility (values tears as natural counterbalance of laughter), and women's strength. Sometimes loves individual men, sexually and/or nonsexually. Commit-

ted to survival and wholeness of entire people, male *and* female. Not a separatist, except periodically, for health. . . . Loves music. Loves dance. Loves the moon. *Loves* the Spirit. Loves love and food and roundness. Loves struggle. *Loves* the Folk. Loves herself. *Regardless.*[41]

To facilitate Celie's exploration of African culture, Walker has one of the main characters serve as a missionary in Africa. This device allows Celie to compare African culture with African- and Euro-American cultures and allows Walker to critique all three. Like Silko and Allen, Walker weaves in a creation myth that serves to show the reader a splitting up of the people as the initial evil. In the Laguna myth, the quarrel of the sister goddesses divided the people, but in Walker's story difference in appearance begins this separation. Through Nettie's letters, Celie learns that in the distant past the Olinka women began to have "colorless" babies, which they first killed and then, when there were too many, drove off into the woods. Thus began the antagonism between "whites" and "blacks." Later the Africans sold their own people into slavery: "The Africans throwed out the white Olinka peoples for how they look. They throwed out the rest of us, all who became slaves, for how us act" (*CP*, 232).

Celie says that the white children were so angry about "being unwanted" that "they gon kill each other off" and "gon kill off a lot of other folk too who got some color. In fact, they gon kill off so much of the earth and the colored that everybody gon hate them just like they hate us today" (*CP*, 232–33). Some of the Africans believe that the whites will become the new "serpents" or scapegoats, that they in turn will be replaced by another group on the basis of how they look or act, and that this scapegoating of a group of people will go on forever. Others, however, "think . . . the only way to stop making somebody the serpent [evil] is for everybody to accept everybody else as a child of God, or one mother's children, no matter what they look like or how they act" (p. 233).

Again, the message is that all people are the children of "one mother" and that by destroying each other we destroy ourselves and the earth. *The Color Purple*, like Silko's and Allen's novels, which go back to the quarrels of Thought Woman's sisters and the people turning away from the Mother, builds on this ancient separation of African peoples to show the parallels in today's world and what must be done by the characters and, by implication, the readers to change to values that are important for continuance. Walker delineates a womanist vision of a journey to healing, and by implication a reformed world. She also shows the reader components of a womanist spirituality.

As a woman in a patriarchal society that has little respect for women and in which worth is often measured by color—the lighter the better—Walker's main character, Celie, with her black skin, becomes what Hurston would call the mule of the world.[42] Her father marries her off to a man looking for someone to care for his four children, keep his house, and serve his sexual needs. She is literally sold into slavery as a beast of burden. Although Nettie urges her to fight back against her male oppressors, particularly her husband, Celie fears that if she does so, she will not survive. Walker shows Celie's situation as the plight of a woman without a community—as long as she is isolated, she cannot move toward Walker's womanist vision. Celie's first step, then, is to develop a supportive community and to see other models of how to be a woman.

The little support that Celie gets comes from other women—her sister before she becomes a missionary in Africa, and her husband's sister Kate, who stands up for her and gets her a new dress. Celie begins to see other models of how a woman can be when she sees a picture of Shug Avery, an independent and notorious woman singer and her husband's lover. She begins to imagine what it would be like to be Shug, "dress to kill, whirling an laughing" (*CP*, 8). Shug is the character who specifically fits Walker's definition of womanist as referring to lesbianism. She is the "woman who loves other women," but who "sometimes loves individual men."[43]

Shug becomes the connection for Celie to her husband on the first night of their marriage: "I think bout Shug Avery. I know what he doing to me he done to Shug Avery and maybe she like it. I put my arm around him" (*CP*, 13). Later, when her husband's father berates her husband for his love of Shug, Celie feels a bond for her husband—they are both in love with Shug: "Mr.____ look up at me, our eyes meet. This is the closest us ever felt" (p. 50). Shug is also the character who has a self-contained strength and capability to go against the values of the community about what a woman should be, loving herself "*regardless.*"[44] Celie follows this model, with Shug as the teacher. For instance, when Celie and Shug are discussing Celie's sexual activity with her husband, Mister/Albert, and Celie tells Shug that she never enjoys it, Shug says that Celie is "still a virgin," implying that if she has never participated in a sexual act and enjoyed it, it is like never having had sex at all. From there Shug proceeds to educate Celie by showing her how beautiful Celie's body is: "Then inside look like a wet rose." Shug helps Celie find her clitoris so that she can "love" herself (p. 69). Celie, connecting the erotic to other bodily activities, remembers the "shiver" she felt when nursing her babies—"Best part about having the babies was feeding 'em" (p. 70).

Shug is also Celie's teacher as to the integrative possibilities of love. Much later in the story, when their husbands have gone to town for the evening, Celie and Shug make love. Again they are discussing Celie's unfortunate sexual experiences with her stepfather and her husband. Celie finally says, "Nobody ever love me." Celie and Shug "kiss and kiss till us can't hardly kiss no more. Then us touch each other. . . . Then I feels something real soft and wet on my breast, feel like one of my little lost babies mouth. Way after while, I act like a little lost baby too" (*CP*, 97). For Celie, her experience with Shug is healing; she finally feels as if someone loves her for herself, and an integration takes place of the various selves that Celie has been—child, daughter, mother, and now, lover.

In Sofia, her stepson's wife, Celie finds another model for being female—that of the warrior woman who will not bow down to physical abuse from the men around her. Sofia is a "strong and ruddy looking" (*CP*, 30) woman who grew up fighting off all the male members in her family. She tells Celie to quit advising Harpo to beat her because she'll "kill him dead before I let him beat me. . . . I used to hunt game with a bow and arrow, she say" (p. 38).

However, a woman as proud and independent as Sofia without the support of a powerful community, money, or whiteness in a patriarchal, racist, classist society is also a danger to herself. By not picking her arguments carefully when she challenges the powers that be, she risks her own survival. Sofia unwisely sasses the white mayor's wife and knocks the mayor down. She ends up in prison. The lesson for Celie and other members of the black community is that fighting back in isolation can lead to discontinuity. Sofia becomes an example of what not to do, but her plight pulls both the men and women in the community together and results in Squeak (Harpo's girlfriend) reclaiming herself. While in jail, Sofia begins to act passively like Celie—"Every time they ast me to do something, Miss Celie, I act like I'm you. I jump right up and do just what they say" (*CP*, 78). The community, valuing who and what Sofia had been and fearing she will go crazy, gathers in Sofia's behalf to see if they can get her twelve-year sentence shortened. As a result of their plan and Squeak's allowing the warden to use her sexually, Sofia is let out of prison and assigned to the mayor's wife as maid. Squeak's brave action on behalf of Sofia also allows her to stand up for herself, telling everyone her name is Mary Agnes, not Squeak. Six months later Mary Agnes becomes a singer in her own right —a free and independent women in the model of Shug.

Sofia's plight also stops Celie from killing Albert. For survival purposes, the warrior woman stance needs to be tempered. As Shug says to Celie when Celie finds herself standing behind her husband Albert's chair with a razor, "Nettie be coming home before long. Don't make her have to look at you like us look at Sofia" (*CP*, 122). Shug supports Celie in helping her turn that murderous intent to sewing and reading Nettie's letters. She helps Celie see that her bond to Nettie is stronger than her need for revenge on Albert for hiding Nettie's letters. "A needle and not a razor in my hand, I think," (p. 125) Celie finally says.

For Celie, the process of going beyond survival to fulfillment and self-integration is linked to having a supportive community of women, and especially to her relationship with Shug.[45] Like Night Swan and Ts'eh in Silko's *Ceremony*, Shug is the link for Celie to the creative intelligence which is the mother, in this case the Black mother. However, Shug is not a spirit being as are Night Swan and Ts'eh, but the result for Celie is similar. Shug's sexual relationship with Celie helps reintegrate Celie—helps to put Celie's mind/spirit and body back together. She teaches Celie that love is possible, and in the process, Shug grows and changes (which the spirit people, Night Swan and Ts'eh, do not). Shug sees how she has harmed others, particularly Annie Julia, Albert's first wife, by keeping "Albert away from home a week at a time" so that Annie Julia would have to "come and beg him for money to buy groceries for the children." Shug also sees that she has treated Celie "like . . . a servant" because she was Albert's second wife (*CP*, 105). As a result of their love, both Celie and Shug grow.

Celie's love for Shug reconnects her with her physical self and the Mother within—an important step to being a self-affirming woman. Christian says that "Shug becomes the mother Celie never had, protecting her from Albert and giving her knowledge about her body and the essential spirituality of the world."[46] However, Celie almost loses that connection when Shug takes a new, younger lover. Celie becomes jealous and unhappy; the color goes out of her life. She does not know that the Black mother, whom Lorde calls "the power which rises from our deepest and nonrational knowledge," comes from within.[47] Celie thinks that because Shug left her that "happiness was just a trick.

. . . Even thought you had the trees with you. The whole earth. The stars. But look at you. When Shug left, happiness desert" (*CP*, 220).

The next step in the journey is to realize that affirmation must come from within as well as from without. During this unhappy time, Celie goes back home and gets reacquainted with Albert, who by this time has come to understand his own inner self—has connected to the Black mother within. Celie and Albert's love for Shug forms a supportive bond for both of them. Both have to learn not to place the inner power outside themselves, for as Lorde says, "[W]hen we begin to live from within outward, in touch with the power of the erotic within ourselves, and allowing that power to inform and illuminate our actions upon the world around us, then we begin to be responsible to ourselves in the deepest sense."[48] This passage is also an illustration of Lorde's view that men also have access to the the Black mother within themselves. Finally, Celie understands that Shug must follow her own journey and love in her own way: "Who am I to tell her who to love? My job just to love her good and true myself" (*CP*, 228).

Walker's portrayal of the relationship between Shug and Celie is as a love in which the each wishes the best for the other, and yet considers his or her own needs. It is not destructive but supportive of all members of the community. While it is sometimes painful, the hurt arises when the inner self is ignored. As Celie says, "[W]e all have to start somewhere if us wants to do better, and our own self is what we have to hand" (*CP*, 230).

Celie's final understanding of her inner power occurs when she realizes that she can be content with her life as it is whether Shug returns or not. Her life will not be as joyful, but it will be enough: "If she come, I be happy. If she don't, I be content. And then I figure this is the lesson I was suppose to learn" (*CP*, 240). Albert, her ex-husband, also comes to a realization of that inner power. He says, "I think us here to wonder, myself. To wonder. To ast. And that in wondering bout the big things and astin bout the big things, you learn about the little ones, almost by accident. But you never know nothing more about the big things than you start out with. The more I wonder, he say, the more I love" (p. 239).

It is also Shug who helps free Celie from the white man's god and teaches her about the god that is in everything, animate and inanimate, and how everything is connected, an important concept in Walker's womanist vision. She tells Shug, "You come into the world with God. But only them that search for it inside find it." Shug says that her "first step from the old white man was trees. Then air. Then birds. Then other people. But one day . . . it come to me: that feeling of being part of everything, not separate at all. I knew that if I cut a tree, my arm would bleed. And I laughed and I cried and I run all around the house" (*CP*, 166–67).

Shug explains that to "praise God" is to like "what you like," to notice "the color purple in a field" is to glory in life, in nature and its beauty (*CP*, 167). Glorying in life extends to making love; Christian calls Celie's and Shug's love an "initiation into a vision of sensual spirituality, which is nature's essence as symbolized in the color purple."[49] This is also the joy that Lorde explains in her essay, "Uses of the Erotic": "And that deep and irreplaceable knowledge of my capacity for joy comes to demand from all of my life that it be lived within the knowledge that such satisfaction is possible, and does not have to be called *marriage*, nor *god*, nor an afterlife."[50]

Like Walker's fictional character Celie, Lorde, who is a black lesbian poet, finds her empowerment through women-bonding. Lorde traces this tradition back both to West Africa and more personally to Carriacou, Grenada, birthplace of her mother and father. She says in *Zami: A New Spelling of My Name*, which is called "a new form, *biomythography*, combining elements of history, biography and myth,"[51] "When I visited Grenada I saw the root of my mother's powers walking through the streets. I thought, this is the country of my foremothers, my forebearing mothers, those Black island women who defined themselves by what they did" (Z, 9).

In her "journey," as she calls it, Lorde has been led by women: "Images of women flaming like torches adorn and define the borders of my journey, stand like dykes between me and the chaos. It is the images of women, kind and cruel, that lead me home" (Z, 3).

At seventeen, when she moves out of her mother's house, it is women who help her find her strength to build upon what she learned from her mother. In the streets of New York, Lorde says, "I found other women who sustained me and from whom I learned other loving. How to cook the foods I had never tasted in my mother's house. How to drive a stick-shift car. How to loosen up and not be lost" (Z, 104). She pays homage to their influence, their strength to help her survive as a young, black lesbian:

> *Their shapes join Linda and Gran'Ma Liz and Gran'Aunt Anni in my dreaming, where they dance with swords in their hands, stately forceful steps, to mark time when they were all warriors.*
>
> *In libation, I wet the ground to my old heads.* (Z, 104)

In *Zami*, Lorde recounts a sexual relationship with a woman, Kitty, in which Kitty becomes for her Afrekete, the "youngest daughter" of "MawuLisa, thunder, sky, sun, the great mother of us all" (Z, 255). Like the passages in Silko's novel *Ceremony*, which recounts Tayo's ritual coupling with Night Swan and Ts'eh, the passage recounting Lorde's sexual relationship with Afrekete is full of references to sky, earth, plants, animals, and in Lorde's case, fruit. As the love-making passages in both Silko's and Allen's stories, the mythic emerges when Lorde writes of making love with Kitty. The mythic is the here and now, and the here and now is the mythic story. Again we see that the story is all one story and part of the whole:

I would turn the corner into 113th Street towards the park, my steps quickening and my fingertips tingling to play in her earth.

And I remember Afrekete, who came out of a dream to me always being hard and real as the fire hairs along the underedge of my navel. She brought me live things from the bush, and from her farm set out in cocoyams and cassava —those magical fruit which Kitty bought in the West Indian markets along Lenox Avenue in the 140s or in the Puerto Rican *bodegas* within the bustling market over on Park Avenue and 116th Street under the Central Railroad structures. (Z, 249)[52]

Lorde and Kitty/Afrekete make love on the roof of Afrekete's tenement and their love-making becomes a prayer:

I remember the full moon like the white pupils in the center of your wide irises.

The moons went out, and your eyes grew dark as you rolled over me, and I felt the moon's silver light mix with the wet of your tongue on my eyelids.

Afrekete Afrekete ride me to the crossroads where we shall sleep, coated in the woman's power. The sound of our bodies meeting is the prayer of all strangers and sisters, that the discarded evils, abandoned at all crossroads, will not follow us upon our journeys. (Z, 252)[53]

After they separate and go their own ways, Lorde says that Kitty/Afrekete left a "print" on her "life with the resonance and power of an emotional tattoo." Here Lorde shows the power of this transforming love: "We had come together like elements erupting into an electric storm, exchanging energy, sharing charge, brief and drenching. Then we parted, passed, reformed, reshaping ourselves the better for the exchange" (Z, 253).

Like Silko's character Tayo, Allen's character Ephanie, and Walker's character Celie, Lorde is empowered by women. Women connect Lorde to women-centered traditions and to the core of her being. She says that all of the women she has "ever loved has left her print upon me" and it was like loving "some invaluable piece of myself apart from me—so different that I had to stretch and grow in order to recognize her. And in that growing, we come to separation, that place where work begins. Another meeting" (Z, 255).

For Lorde, Afrekete, MawuLisa's "youngest daughter," is the "mischievous linguist, trickster, best-beloved, whom we must all become" (Z, 255). Becoming the Goddess and loving the Goddess, loving part of the self, is another version of finding the Goddess within the self and, in Allen's words, of "walking in the ancient manner, tracing the pattern of the ancient design" (*WOS*, 209). It is also Walker's acknowledgment that in cutting a tree we bleed—an acknowledgment of the connectedness of all.

Part of walking in the ancient way of the Goddess is a discovery and celebration of the body in its many erotic capacities and its connectedness to everything else. For women, the maturing of the body from childhood to womanhood was an especially important event celebrated in many holistic cultures. For instance, even in the more patriarchal African Olinka society in which Walker's Nettie functions, this is the time young women were ritually scarred or the time of cicatrization, part of a ritual to mark their coming into womanhood. Recreating a celebration ceremony for today's readers, Lorde recounts her coming into womanhood and the accompanying ceremony in a beautiful, sensual passage in *Zami*. She says when her mother discovered that Lorde had begun to menstruate, "[w]hat then happened felt like a piece of an old and elaborate dance between my mother and me" (Z, 76). Although her mother responded to this event with the usual dire warnings about watching yourself around boys, there is also a sense that something wonderful has happened:

> It was the lurking of that amused/annoyed brow-furrowed half-smile of hers that made me feel—all her nagging words to the contrary—that something very good and satisfactory and pleasing to her had just happened, and we were both pretending otherwise for some very wise and secret reasons. I would come to understand these reasons later, as a reward, if I handled myself properly. (Z, 77)

When Lorde's mother leaves to run an errand, Lorde conducts a ritual celebration of her own by preparing the spices with a mortar and pestle for rubbing into the beef for dinner. This ritual, with its sensuous accompanying movements, allows her to appreciate fully the momentousness of the occasion:

> My body felt new and special and unfamiliar and suspect all at the same time.
>
> I could feel bands of tension sweeping across my body back and forth, like lunar winds across the moon's face. I felt the slight rubbing bulge of the cotton pad between my legs, and I smelled the delicate breadfruit smell rising up from the front of my print blouse that was my own womansmell, warm, and shameful, but secretly utterly delicious. (Z, 77)

As she grinds the spicy mixture, she establishes a voluptuous rhythm in response to the "heavy fullness at the root of me that was exciting and dangerous" (Z, 78). She feels a "vital connection . . . between the muscles of [her] . . . fingers curved tightly around the smooth pestle in its insistent downward motion, and the molten core of my body whose source emanated from a new ripe fullness just beneath the pit of my stomach" (Z, 78). The connection acts as an "invisible thread, taut and sensitive as a clitoris exposed, stretched through my curled fingers up my round brown arm into the moist reality of my armpits. . . . The thread ran over my ribs and along my spine tingling and singing, into a basin that was poised between my hips, now pressed against the low kitchen counter" (p. 78).

In Lorde's description, the basin becomes "a tiding ocean of blood beginning to be made real and available . . . for strength and information" (Z, 78). She responds to the "jarring shocks of the velvet-lined pestle, striking the bed of spice" as assaults. Her movements grow more and more caressing until she stands "dreamlike," her "body . . . strong and full and open, yet captivated by the gentle motions of the pestle, and the rich smells filling the kitchen, and the fullness of the young summer heat" (p. 79). This is the ritual celebration of the body, the body as woman, and its connection to everything around it—another kind of integration. It is also acceptance of womanness, of connection to other women, and the erotic potential in this, and the connection to one's mother. Lorde says, "[A]fterward when I was grown, whenever I thought about the way I smelled that day, I would have a fantasy of my mother, her hands wiped dry from the washing, and her apron untied and laid neatly away, looking down upon me lying on the couch, and slowly, thoroughly, our touching and caressing each other's most secret places" (p. 78).

Years later when speaking of how consciousness of the body and her efforts to fight cancer fit into "political work," Lorde says, "I respect the time I spend each day treating my body, and I consider it part of my political work. It is possible to have some conscious input into our physical processes—not expecting the impossible, but allowing for the unexpected—a kind of training in self-love and physical resistance."[54]

Furthermore, reminding us again how everything is connected, she says:

> Visualizing the disease process inside my body in political images is not a quixotic dream. When I speak out against the cynical U.S. intervention in Central America, I am working to save my life in every sense. Government research grants to the National Cancer Institute were cut in 1986 by the exact amount illegally turned over to the Contras in Nicaragua. One hundred and five million dollars. It gives yet another meaning to the personal as the political.[55]

For Lorde, the inner war parallels the outer. She is, to borrow a phrase from Allen, a "word warrior,"[56] using the word as her weapons for life against those allied with death: "For me, living fully means living with maximum access to my experience and power, loving and doing work in which I believe. It means writing my poems, telling my stories, and speaking out of my most urgent concerns and against the many forms of anti-life surrounding us."[57]

In this sense, to find the Goddess within one must often first confront spiritual and physical illnesses, which signal the disharmony or dis-ease of separation from the Goddess or oneself. To integrate, one must seek healing and perform rituals. Lorde says that when she is "in touch with the erotic" she is "less willing to accept powerlessness, or those other supplied states of being which are not native to me, such as resignation, despair, self-effacement, depression, self-denial."[58] This implies an integration of spirit and body. Thus the reader sees Tayo, Ephanie, and Celie struggling to re-integrate the spiritual and physical. The separation of spirit and body often manifests itself in disease or physical illness and can also be a necessary step to cleansing the body of dis-ease, as symbolized, for instance, by Tayo's vomiting.

Walker, like Lorde, connects physical illness to spiritual illness, thereby reinforcing the connection between the spiritual and the physical. For instance, Celie finds that for over a month she has difficulty sleeping. She finally understands she has sinned "against Sofia spirit" (*CP*, 37). She had told Harpo to beat Sofia if he wants to control her. When Sofia confronts Celie, their discussion leads to an understanding between them—that Celie is jealous of Sofia because she fights back, and that Sofia feels sorry for Celie because Celie "never stand up for herself" (p. 38). They form a bond, begin piecing a quilt together, and Celie is a step closer to her own empowerment. This is also the beginning of politics for Celie. She begins to extend the personal into the political. Her understanding goes from "I should not put up with this treatment" to "no woman should put up with this." This particular insight culminates in her integration of her politics with her personal life, and she leaves with Shug to begin a life together. This integration is a step on her journey to wholeness.

Another example of how illness is connected to spiritual health in *The Color Purple* is shown in Harpo's eating disorder. When he finds out that he is not big enough to beat Sofia into submission, he begins to eat constantly—presumably to make himself bigger than Sofia. Eating becomes an obsession. When Celie confronts him about his behavior and points out that his own father, whom he has been trying to imitate, does not control Shug, the love of his life, Harpo vomits. That is the end of his eating disorder. However, he does not get in touch with his inner self enough to prevent Sofia from leaving him. She is only able to remember how he continually tried to control her, even when they are making love: "Once he get on top of me I think bout how that's where he always want to be" (*CP*, 59).

In another example of bodily sickness caused by spiritual illness, Nettie understands that Corrine, a black missionary with whom Nettie lives, will die unless Corrine can rid herself of the terrible suspicion that her husband has cheated on her with Nettie. In her suspicion, Corrine has even closed herself off from her children. Corrine has cut herself off from her community, denying her connections to everything and everyone. Although Corrine's belief in her husband and Nettie is restored, she dies anyway. She had "erase[d] herself, her spirit" (*CP*, 199), as Nettie puts it, for too long.

In both African and Laguna cultures, there are those who do willful harm in their acts and words. In African culture, those who act against the good of the community for their own gain are called wizards. The punishment for this is extinction—destruction of the body by burning or throwing it to the hyenas so that the person will cease to exist. A wizard is able to destroy "the life force" of people and make them do the wizard's bidding.[59] Silko, too, documents wizards or witches in her book, *Ceremony*, as those who have succumbed to the lust for power and work harm on the community. Thus the young veterans who return from World War II to Laguna turn their backs on their community to pursue the status they had had as soldiers in uniform. Out of their rage at having lost this status, they do the work of "the witchery" and try to draw Tayo into it as well. It is fitting that the culminating scene which shows the veterans acting out this rage against their own people takes place at the abandoned uranium mine from where the destructive component of the atom bomb came. The atom bomb symbolizes the ultimate lust for power, and those who control it do the work of the witchery. The ultimate harm to the community is its extinction.

In *The Color Purple*, Walker shows that words in the form of curses can also affect physical well-being. When Albert, Celie's husband, refuses to give her the letters from her sister, Celie curses him:

> I curse you, I say. . . . Until you do right by me, everything you touch will crumble. . . . [E]verything you even dream about will fail. . . . Every lick you hit me you will suffer twice. . . . The jail you plan for me is the one in which you will rot. . . . Anything you do to me; already done to you. . . . Then I feel Shug shake me. Celie she say. And I come to myself. (*CP*, 175–76)[60]

The power of these words is such that Albert shuts himself in his house, does not eat or clean himself, and hears things so that he is unable to sleep. The symptoms do not improve until Albert sends Celie the rest of her sister's letters. Then he seems like a changed man, and Sofia says Albert "act like he trying to git religion" (*CP*, 189). According to Walker, in an article in *Mother Jones*, "Only justice can stop a curse."[61] When Albert gives Celie the letters, justice is done, so that Albert is freed from Celie's curse.

Both Allen and Silko show that curses can be stopped, particularly those curses that are a misuse of the power of words by wizards or those wishing to harm the community for their own personal gain. In Silko's novel *Ceremony*, Tayo's healing brings the rain and heals the community. As Silko says, the witchery "is dead for now" (*C*, 274). In Allen's novel *The Woman Who Owned the Shadows*, Ephanie fears that she is cursed, that she is a harm-doer: "Ephanie understood the ancient nightmares, felt the great slab lowered on witches to unbend their maniacal minds. Longed for such a stone pressing on her own chest, to stop the ache centered there, longed for the certain recognition of her own death in that condemnation" (*WOS*, 212). But part of her journey is to discover that the image created by the words of a curse or witchery is only one alternative for the future: "There are no curses. There are only descriptions of what creations there will be" (p. 212). It is the responsibility of humans to use their creative intelligence to express in words their understanding of the relationships between people, things, and events that shape the future.

In *The Color Purple*, Walker shows how this responsibility can work through the power of words. She has Celie use the written word as her medium. As Celie develops her creative intelligence—her understanding of the relationships among people, things, and events—which is also the power of the erotic, and expresses it in words, her life begins to change for the better. She discovers her own power and uses it, as when she curses Albert. Discovering the value of relationships, she bonds with other women, further empowering herself. Her letters to God change to letters to Nettie when she abandons the idea of God as an old white man with a long white beard, and sees that "God" is really everywhere and in everything. She turns her anger and frustration into creativity and joy. By sewing instead of slashing Albert with a razor, she is able eventually to develop a folk-pants business in which the actual making of pants gives her great joy—the joy of the power of the erotic, doing something with all one's being. In Nettie's letters from Africa, she learns about her African heritage, giving her some pride in being black and some alternatives to Euro-American culture, and she further extends her sense of connectedness.

She learns about different traditions for men and women, and uses some of them to create her own womanist perspective. For instance, she discovers that "Olinka men make beautiful quilts" (*CP*, 159) and that men and women in Africa both wear long robes or "dresses" (p. 230). She makes use of these ideas when she questions why only men should wear pants and why men do not sew. She makes pants that "anybody can wear" (*CP*, 230) and teaches Albert to sew. On the other hand, she learns that some women in the African tribe in which her sister lives still undergo cicatrization, "scarring or cutting of tribal marks" done on their faces, and clitoridectomy performed as "a way the Olinka can show they still have their own ways . . . even though the white man has taken everything else" (p. 202).[62] This knowledge helps her understand her daughter-in-law's scarring when Celie finally meets her, and it deepens her sense of relationship.

She also learns that in this tribe, a woman's situation is much like her own was with her father. The men give orders to the women, but don't listen when the women are speaking. Nettie says that "the women also do not 'look in a man's face' . . . a brazen thing to do. They look instead at his feet or his knees. And what can I say to this? Again, it is our own behavior around Pa" (*CP*, 137). She vows that she will no longer continue in this tradition, and she forms a new kind of relationship with her ex-husband in which they become equals and friends.

Despite the similarities of the two patriarchal systems, Celie does discover some differences between the positions of women in African and Euro-American cultures. From these differences she can draw strength and use them in building her new woman-centered culture, particularly the ideas that women can own and care for their own property and find emotional fulfillment with other women. She finds that women in polygamous marriages have their own individual huts and their own fields. They spend most of their time with other women and develop close relationships to the other wives: "Their lives always center around work and their children and other women. . . . They indulge their husbands, if anything" (*CP*, 141).

Women can also gain access to the status of men by being widowed, having borne many sons, or being born into a wealthy family, among other ways. In *The Color Purple*, the wealthy, white, English woman Doris Baines, who comes to Africa as a missionary to avoid marrying and to be able to write books in peace, has such a status. The chief gives her a couple of wives, whom she educates in England and then marries off to some men of the tribe. In African culture, this situation is known as "giving the goat to the buck," and any children born to the wives belong to the woman "who is the nominal husband."[63] This situation is a way for a wealthy woman to start a compound or relationship group, which is based on having descendants. The children "come under the control of" the woman's heirs after her death.[64]

Unlike Lorde, Celie is never able to connect with the goddesses of African belief because everything she learns about Africa is through Nettie, and Nettie's patriarchal Christianity prevents her from learning about African religion and relaying information about the goddesses to Celie. Walker corrects this situation in her next novel, *The Temple of My Familiar*.[65] Nettie's basic Christianity doesn't seem to change much with her African sojourn, but being a missionary in Africa has allowed her to do things that many women of her time were not able to do—travel and have access to some education and independence.

However, by learning about her African heritage and thinking about her African-American life, Celie is able to enlarge her worldview and realize that she is not "the center of the universe" (*CP*, 143), which is how Nettie says the Africans and white people think of themselves. She can see that she is connected to an ancient culture that is not inferior to white culture, and this is an important aspect in Celie's growth. She sees that the scapegoating of whites and others that some Africans persist in denies their connectedness to them, as does the behavior of the whites toward blacks. At the end of the novel, when she is reunited with her sister Nettie and her children, she sees that they are all part of the whole. The difference in customs matters little; what matters is that they are all together; they are a community. As Celie writes about her new daughter-in-law, Tashi:

> What your people love best to eat over there in Africa? us ast.
> She sort of blush and say *barbecue*.
> Everybody laugh and stuff her with one more piece. (*CP*, 244)

Walker continues delineating her search for a woman-centered spirituality in *The Temple of My Familiar (TF).* In fact, *Temple* has puzzled many critics because it has very little conventional plot. Each of Walker's many characters is on a spiritual journey to wholeness, helped by one another and the "voices of the ancestors," who appear in various forms and, as one critic has said, lead "relentlessly" back to the "Black/Brown African Goddess."[66] One of the characters says that people are "only related to those with whom you are in spiritual progression" (*TF*, 180–81), and this seems to be the key to this novel—each character is in spiritual progression to the other.

Walker shows "a walking in the ancient way" of the ancestors, which is a different experience for each character, depending on his or her current situation. The reader follows the spiritual journeys of, among others, a black history professor, Suwelo, and his estranged wife, Fanny, granddaughter of Celie from *The Color Purple*. Lest white feminist academics become too complacent, Walker creates Fanny as an ex-women's studies professor who left academia because of racism. Suwelo's journey is facilitated by Miss Lissie, an elderly, sassy black woman who is able to teach Suwelo through her knowledge of the ancestors emanating from the Black mother of Africa. Miss Lissie remembers some of her many reincarnations and, through them, the destruction of the goddess-worshipping cultures, a result of the envy and greed of both black and white men that led to their patriarchal cultures. Miss Lissie even remembers the final split between white and black women, which took place during the witch burnings of the Inquisition, when the daughters of the Moors were destroyed in Spain—the daughters who had hoped that the African "Great Mother, Creator of All, Protector of All, the Keeper of the Earth. *The* Goddess" could continue to be worshipped in the guise of the Black Madonna (*TF*, 267).

One of the things Suwelo learns is that sexual expression is sacred and that it is a "superficial, ultimately fraudulent act . . . to sleep with a person you did not really know" (*TF*, 131). Suwelo is particularly threatened by lesbians, and he shows some envy for the power of women, one of Walker's major concepts in the novel. Walker also illustrates womanist principles through her lesbian characters and seems to equate both womanist and lesbian with walking in the ancient way of the Goddess. Suwelo says about the lesbians he has seen in San Francisco:

> Beautiful, beautiful women, quite a lot of them, though some of them didn't look so hot. Just seeing them on their outings together, climbing the hills, sunning in the parks, eating noisily at the largest tables in restaurants in Berkeley, made you want to cry. They'd *left* us! Hell, those bitches were so tough, they'd left *God!* This was when they were just discovering the Goddess, and it was all the time Goddess this and Goddess that. I once asked a black woman on the street where the new bus stop was—the city was repairing the old bus stop part of the street we were on—and she just looked at me, shrugged, and said an easy "Goddess knows!" It blew me away. (*TF*, 241)

Miss Lissie's response to this is: "Men are dogs" (*TF*, 242, 247). Miss Lissie, true to Walker's definition of "womanist," has loved individual men, but in addition to being "outrageous, audacious, courageous . . . [and] willful,"[67] she has also loved other women. For instance, in one of her lives, she had lived in a harem with hundreds of other women and an old master too "sickly" to do anything to the women (p. 105). She had two lovers, a woman named Fadpa and a eunuch. When Lissie and Fadpa were 96 and 103, they were given their freedom and spent the rest of their lives together. Lissie is one model of a "womanist," the woman unto herself, which other characters are struggling to become in the way in which Lorde struggles to become Afrekete. Not only do black women in Walker's novel undertake this journey, but Walker shows the reader that white women undertake the journey as well: A white woman character is also drawn to Africa and the principles of the Goddess while researching the life of her great-aunt.

Fanny's journey is facilitated by "spirit lovers"—another version of Lorde's being ridden by the gods or "spirit possession." Whereas Lorde's spirit possession is always by a female spirit, Fanny's spirits (and Walker's as well) are just as often male. Fanny says of her possession:

> They open doors inside me. It's as if they're keys. To rooms inside myself. I find a door inside and it's as if I hear a humming from behind it, and then I get inside somehow, with the key the old ones give me, and are, and as I stumble about in the darkness of the room, I begin to feel the stirring in myself, the humming of the room, and my heart starts to expand with the absolute feeling of bravery, or love, or audacity, or commitment. It becomes a light, and the light enters me, by osmosis, and a part of me that was not clear before is clarified. I radiate this expanded light. Happiness. (*TF*, 186)

Walker also documents the rituals and celebrations of life of indigenous peoples that ensure continuance—the cooking of a gumbo, the singing of the songs of the ancestors, the making of feathered capes, and the weaving of "the tribal cloth, the magic of which is that as long as it is woven, the tribe exists, as long as you know how to weave it, so do you" (*TF*, 230–31). These "arts" are the "bearing witness," the "saying yessiree to the life spirit," the refusal of which can have similar consequences to those experienced by Allen's Ephanie when she does not follow the way of the medicine women as directed by her spirit guardian. For instance, Hal, a painter, becomes blind when he does not use his gift of truly seeing the beauty of life and recording it in his painting (p. 60).[68]

Like Silko and Allen, Walker connects all stories: "Well, you see how to me all daily stories are in fact ancient, and ancient ones current" (*TF*, 173), but these stories need to be put together "in some kind of pattern . . . [to] be understood in the present" (p. 102). That is what Walker is attempting to do in *Temple,* to bring the fragmented remains of Afracentric culture that focus on the Goddess together in a pattern that contemporary readers can understand. Instead of giving readers one journey or pattern to follow—as do Allen in *The Woman Who Owned the Shadows* and Silko in *Ceremony*—she gives us numerous patterns to piece together in a crazy quilt of a novel. The novel even contains a "gospel" according to Shug, who forms a church with Celie. It is no wonder that some critics could not understand *Temple* as a novel, for Walker has crossed the boundary between genres, eliminating the boundaries between the sacred and secular, between mind and body. Walker, like the other women in this study, also expresses concern about the destruction of the earth. For Walker, this apprehension is directly connected to the destruction of Africa. She says through Miss Lissie: "You cannot curse a part without damning the whole. That is why Mother Africa, cursed by all her children, black, white and in between, is dying today, and, after her, death will come to every other part of the globe" (*TF*, 198).

In *The Color Purple* and *The Temple of My Familiar*, then, Walker traces spiritual journeys to wholeness through her characters. Using the West African tradition, Lorde and Walker show the reader visions of possibilities for the future—Lorde's vision uses African goddesses and Walker's creates a vision, rooted in keeping "alive in us the speech and the voices of the ancestors."[69] And the voices Walker wants us to hear are particularly female—"womanist." As Walker says, "For if and when Celie rises to her rightful earned place in society across the planet, the world will be a different place."[70] Both women are powerful poets who, as Jahn says, use the word "to create images upon images,"[71] transforming the words as well as themselves. In this way, the future can be transformed. Lorde's personal journey recounted in *Zami* and in her poetry, and the journeys to wholeness undertaken by the main characters in the novels *The Color Purple, The Woman Who Owned the Shadows,* and *Ceremony,* culminate in the realization of their connection to the Mother or the female principle, and therefore their connection to everything, animate and inanimate. As Celie says in the circular greeting in her last letter: "Dear God. Dear stars, dear trees, dear sky, dear peoples. Dear Everything. Dear God" (*CP,* 242).

FOUR

Revisioning Celtic Traditions: Starhawk, Priestess of the Goddess, and Marion Zimmer Bradley's *The Mists of Avalon*

"Grand Grand Mother is returning"
JUDY GRAHN

A THIRD strand of the female principle in American culture can be found in the contemporary practice of witchcraft as a religion by feminists[1] such as Starhawk (Miriam Simos). Starhawk is a therapist with a Master's degree in psychology from Antioch University and the author of several nonfiction works, including *The Spiral Dance: A Rebirth of the Ancient Religion of the Great Goddess (SD); Dreaming the Dark: Magic, Sex and Politics (DD);* and *Truth or Dare (TD);* she is also a priestess in the Celtic Faery tradition of the Old Religion.[2] Her background is Jewish, and she was born in St. Paul, Minnesota. She also teaches at Antioch University West in San Francisco, writes poetry and fiction, gives lectures, and works as a peace activist. As a friend says of her, "I experience Starhawk as being ordinary, just like you and me."[3]

In the previous chapters, we have looked at the female principle in Laguna Pueblo beliefs and in West African traditions as they are expressed in contemporary literature. Starhawk, however, is not primarily a writer. As a priestess and witch, she actively conducts rituals for participants concerned about self healing and the healing and empowerment of the earth.[4] Starhawk's focus is on the Goddess in all, especially in women. She directs many all-women rituals, though occasionally men can also participate. If we examine Starhawk's teachings today and what we can recover of the Celtic Faery tradition from the past, we discover that they have much in common with both the Laguna and West African traditions.

Scholars disagree as to whether a witchcraft tradition has been passed down from ancient times. For instance, Norman Cohn has summarized the various theories concerning witchcraft up to the contemporary witchcraft movement and concludes that a witch cult never existed, that it was essentially manufactured by the Inquisition.[5] The contemporary witch movement, however, claims otherwise. As Starhawk notes about her own research into witchcraft, the information is confusing. Depending on their approach, some studies concentrate on the persecution of witches and other so-called devil worshippers, while others argue that these women were not witches but simply fell afoul of the authorities.[6] The identification of witches as satanists seems to be a historical approach, while the identification of witches with sorcery seems to be an anthropological one.[7] Some, like anthropologist Margaret Murray, believe that many of those who were persecuted in Europe and in America were actually practitioners of what Murray calls "ritual witchcraft . . . or the Dianic cult," which, according to Murray, was "the ancient religion of Western Europe."[8] Although most scholars refute much of Murray's work in this area, religious historian Mircea Eliade does credit Murray with "emphasizing the persistence of pagan folk practices and beliefs centuries after the introduction of Christianity"[9] and points to an area worthy of further study that was not under rigid ecclesiastical control—Romanian folklore traditions that support the concept of a pre-Christian witch religion.[10]

The information is confusing in part because very little was written down by the Celts, who Jean Markale says were the repository of the remnants of the Goddess Religion.[11] The Celtic legends were primarily recorded by medieval Catholic monks who in all likelihood altered the stories somewhat to fit Christian concepts. Despite this drawback, these legends remain the most fruitful source of understanding Celtic beliefs. Observations by classical writers need to be judged carefully as to their reliability.[12] The so-called source book of witch activities and beliefs, the *Malleus Maleficarum* ("The Hammer of the Witches") was published by two Dominican Inquisitors in 1484.[13] However, according to Jeffrey B. Russell, there was no English translation of the *Malleus* "until modern times," and therefore accusations against so-called English witches differed greatly from those on the continent. The English witches were usually accused of causing harm instead of being sexually perverse, able to fly, and capable of other such activities as recounted in the *Malleus*.[14]

Consequently, there are numerous problems for the witchcraft investigator—problems that are similar to the problems one encounters by looking at anthropological accounts of Laguna and West African cultures. In tracing yet another thread of woman-centered spirituality, I am not attempting to prove or disprove the authenticity of the Celtic Faery tradition. Rather, I will connect it to what is known about Celtic religious tradition, mostly through the "mythological thinking" shown in manuscripts and in oral tradition, and thereby try to elucidate the contemporary beliefs and lesbian sensibilities of feminists who practice witchcraft or connect to Celtic traditions. Although the Celts had no unified political organization, there was what Proinaias MacCana calls "a highly developed sense of cultural affinity among the learned classes."[15] They were identified as Celtic "by their language, their shared characteristics, and their mode of life, as well as by their geographical location."[16] The druidic organization also transcended political rivalries to foster "an ideological unity."[17] These are the things that allow one to speak "of one Celtic mythology."[18]

Today's witches such as Starhawk and Z. Budapest[19] appropriate Murray's thesis that witchcraft was the ancient religion of Western Europe which worshipped the Goddess and her consort, the Horned God. The religion as practiced today has nothing to do with the devil and evil, since contemporary witches do not believe in the Christian God or the Christian devil. As Margot Adler says about witchcraft in her study of contemporary "neo-paganism": "The Witch . . . is an extraordinary symbol—independent, anti-establishment, strong, and proud. She is political, yet spiritual and magical. The Witch is woman as martyr; she is persecuted by the ignorant; she is the woman who lives outside society and outside society's definition of woman."[20] She has, in other words, the characteristics assigned to the lesbian. She is the woman not under the control of men, the woman unto herself.

In spite of this, witches are generally thought of as satanists; this image is supported by portrayals of witches in contemporary horror movies and novels. "Witch," like "lesbian," has long been a word used negatively against women—to accuse them of foul crimes in ancient as well as modern times, to force them to conform to society's mores. However, contemporary witches refuse to give up the word, connecting it to the Anglo-Saxon stem, *wicca* or *wicce*, "to bend or shape,"[21] and identifying "with 9 million victims of bigotry and hatred." To be a witch is "to take responsibility for shaping a world in which prejudice claims no more victims" (*SD*, 7).

Contemporary witches believe that the Great Goddess, as she is called today, was worshipped not only in Western Europe but in many other parts of the world and was known by many names. In *The Spiral Dance*, Starhawk records a version of "The Charge of the Goddess," which is part of a ritual common to almost all branches of contemporary witchcraft. Many scholars trace "The

Charge" back to Charles Godfrey Leland in his *Aradia, or the Gospel of the Witches* (1899), rather than to ancient Goddess worship.[22] Whether Leland's material was authentic or not, "The Charge" still appears in contemporary witchcraft, and Starhawk's version lists some of the names by which the Goddess has been known: "Artemis, Astarte, Dione, Melusine, Aphrodite, Ceridwen, Diana, Arionshod, Brigid . . . ."[23] Archaeological evidence shows that goddesses, either as primary or secondary figures, were also worshipped in the Middle East, in Egypt and surrounding areas, as well as in Mediterranean cultures.[24] As far as the Celtic tradition is concerned, MacCana comments that for the Irish, at least, "the ruler of the supernatural realm is a goddess rather than a god, precisely as in those early years. Irish tales . . . represent the otherworld as 'the Land of Women'. . . . It is evidently an old tradition and one which proved remarkably tenacious, and it seems to confirm that the notion of a great goddess who was the mother of the gods is a basic element of insular Celtic mythology."[25] It is to this tradition to which Starhawk claims to adhere.

Although there are other witchcraft traditions, Starhawk claims to have been instructed in the Faery tradition of Britain by a teacher in San Francisco (*SD*, 11). This tradition, like all witchcraft traditions, is primarily oral, like those of the Laguna and West African tribes. Witchcraft traditions were rarely written down until recently, but one such recording was made in 1973 by Lady Sheba in her *Book of Shadows*, a collection of rituals that seem to be in the Gardnerian tradition.[26] According to Sheba, her book is a copy of a witch's private book usually written out in longhand, kept especially while the rituals were being learned, and generally guarded with much secrecy. Although there is controversy over whether such writings are authentic or not, the point is that most witches have taken the fragments of whatever traditions they believe they have found and are shaping them themselves—"using past sources for inspiration but mixing them with modern creativity."[27]

Starhawk says that her tradition goes back to "the Little People of Stone Age Britain" and that since a good portion of the Faery tradition is still unrevealed, "many of the rituals, chants, and invocations come from our creative tradition" (*SD*, 11). She, like the others we have studied, especially Lorde and Walker, is using elements she believes to be traditional, but is also embellishing, combining, and creating new worship forms.

Despite the fact that there are different witchcraft traditions, Starhawk and other practitioners, such as Leo Martello and Doreen Valiente, note that the basic tenets are much the same from tradition to tradition.[28] While some of these principles occur in mainstream American religions, this combination of basic tenets seems to be unique to the Goddess Religion. One of these basic tenets is that there is no outside authority, only an inner authority.[29] Practitioners of witchcraft learn to cultivate this inner authority and do not look to someone or something outside themselves to give them the truth. Like the Laguna and West African traditions, there is no separation of body and spirit in witchcraft. The Goddess, who is the symbol of the life force in all things, is all. She is the "absolute reality" that cannot be fully known and must therefore be "felt or intuited—represented metaphorically in literature, poetry, ritual, and the dance" (*SD*, 7). About the Goddess, Starhawk says:

> The primary symbol for 'That-Which-Cannot-Be-Told' is the Goddess. The Goddess has infinite aspects and thousands of names—She is the reality behind many metaphors. She *is* reality, the manifest deity, omnipresent in all of life, in each of us. The Goddess is not separate from the world—She *is* the world, and all things in it: moon, sun, earth, star, stone, seed, flowing river, wind, wave, leaf and branch, bud and blossom, fang and claw, woman and man. In Witchcraft, flesh and spirit are one. (*SD*, 8)

Another basic principle is that although the "Goddess is immanent, . . . She needs human help to realize her fullest beauty.

The harmonious balance of plant/animal/human/divine awareness . . . must constantly be renewed" (*SD*, 11–12) through ceremonies conducted by witchcraft participants. This is a similar concept to that found in both Laguna and West African cultures. In Laguna culture, the task of the individual is to contribute to the good of the group by maintaining the proper connections to the tribe and everything around it through the rituals of daily life, which include, for instance, offerings to ensure that the rain clouds will come and the crops will grow. In West African cultures, the task of the individual is to use the words or "active intelligence," as scholar Janheinz Jahn calls it, to activate the life forces in everything.[30] Therefore in all three cultures, human beings are seen as being in a reciprocal relationship with the divine.

In witchcraft, the individual witch, either male or female, "is a 'shaper,' a creator who bends the unseen into form, and so becomes one of the Wise, one whose life is infused with magic" (*SD*, 7). In this context, magic is defined as "the art of changing consciousness at will," and has its basis in the belief that there is "an ordered coherent universe in which all parts are interrelated."[31] Starhawk relates magic to the age-old techniques practiced by shamans who "could attune themselves to the spirits of the herds, and in so doing they became aware of the pulsating rhythm that infuses all life, the dance of the double spiral, of whirling into being, and whirling out again" (p. 3).

Not only does witchcraft see all things as connected, but it also sees everything as swirls of energy, flowing in and out of one another. This explains in part how witches see themselves as shapers of reality, for if one envisions everything including oneself as made up of these energy swirls, then it is not difficult to envision moving them or changing them in combination with one's own swirls. This is the art of changing consciousness at will—of going from the fixed "linear" reality to the inner swirls. Starhawk explains:

> The mythology and cosmology of Witchcraft are rooted in that "Paleolithic shaman's insight": that all things are swirls of energy, vortexes of moving forces, currents in an ever-changing sea. Underlying the appearance of separateness, of fixed objects within a linear stream of time, reality is a field of energies that congeal, temporarily, into forms. In time, all "fixed" things dissolve, only to coalesce again into new forms, new vehicles. (*SD*, 18)

Magic, then, involves focusing on "swirls of energy." The practitioner uses a consciousness that sees the world in "patterns and relationships rather than fixed objects" (*SD*, 20). For instance, in Silko's *Ceremony*, when Betonie, the Navajo medicine man, diagnoses Tayo's illness, he looks for patterns—how Tayo fits into the pattern of what is happening around him—and his cure also has to do with patterns. In this case, even the pattern of the stars has to be right: "He was drawing in the dirt with his finger. 'Remember these stars. . . . I've seen them and I've seen the spotted cattle; I've seen a mountain and a woman' " (*C*, 160). The altered or heightened consciousness of the shaman or the witch is achieved by severe and extended training and work. Starhawk says that this heightened awareness can often be achieved during ritual when the right hemisphere of the brain, which is involved with intuitional, comprehensive knowing rather than linear thinking, is in use (*SD*, 19).

Because of its emphasis on the lack of separation between spirit and matter, flesh and intellect, witchcraft can also be seen as a religion that is close in spirit to American and African tribal religions in its reverence for the earth and all life.[32] Currently some Native American peoples are attempting to connect to non-native peoples who hold similar beliefs. For instance, in her investigation of neo-paganism, Adler comments that the *Akwesasne Notes*, "A Journal for Native and Natural Peoples," published by the Mohawk Nation, "came to embrace a viewpoint more universal than Native American traditionalism"—a wanting to discover how to "free oneself from consumer culture."[33] Allen points to the similarities among Native American groups and gynocentric pre-Christian European tribes, the last remnants of which could be found in the British Isles.[34]

To witches, to do harm is to misuse power, as it is in both the Laguna and West African traditions. Witches believe that whatever "you send" or cause to happen will return to you threefold; therefore they are very careful not to cause harm.[35] In these religions things and people are seen as "interdependent and interrelated and therefore mutually responsible. An act that harms anyone harms us all" (*SD*, 12). One example of this belief in interdependence from Silko's *Ceremony* is Tayo's worry that he has caused the drought in his land because he cursed the jungle rain while he was at war. In Walker's *The Color Purple*, Celie illustrates another facet of the principle of connection when she curses Albert, saying that until he does right by her, everything will go wrong for him. He has harmed her and by act of will she turns his harm on himself.

To Starhawk, the Goddess is "power-from-within," which is opposed to "power-over"—the domination that fuels wars and will lead to annihilation (*DD*, 3). Her concept of the Goddess as power-from-within or "*immanence*—the awareness of the world and everything in it as alive, dynamic, interdependent, interacting and infused with moving energies: a living being, a weaving dance" (p. 9) is also present in Lorde's Black mother and in Silko's and Allen's Thought Woman. Starhawk also describes the Goddess as "the power of the low, the dark, the earth; and our lives, and our passionate desire for each other's living flesh" (p. 4). Lorde's Black mother or power of the erotic "is a resource within each of us that lies in a deeply female and spiritual plane, firmly rooted in the power of our unexpressed or unrecognized feeling,"[36] while Allen's Thought Woman is "the creative power of thought" that produces "mountains, lakes, creatures, and philosophical/sociological systems."[37] Silko depicts her more personally as the originator of the story Silko is telling. The story is held in Thought Woman's mind while Silko is telling the story —therefore encompassing all while Thought Woman is all. Starhawk's Goddess, Lorde's Black mother, and Silko's and Allen's Thought Woman are all aspects of the female principle, which Starhawk and others point out has been revered through time. She is the source of all creative energy, and as Starhawk says, She "does not rule the world; She is the world" (*SD*, 9).

Because the female principle is seen as the life force, it is present in both males and females. Silko and the others also note that this power is part of every human being, but in Euro-American society men are taught not to recognize this power within themselves. Susan Griffin, in *Pornography and Silence,* has argued that men project this power onto women, seeing women as irrational, uncontrolled nature and thereby seeing themselves as rational and in control.[38] Women, if they are seen as giving birth, are also seen as giving death—as devouring mothers. Men are thus able to see death as outside of themselves. The effect of this split is to make both men and women less human, less able to develop fully. In the Goddess Religion, these concepts are not only reversed, but they are changed. Men are identified with death, but this is not negative. Death necessarily bounds otherwise unlimited creation, and death and life form a cycle that allows change and new life.

In witchcraft as in the Laguna culture, to be in balance is to encompass opposites—light and dark, death and birth, male and female. Starhawk explains: "Unchecked, the life force is cancer; unbridled, the death force is war and genocide. Together, they hold each other in the harmony that sustains life, in the perfect orbit that can be seen in the changing cycle of the seasons, in the ecological balance of the natural world, and in the progression of human life from birth through fulfillment to decline and death—and then to rebirth" (*SD*, 27).

The Celtic tradition, in which there was less separation of male and female roles, is a model for spiritual/social roles for today's witches. As Marie-Louise Sjoestedt notes in her examination of the gods and goddesses of the Celts, many of the major gods and goddesses had both nurturing and warlike qualities compounded in the one deity; there was not the separation of function or type that one seems to find in Roman or Greek gods, for instance. The result of this lack of separation seems to be echoed in Starhawk's words. In addition, the deities often come in groups of three such as the three sisters (Morrigna), giving a complex view of possibilities. The fact that there were many Celtic goddesses of war and that women such as Queen Boudica, who led a revolt of the Britons against the Romans in A.D. 61, fought in battles seems to show that the Celts were less rigid about the parts women could play in Celtic society than, say, the Romans.[39] Indeed, while conducting individual ritual healing sessions, Starhawk often takes the participant on a symbolic journey, using storytelling techniques and drawing on Celtic symbols and content in which women did battle with evil just like men.[40]

As Markale notes, "There is evidence, throughout the Celtic legends, of women taking an unrestricted part in public life. There are queens, princesses, priestesses, prophetesses, maids, servants, peasants, workers, educators, warriors, horse-women."[41] The variety of women's roles could be explained by and was also reflected in the abundance of attributes that each Celtic goddess had. MacCana explains the differing attributes, some contradictory, identified with each Celtic goddess, such as "maternal, seasonal, warlike, young or aged, beautiful or monstrous" as within her role as being "primarily concerned with the prosperity of the land: its fertility, its animal life, and (when it is conceived as a political unit) its security against external forces."[42] Therefore, since the Goddess in each guise is acting to fulfill this role, the picture that emerges is complex and not the simplistic one we have been taught to expect.

Lesbian writer Judy Grahn has also been exploring the roles of women in ancient Celtic culture and what these might mean for today's lesbian. In fact Grahn traces the word "dyke" back to

Boudica, the first-century Celtic queen who led a successful revolt against the Romans in what is now England. Grahn proposes that Boudica's name could have been a title, meaning "bull-slayer-priestess." As leader of her people, Boudica might have performed the sacrifice of the sacred bull or cow on "special sacred embankments, 'dykes,' " a ritual to impart life-giving blood power to the priestess and people.[43] Grahn also speculates that Boudica was lesbian, noting that as a warrior queen, she would have followed the customs of the warrior men, who were known to the Romans for their homosexual practices.

Grahn asserts that the Celts came to what is now Great Britain and took the "spirit-worshiping, the woman-oriented ways" of their predecessors, the Faery folk, into Celtic culture.[44] For Euro-American women seeking a woman-centered spiritual heritage, Celtic traditions offer real possibilities. Like Paula Gunn Allen, Grahn proposes a sacred calling for lesbians, but this time connected to Celtic and European traditions. According to Grahn, besides its connection to Boudica, "dike" means "balance, the path," also being the name of a Greek goddess whose "function was natural balance, the keeping of the balance of forces."[45] Like Native American lesbians or the "ceremonial dykes"[46] of whom Allen writes, Grahn says lesbians follow the same paths as "shaman/priest ancestors . . . whether we consciously know it or not."[47] Grahn sees contemporary lesbians as acting to promote balance: "We are forced to the cusp between psychological worlds, between the objective and subjective in an individual life 'giving' us a particularly balanced position from which to view our society," allowing "us to make a balance between what is considered male and female" in our own lives. In turn, contemporary lesbians can serve as models for a more balanced way of life.[48]

Grahn also ties lesbianism into the Old Religion of the witches, noting that the rites celebrating the mysteries of Demeter and Persephone ("the Kore, . . . the Maid, the unmarried one, the Dyke")[49] had lesbian elements. This same rite is featured in many wiccan traditions today.[50]

In the Goddess Religion, language is important, just as it is to both Laguna and West African cultures. Witches use symbolic, metaphoric, and imagistic speech to cast spells. Like the scholar Janheinz Jahn, Starhawk believes that poetry is "itself a form of magic. . . . Spells and charms worked by Witches are truly concrete poetry" (*SD*, 110)[51]—poetry aimed at bringing measurable results. Because the Goddess is "That-Which-Cannot-Be-Told," symbols and metaphors suggest her representation. Christine Hartley, author of *The Western Mystery Tradition*, believes that the best way to understand the teachings of the tradition is to read poetry and fiction by those who are trained in the tradition and who are trying to convey some of it to their readers. She writes: "The teachings of the Mysteries, being largely in the form of symbols, can often best be conveyed and concealed in fiction where the characters can be made to work out their problems in a manner which makes it easy for the average intelligent person to understand and appreciate them. There are many esoteric truths which it is easier and more suitable to convey under the guise of story."[52]

Story, then, is as important to witches as it is to Laguna and West African cultures. It conveys the teachings that connect its participants to one another and to the world around them and helps them to understand the truths of other lives and to see patterns, not just to describe linear reality. Because of the importance of story to the understanding of esoteric truths, it seems particularly appropriate to examine Marion Zimmer Bradley's novel, *The Mists of Avalon (MA)*, which portrays the Celtic legends of Arthur and his sister, Morgaine, from the perspective of the Goddess Religion.

In her acknowledgments, Bradley cites as sources Starhawk and *The Spiral Dance*, Margaret Murray, Christine Hartley, and Dion Fortune, as well as others connected with what is now called the Goddess Religion. The Arthurian legends are particularly appropriate because they go back to the stories of Ceridwen, the Celtic Goddess, and her cauldron of plenty. Ceridwen is considered a primary aspect of the Goddess by those practicing in the Celtic Faery tradition. By looking at the portrayal of Ceridwen and Bradley's reconstruction of the Celtic world, we can come to understand Starhawk's current practices better. As Starhawk tells us: "In early Celtic myth, the cauldron of the Goddess restored slain warriors to life. It was stolen away to the Underworld, and the heroes who warred for its return were the originals of King Arthur and his Knights, who quested for its later incarnation, the Holy Grail" (*SD*, 83–84).[53]

The Mists of Avalon is not a lesbian novel in the conventional sense. However, in the sense of being woman-centered, it turns around the traditional Arthurian tales, focusing on the women and giving the reader a glimpse into how a woman-centered culture might have functioned (not without problems, as any participant in a lesbian/feminist organization has found). It portrays strong women who are in control of their own lives and those who attempt to control their own lives while immersed in the ever-growing patriarchy—a tale of co-optation and treachery with which contemporary lesbians are very familiar. The very acknowledgment of the possibility of a woman-centered culture makes this novel special.

The Mists of Avalon is unique in yet another way. Women-centered cultures, including the Native American cultures that fall into this group, place little emphasis on with whom one is sleeping. Roles are tied to occupational functions or, as Evelyn Blackwell puts it, "Individuals possessed a gender identity, but not a corresponding sexual identity, and thus were allowed several sexual options."[54] Thus *The Mists of Avalon* shows the reader sexuality in the woman-centered culture in Avalon expressed in terms of occupational or sacred function. Morgaine's gender identity was tied to being a priestess, but whether she slept with men or women had to do with whether she was performing a ritual using the sexual power of either at the time or, if she was not, just her preference at the moment. Like some Native American culture dreamers, if Morgaine had felt she was directed by the Goddess whom she served to sleep only with women and to use only that kind of sexual power—lesbian sexual power—in rituals, one could imagine she would have done so, as do the participants in the feminist Dianic tradition today. This is very different from the Christian concept of gender and sexuality as one and the same thing.

Judy Grahn's novel *Mundane's World,* which recovers the ordinary as magical, operates on the same principle. In the novel's woman-centered culture, characters are not identified by sexual orientation, but by their clan identification, which also is tied to an occupation. For instance, those of the Tortoise clan are farming people, the Bee clan are the architects of the city, and the Snake clan are responsible for maintaining the ceremonies of the group and for healing. Some of the women characters sleep with men, some with women, but they are known by their occupation/clan affiliation, the clans being headed by women, with the sons and brothers living together in a men's quarter, with their lovers' clan, or their mothers' clan.

The point is that even writers who identify themselves as lesbian and who generally write explicitly lesbian literary pieces envision a woman-centered culture in which sexual orientation is not a primary concern, but in which woman-centeredness is the focus. In both *Mundane's World* and *The Mists of Avalon,* a woman-centered culture is portrayed as having women who are in control of their own lives and not under the control of men, regardless of who they sleep with—the definition of lesbian I am using here. The other part of the definition is women who are emotionally centered in other woman—a characteristic displayed more in Grahn's novel than in Bradley's. In that respect, Bradley's novel can be instructive as we watch the characters become coopted by the emerging patriarchy of Britain.

Another reason that looking at *The Mists of Avalon* can be helpful is that since it uses "witches" as positive main characters —Morgaine and others involved in the Goddess Religion—it not only turns upside-down the traditional tale that Arthur's sister, Morgan le Fay (Morgaine), was evil, but it also reverses the traditional idea that witches are evil. Therefore, the novel can help us overcome some of the prejudices built into the very word "witch." The book can also help us see how a conquering tradition often works to absorb existing traditions and to label that which it cannot absorb as evil or mere superstition.[55]

The Mists of Avalon is a novel about the transition between the Old Religion and Christianity in the British Isles, and it takes place during the time that Arthur becomes king. The story follows the lives of three sisters, Morgause, Igraine, and Viviane, and their children. There is a great difference in the ages of the sisters, and at the beginning of the novel, they can be seen as the three cyclical aspects of the triple Goddess—the maiden, the mother, and the crone or wise woman.[56] As the reader discovers, the Goddess is especially in every woman because women "embody" the Goddess and every woman is the Goddess, and so we follow each woman through the phases in the life of the Goddess (*SD*, 12).[57] At the beginning of the novel, Morgause is a girl just coming into womanhood, while Igraine is a mother married to a Christian man, and Viviane, many years their senior, is the High Priestess of the Old Religion on the Isle of Avalon. It is primarily upon Igraine's children—Arthur, who becomes king, and Morgaine, destined to become High Priestess—that the story focuses. The tale is told from Morgaine's perspective, through her ability to get inside the minds of the other characters, particularly the other women in the story, such as Gwenhwyfar, the Christian girl who becomes Arthur's wife, and to recall events both past and future.

In the Goddess Religion, place is an important concept, as it is to the Laguna Pueblo and other tribal groups. However, as in the African-diasporic traditions, those who follow the Celtic way of the Goddess are separated from their tradition in time and space. In the Celtic Faery tradition, place often becomes a function of altered consciousness. Those who have the skills to alter their consciousness may be able to wander in and out of worlds, as Bradley portrays in *The Mists of Avalon*. As Morgaine, the reader's guide in the novel, says: "For at that time the gates between the worlds drifted within the mists, and were open, one to another, as the traveller thought and willed. For this is the great secret, . . . that by what men think, we create the world around us, daily new" (*MA*, ix).

In *The Mists of Avalon,* several worlds are portrayed: one is the Avalon of the Lady of the Lake, who is the High Priestess and representative of the Goddess on earth. At the time in which the novel takes place, Avalon has become part of the druidic mysteries and the priestesses cooperate with the druids, who are from a newer tradition.

Another world is the realm of the Castle Chariot, where time seems to stand still. This realm seems to be connected to the Goddess in her most elemental form—as blind, cyclical nature, neither good nor bad but life-sustaining, a force that has no name. When Morgaine wanders into the realm of Castle Chariot, the dark lady she meets there tells her: "I am not the Goddess, Morgaine, nor even her emissary. My kind know neither Gods nor Goddesses, but only the breast of our mother who is beneath our feet and above our heads, from whom we come and to whom we go when our time is ended. Therefore we cherish life and weep to see it cast aside" (*MA*, 225).

This aspect of the Mother is also present in Silko's *Ceremony.* Silko weaves in a section that is not really part of the plot—a section about a young child and his mother in the shacks of Gallup (*C*, 114–18). In an interview, Silko has said:

> The section is about the little child and his relationship to his mother. It also relates to Tayo because his mother comes and goes like the kid's mother. Tayo lost his mother when he was very young, so the child's mother becomes a metaphor for his mother and the mother of creation. The Laguna story that I follow is about the mother creator, and it's uncorrupted by Christianity. The mother in the Gallup section has her own kind of momentum and her own way. . . . [W]hen the little boy is

waiting for his mother to come back, he doesn't feel as rotten as the outward appearance of his life shows. He's been loved. It all comes together in the end, his being loved, the mother, the creator.[58]

Beyond Avalon and the realm of the Castle Chariot are other places, such as the lost island of Atlantis and the Land of Eternal Youth, which figure both in Bradley's fictional account of the Celtic Faery tradition and in contemporary witches' understanding. Christine Hartley, in *The Western Mystery Tradition*, recounts the legend—first recorded by Plato and a part of the esoteric traditions—of the lost Island of Atlantis on which there was a great temple. When the island sank into the sea, priests fled to Britain to maintain their traditions. Bradley uses this legend in the visions of both Morgaine and her mother, Igraine. Morgaine sees "the great temples of Atlantis now drowned forever between the covering oceans, . . . new worlds rising and setting . . . and silence and beyond the night the great stars wheeled and swung" (*MA*, 167). As she prepares for her part in the Great Marriage of the king to the land, Igraine remembers a former life at Atlantis that she shared with Uther, whom she eventually marries in her current life: she remembers "the *other* Uther, the Uther she had known at the ring of stones outside time and ordinary place; the priest of Atlantis with whom she had shared the Mysteries" (p. 75).

According to Starhawk, in the contemporary traditions of witchcraft, death "is a stage in the cycle that leads to rebirth. After death, the human soul is said to rest in 'Summerland,' the Land of Eternal Youth, where it is refreshed, grows young, and is made ready to be born again. Rebirth . . . is seen as the great gift of the Goddess, who is manifest in the physical world. Life and the world are not separate from Godhead; they are immanent divinity" (*SD*, 27).[59]

In *The Mists of Avalon,* the Isle of Avalon itself becomes this Land of Eternal Youth in legend, "lost forever in the mists of the Summer Sea" (*MA*, ix), after Christianity forces the island to retreat. Morgaine takes the dying Arthur away in the barge "to the true Holy Isle in the dark world behind our own" (x) where the peasants believe he lies sleeping.

This magical island of women (in all the stories, it is women who take Arthur away to a land in which a woman reigns) is not a recent invention but is mentioned by ancient Greek and Latin writers. For instance, Jean Markale quotes Pomponius Mela (III, 6) who says: "Facing the Celtic coasts lie a group of islands. . . . Sena in the British Sea (the Channel) . . . was renowned for its Gallic oracle, whose priestesses . . . were said to be nine in number." These priestesses had power over the weather, could change the form of animals, heal those stricken by "incurable" diseases, and foretell the future. They attended only with those who came "over the sea expressly to consult them."[60]

The soul's resting place is also called "the Land of Faery." According to Doreen Valiente, a contemporary practicing witch, the Land of Faery is a place that exists "in another dimension co-existing with the world we can see with mortal sight."[61] She notes that the Land of Faery can sometimes be visited in dreams and remembered in fragments. In a 1911 study, W. Y. Evans-Wentz claimed that the "Fairy-Faith" was still practiced in the British Isles. He recorded an interview with an Irish seer who claimed to see "opalescent beings" who "belong to the heaven world" and "shining beings" who "belong to the mid-world."[62] Evans-Wentz summarizes his findings: "[The Sidhe] are described as a race of majestic appearance and marvellous beauty, in form human, yet in nature divine. The highest order of them seem to be a race of beings evolved to a superhuman plane of existence . . . and are the race known to the ancient men of Erin as the Tuatha De Danann [Children of the goddess Dannu]."[63] Indeed, Irish mythology recounts the tales of the withdrawal of the people of the Goddess "into the hills and down into the earth, or to mysterious islands beyond the horizon" after being defeated by the sons of Mile, the Gaels.[64]

Justine Glass, in a study of contemporary witchcraft, comments that witches believe that the Goddess will allow them to be reborn among those they love if they deserve it. Witchcraft is often seen as hereditary, and practicing witches are seen as those who also practiced witchcraft in other lives.[65] Even though this belief does not accord with the findings of Celtic scholars, Bradley follows this tradition in *The Mists of Avalon* when she has characters remember former lives in which they served the Goddess and when she uses a title such as the Merlin and variations of the name, Morgan Le Fey. In the witchcraft tradition, these names are generic names or titles for those who serve the Goddess rather than names for specific individuals (like the name Yellow Woman in the Laguna tradition). That is not to say that individuals with those titles or names could or did not exist, but it is their mythic function that is most important in the witchcraft tradition. Hartley points out that the names of Arthur (the Sun God),[66] Merlin ("man from the sea . . . the first source of all life"), and Morgan ("woman from the sea . . . the Word, the life-giving Force")[67] are names that recur cyclically in the Celtic legends whether or not they are names of historic persons.

The Mists of Avalon portrays several places that coexist at the same time and even at the same place. Avalon, Glastonbury, and the fairy country all occupy the same time and site, but which one can be seen and visited depends on techniques of consciousness. Gwenhwyfar, who later becomes queen to Arthur, wanders into Avalon by mistake while playing outside her convent school in Glastonbury. According to Morgaine, who finds the girl and helps her cross again to the other place, her ability to come into Avalon unbidden and untrained shows the possession of some natural powers. Morgaine says it often happens "in spots of concentrated power" that "the veil" of mists between the places thins, but it is unusual for a person to be able to cross over rather than just to see across (*MA*, 157).

Many have tried to locate the site of Avalon or the Other World, placing it as the Isle of Aval in Brittany, the Isle of Man in Great Britain, or the abby of Glastonbury in the marshland, which is neither water nor land but both. However, as Markale notes, "such attempts have little point, because the island in question is outside the time and space of the living world."[68]

Studies of ancient Celtic religion and its remnants and *The Mists of Avalon* also discuss another aptitude—"the sight." Generally this seems to be a sort of sixth sense that can be developed with training, but that often seems to occur naturally in those who have a Celtic heritage. Therefore, in *The Mists of Avalon,* we see Morgause, Igraine's sister, using her powers without training; the difference in her use from others such as Morgaine in the novel is that she uses the sight for her own benefit and with no ethical standards. The suggestion is made that without the ethical standards imparted by the Goddess Religion—the training—the sight may be misunderstood and misused. Morgaine is asked to make spells and charms for Gwenhwyfar, but she balks at this, for she does not see herself as a purveyor of charms and spells but as one working for a larger good—the will of the Goddess.

Another way in which Bradley's *The Mists of Avalon* accords with Starhawk and the Celtic Faery tradition is in its identification of the druids as the surviving repository of the earlier Goddess Religion but, ultimately, as its betrayer. For instance, in discussing the Celtic tradition, Jean Markale refers to an old tale, from Ireland from A.D. 1200, in which a handsome man is lured away to the depths of the sea or across the sea to a land of women. Markale interprets this tale as harkening back to "an earlier age when women had powers lost to them even in Celtic societies."[69] Like the Avalon at the end of Bradley's novel, the women in the story are banished or control a land out of sight of ordinary mortals. They are, according to Markale, "reflection[s] of the goddess of ancient, pre-patriarchal societies, the *Magna Mater,* who haunts every corner of life, but reveals herself only reluctantly" and are even then in "conflict . . . with the established religion."[70] The story reads:

Ireland, *The Story of Condle the Red*

A woman dressed in the most beautiful clothes appeared to Condle, son of King Conn of the Hundred Battles. He alone could see her, though everyone else could hear her. When the King's Druid cast a spell that drove her away, Condle remained sad and silent for a month, eating nothing but an apple the woman had left him. Then she appeared to him again and invited him to come with her to the "Land of Promise inhabited only by women", in the strange world of the *sidh*, which is underground or over the sea. Despite the Druid's efforts, Condle left his father and family and sailed away in the fairy's "glass boat" never to be seen again.[71]

A Christianized version of the story illustrates the overthrow of the religion of the druids as well, but the women remain on their island and are still a danger to the established order—the young man ultimately disappears into their realm, as Markale interprets it. Similarly, at the end of *The Mists of Avalon*, the Great Goddess lives on in her aspect as the Virgin Mary. The Christianized version reads:

Brittany, *The Story of Guengualc'h*

Some young people returning from their studies were walking along the river bank in the valley of Trequrier. One of them, nicknamed Guengualc'h ("White Falcon") because he was so handsome, fell silent. When his friends tried to ask him a question there was no reply, and turning to look at him, they realized he had disappeared. They searched the river-bank in vain and, finally, in despair, called upon St. Tugdual for help.

"Immediately the young man rose to the surface of the river, with a silk sash tied to his right foot." He told how the "ladies of the sea" had taken him away and lured him under the rocks. He had been rescued by a venerable old man (St. Tugdual). "At the sight of the prelate, the nymphs had fled, but one of them forgot to untie her sash." They all offered up thanks to St. Tlugdual for having rescued Geuengualc'h who had been "temporarily deluded by the Devil". Guengualc'h "went to confession, took Communion, and, exactly a year to the very day after the Devil had led him astray, he left this world" (Vita *Santi Tulguali Episcopi*, 33, twelfth-century MS. in the Bibliothèque Nationale).[72]

Justine Glass explains that the witches worked with the druids when druidism was the official religion of Britain. Contemporary witches believe that Stonehenge, which predates the druids, was originally consecrated to the Great Goddess and that Stonehenge is "symbolic of the female principle."[73] According to her, "For about two thousand years, the witches were the priestesses of the community or village; performing rites for bringing prosperity to the land and to the people; acting as seers, healing men and animals in return for food and shelter."[74]

Bradley also shows how the religion of the Celts was absorbed into Christianity. An example is the goddess Brighid, who becomes St. Brigid. MacCana comments that "no clear distinction can be made between the goddess and the saint and that in all probability Brighid's great monastery of Kildare was formerly a pagan sanctuary."[75] MacCana says that originally "Brighid" was a term meaning "exalted one," and the term was also used for a goddess in Britain—Briganti, the exalted one. This goddess also gave her name to rivers: Ireland's Brighid, Wales' Brant, and England's Brent.[76]

In *The Mists of Avalon*, Bradley shows the reader a Britain in which there are four groups vying for survival: (1) the remnants of the older tribes, "the Goddess peoples," who Starhawk explains "were known as the Sidhe, the Picts or Pixies, the Fair Folk or Faeries" (*SD*, 4); (2) the Celts, who won over the older tribes, but who had incorporated much of the old Goddess Religion into the practices of the druids (p. 4); (3) the Christians; and (4) the Saxon invaders who were trying to take over Britain. Bradley shows the reader the period in Britain during which the druids, the remaining powerful force connected to the worship of the Goddess, are being overcome by Christianity. She gives us a good picture of the beliefs of the two conflicting religions and the adaptation by Christianity of many Old Religion rites and places of worship. Furthermore, the novel portrays the evolution of the Old Religion from the rituals of the tribes, the customs of the people, and the fairyland of the Dark Lady into druidic practice, as well as the intermingling of many beliefs. As Queen Morgause, sister of Igraine, says about her subjects: "To tell the truth, most of them care not whether the God of this land is the white Christ, or the Goddess, or the Horned One, or the Horse God of the Saxons, so long as their crops grow and their bellies are full" (*MA*, 212).

The function of the male druids and the priestesses of Avalon in *The Mists of Avalon* is important to understanding the ethical system of today's witches and how that system could be perverted. The druids or the Merlin seems to be the connection to the courts, to the outside world, and the High Priestess is the connection to the Goddess herself. It is the Merlin who tries to work out compromise with the Christians, to work out a way of coexisting, while it is the High Priestess who tries to maintain the old ways. Many have acknowledged that it is usually the women who carry on the traditions in a tribal society,[77] and here we see this pattern repeated. The question of whether a tradition is compromised by the attempts to coexist is one which continues to be argued, but failure to adapt also can lead to extinction.

In Silko's book *Ceremony* a major theme of the novel is the failure of the Laguna society to change, to adjust to the different circumstances in which they find themselves. They are caught in a system controlled by Euro-American values that is not of their making. The young men go off to a world war the scope of which could never be imagined. The Lagunas are a peace-loving tribe for whom war was seen as an abnormal activity. Before a tribal member who had killed in warfare could come back into the village, he had to be purified by the medicine men in rituals constructed especially for that purpose. But these rituals could not work for those involved in a world war. Hence a new ritual, a new way of seeing in order to put the pieces back together, had to be enacted for Tayo and others who came back from the war. Those who clung to the old rituals were doomed to be unsuccessful.

One of the differences between what happens in *Ceremony* and *The Mists of Avalon* involves this very principle. The High Priestesses as representatives of the Goddess attempt to carry on with the old rituals to create wholeness—to bring people back to the Goddess, but they never are able to put the pieces together to create new rituals. Rather than create positive rituals for union, they continually attempt to manipulate forces and people to fit into the little piece of the whole which they see. Like Tayo's old medicine man, Ku'oosh, they cannot understand the forces outside the immediate community well enough to conduct rituals for healing. Viviane has Arthur go through the ancient traditional testing of the King Stag and then mate with his own sister, Morgaine, as the Spring Virgin and representative of the Goddess. The ancient ritual had worked before and appears to work this time, but Viviane should not have used Morgaine as the Spring Virgin because in the Christian world in which Morgaine also lived, to sleep with Arthur, her brother, was incest, and the ritual Viviane prepared did not encompass this aspect of the changing world. The ritual ignored this powerful aspect of the situation, which later skews the results. Witchcraft is not a religion in which the ends justify the means. Do no harm and then do as you will is a basic tenet. Therefore the positive working of forces is stressed. In this case, although Viviane has many misgivings about using Morgaine in the ritual and fears Morgaine will come to hate her, Viviane persists anyway.

The Mists of Avalon also demonstrates the altered consciousness of being connected with the Goddess and what can happen when people turn away. Toward the end of the novel, a vision of the Holy Grail appears in Arthur's Great Hall to the peasants, knights, and ladies of the court. The Holy Grail, as has been noted before, is a version of Ceridwen's cauldron of plenty, from which all comes and in which people are rejuvenated. Markale also explains the cauldron or grail as "the uterus of the mother goddess."[78] Each viewer of the grail sees whatever his or her own faith allows him or her to see—much like the stories told by those who die momentarily and then are brought back to life. The peasants who have been invited into the hall for the celebration find on each plate what each likes the best, as in the old Celtic legends. Gwenhwyfar sees the Goddess herself, who tells her: "*Before Christ ever was, I am, and it was I who made you as you are. Therefore, my beloved daughter, forget all shame and be joyful because you, too, are of the same nature as myself*" (*MA*, 775).[79]

Most of the knights see the chalice of Christ borne by a maiden in white, but because they have turned away from the Goddess, there is a kind of retribution in this vision. Instead of seeing the vision as a cup of plenty, peace, and joy brought by the Goddess and connecting with the divine within themselves, the knights see it as the chalice of Christ and as something to be possessed. They do not feel that they are part of God, but see God as outside themselves, something to be sought after. Most follow this magical symbol of what should be fruitfulness to their deaths, in a frenzy to possess it. As Gwenhwyfar says of Lancelet's proposed quest, "So it had come to him, too, that great joy? But why, then, did he need to go forth to seek it? Surely it was within him as well?" (*MA*, 777).

Bradley shows that by the time of Arthur, Christianity had become a religion of ascetics; it did not value the land nor the female principle symbolized in the Goddess. As Kevin, the Merlin of Britain, says of some of the Christian bishops, "In their pride [they] see the Creator only as the avenging Father of Soldiers, not also as the loving Mother of the fields and the earth" (*MA*, 726).[80] Christianity had banished the joyous, raucous celebrations of fertility and life, of the gifts of nature and the Goddess, and kept only the love of blood in warfare. According to Jean Markale in her examination of the various versions of the grail quest, traditional elements associated with the grail are:

> *vengeance by blood,* after some action that has shaken the balance of the world and led to the infertility of the kingdom; *the impotence of the king* who can no longer rule; *ritual sacrifice,* whether human or animal or though simple substitution of the victim or offering; *task* inflicted on these who set out on the Quest; *female characters* who belong to a fairy world and guide those who take part in the Quest; and the *queen, princess or empress* who controls the drink of power and sovereignty, which is given only to the man who has overcome all the tasks.[81]

Markale asserts that long before the myth of the grail was absorbed into Christianity, the search for the grail was the search for woman—the quest for the Goddess overthrown by male gods. Only when her youngest son kills the usurping father will she rise from her other world to restore harmony.[82]

Lancelet is an example of what has happened to many of those who had come under the influence of Christianity. Son of Viviane of Avalon and born of the Great Marriage (the spring rites), he was raised in Avalon until he was sent to fosterage in Brittany.[83] At the time of the vision, he is at war with himself; he cannot trust what he has seen in the Great Hall. He fears it is some trick of his mother and must seek it out for himself. He cannot accept what has been given. He doubts the female principle within himself and must place it outside. Partly this is because of the mistrust he feels for a mother who is representative of the Goddess and who has manipulated things in a way harmful to him and others, but it is also a result of his allegiance to the patriarchal ways of Christianity. As he previously had said to his mother, "I have lived in a world where men do not wait for a woman's bidding to go and come" (*MA*, 146).

The women of Avalon have also strayed from the way of the Goddess. Morgaine, in her turn, has worked for the hurt of others. In a desperate attempt to conserve what she sees as the fading influence of the Goddess and to punish Arthur for his complicity with Christianity, she tries to replace the king with her priest and lover, Accolon. Morgaine questions whether she must lie and lure Arthur into the Fairy Land to serve the Goddess: *"Oh, as a maiden in Avalon I was so proud that I spoke only truth! Is it queencraft, then, to lie, that I may serve the Goddess?"* (*MA*, 729). When Morgaine has Excalibur, the sword, taken from Arthur while he sleeps in the Fairy Land, she has the choice of returning it to the Goddess and letting both Arthur and Accolon strive for the kingship unaided by Avalon's magic. Earlier, Kevin the Merlin had warned her against setting her "own will and pride and ambition for those" she loved above the Goddess, but she does not heed him and gives the sword to Accolon despite her own misgivings, since she believes that "without Excalibur, there was no way Accolon could reign as the new King from Avalon" (p. 734). Her own pride and ambition get in the way of her decision: *"When I am Queen, this land shall be at peace, and the minds of men free, with no priests to tell them what they must do and believe"* (p. 734).

Later she retreats to Avalon to be healed and comes to understand that her plans had been madness: "There at last I could mourn for Accolon—not for the ruin of my hopes and plans. . . . I could see what madness they had been; I was priestess of Avalon, not Queen" (*MA*, 757). *The Mists of Avalon*, then, illustrates the witches' belief, as does Silko's *Ceremony* for the Laguna, that the turning away from the Goddess, the Mother, results in illness and a sick society. This is an illustration of what Starhawk would call the use of "power-over" rather than "power from within" (*DD*, 1–14)—the difference between the role of queen of Christian Britain and priestess of Avalon.

In *The Mists of Avalon* and in the witchcraft religion, sexuality is sacred, and many of the old rites used the sexual act to raise and channel energy. Justine Glass cites "The Sacred Marriage" as an example. She says that the purpose of the Sacred Marriage was "to give power to the god" and "to create a contract, through this power, between the god and his worshippers."[84] The sexual act was not for the pleasure of the participants.

In *The Mists of Avalon,* Bradley explains the concept of the fertility ritual for the Goddess and the Horned God (also the sun god) that was enacted at the great festival of Beltane on May First. At this time the High Priestess and her priest participated in a ritual sexual union in order that the fields might be fertile and in acknowledgment that "she who works, silently and alone, at the heart of nature, cannot work her magic without the strength of Him who runs with the deer and with the summer sun draws forth the richness of the womb" (*MA*, 677).[85]

Doreen Valiente, a contemporary practicing witch, acknowledges that one of the main purposes of today's witchcraft is to ensure fertility through its rituals.[86] However, she notes that today the idea of fertility has evolved into a consideration of the fertility of the mind and the spirit. According to her, "The spirit of the old rites . . . continues; but in a higher form. The concern is not so much with literal fertility as with vitality, and with finding one's harmony with Nature. In this way, people seek for a philosophy of life which bestows peace of mind, as well as physical satisfaction."[87]

As in the Laguna Pueblo traditions and the African-diasporic traditions, the erotic and sexual activity can be important links to spirituality and to the Goddess. In *Dreaming the Dark*, Starhawk devotes a whole chapter to "Sex and Politics." She refers to Audre Lorde's power of the erotic, agreeing with Lorde that "the erotic can become the bridge that connects feeling with doing; it can infuse our sense of mastery and control with emotion so that it becomes life-serving instead of destructive. In the dialectic of merging and separating the erotic can confirm our uniqueness while affirming our deep oneness with all being. It is the realm in which the spiritual, the political, and the personal come together" (*DD*, 138).

Starhawk sees the erotic as capable of healing, if only temporarily, the mind/body split. It can lead an individual to ask, "What do I, at my root, at my core, desire?" (*DD*, 141). With proper attention to his or her erotic desires, "that power which arises from our deepest, non-rational knowledge,"[88] an individual can begin to integrate the various selves which Starhawk sees as split asunder in our culture. If people understand that sex is a kind of energy and therefore power, they can begin to see that same energy and power in nature around them and reestablish their links to the earth. Starhawk says: "Sex is energy. What gives the physical exchange its excitement, its intensity, is the movement of vital energy, an energy not limited to human beings, but present in earth, air, water, fire, in plants and animals, in all living things. Understanding that the erotic is energy opens up the potential for an erotic relationship with the earth" (p. 143).

Starhawk also points out that in loving someone else, people love themselves. In this way, sexual acts can be a kind of healing, especially if they allow people to see themselves as connected and whole. About this process she says:

> It seems that sexuality can be a process of mirroring. Self reflects self in the water; in the motions of hands, lips, tongue, genitals; in the thrust and arch of bodies; in attraction; in conversation; in growth and change. Mirroring, we take another into ourselves and become changed by that other. Being mirrored, we are acknowledged, our beings are recognized; we feel our own impact. Mirroring and being mirrored, we create a reverberation, the hum and throb of an energy that lifts us in waves of emotion and sensual pleasure. (*DD*, 136)

According to Starhawk, if people are genuinely listening to their innermost selves, they know that sexuality and the power of the erotic need not be limited to partners of the opposite sex. She says that we therefore need "to stop defining ourselves in terms of our sexual partners, to realize that the richness of sexual attraction and expression lies in its hues, its infinite shadings, and only our cultural estrangement restricts us to the three primary colors [lesbian, gay, or straight]" (*DD*, 142). It is this "richness of sexual attraction" which *The Mists of Avalon* portrays, not privileging one kind of sexual activity over another.

The function of sexuality, then, can be to connect the individual to others and to the earth, to institute change and growth, to heal in helping people love themselves and others. This is precisely what happens in *Ceremony* in Tayo's relationship with Night Swan and Ts'eh. These women are, as Native American writer Linda Hogan says, "spirit people,"[89] and function as aspects of Thought Woman to heal Tayo by connecting him to the earth and to the female principle. He feels himself loved and can then extend that love to the earth and those around him. He can again grow and change. A similar process happens for Celie through Shug in *The Color Purple.* Shug is not a spirit person or aspect of the Goddess in the same way as Night Swan or Ts'eh is, but the result for Celie is the same. She feels loved and this love extends to everything around her; she feels connected; the joy of "the color purple"—nature's brazen acknowledgment of joy and passion mirrored in the wildflowers—flows through her, and the long process of healing begins to take place.

In *Zami,* Lorde describes her sexual relationship with Kitty, who takes on the aspect of the Goddess, Afrekete. This sexual relationship becomes a ritual and acts in the same way for Lorde as it does for Celie and Tayo. It also allows her to see aspects of the Goddess in herself and in others or to discover, as Starhawk and practitioners of witchcraft say, that she *is* the Goddess. According to the witchcraft tradition, this is the highest point of initiation into the Mysteries and one of the most difficult—to see that God or the Goddess is not outside oneself, but that one is the God. This is the ultimate connection.[90] In a woman-centered tradition, women discover that they are the Goddess in a way that they cannot in other male-centered traditions. In fact, scholar Charlotte Spivack suggests that *The Mists of Avalon* goes even further than just showing characters who embody the Goddess; she says that "above all *The Mists of Avalon* addresses the woman reader as the goddess incarnate."[91] In this way the novel also becomes a curing ceremony like the novels of the others we have discussed—changing the world view of women and allowing them to see themselves as embodiment of the sacred.

In *The Mists of Avalon*, Morgaine finally comes to this insight:

> And now she knew why she had never again caught sight of the queen within the land of Fairy.
>
> *I am the queen now.*
>
> *There is no Goddess but this, and I am she. . .*
>
> *And yet beyond this, she is, as she is in Igraine and Viviane and Morgause and Nimue and the queen. And they live in me too, and she. . .*
>
> *And within Avalon they live forever.* (*MA*, 815)

Sexual relationships play an important part in *The Mists of Avalon*. There is the Great Marriage—the marriage of the king or queen to the land in which Morgaine officiates as the Spring Maiden and representative of the Goddess, while Arthur is the King Stag and the representative of the Horned God, consort of the Goddess. In the old rites recorded by many scholars, this rite was believed to release energy to ensure fertility for the land and people.[92] It signified the direct connections between the ruler, the Goddess, the land, and fertility. Fertility was renewed by slaying (or later, symbolically slaying) the ruler or his or her representative before the powers of fertility waned. The new ruler then "married the land" or was "ritually united with the sovereignty of the territory," usually a person who represented the Goddess or the Horned God.[93] In Celtic mythology, the state of the kingdom reflected the worth of the ruler. A ruler "who is blemished in . . . conduct and character or in his [or her] person" must be "deposed."[94] These rites are an example of what Glass refers to when she comments that sexual rituals were for the power of the Goddess and not for the pleasure of the individuals.

A second kind of sexual ritual is the one performed by Nimue with Kevin, the Merlin of Britain, in revenge for what is seen as his betrayal of the Goddess and of Avalon. She consummates their relationship in the dark of the waning moon, thought to be a time to work evil magic rather than good. This ritual binds him to her in what Starhawk would describe as the use of "power-over" another rather than the use of "power-from-within." Power-over is a misuse of the erotic and a violation of that mirror relationship in which the lovers are mirrored in one another and grow and change. Though Nimue uses the erotic to harm, she does not escape from the hurt she causes; what she "sends" returns to her: "For an enchantment to be total, it must involve both enchanter and enchanted, and she knew with a spasm of terror, that this spell she was weaving would work on her too, and rebound on her" (*MA*, 787). And so it does; after she delivers Kevin over to his death, she drowns herself, unable to bear the guilt of her part in his betrayal.

A third kind of sexual relationship is that in which the lover is changed, grows, is connected to the self, other, and nature, and thereby is healed. Morgaine has three such relationships—one with Kevin, one with Accolon, and one with Raven. In her relationship with Kevin, she finds he accepts and loves her for who she is, not as priestess or queen but as herself. In turn, she accepts and loves him, not caring about his broken body or that he is the Merlin of Britain. Her sexual relationship with Kevin is a healing one for Morgaine: "*This is the first time really, that I have done this of my free will, and had the gift taken simply, as it was offered.* It healed something in her" (*MA*, 417)—making up somewhat for Viviane's betrayal of her in the sexual rites with her brother Arthur.

Morgaine's sexual relationship with Accolon restores her connection with the Goddess. In this powerful sexual ritual, she again becomes priestess of the Goddess: "Even as we lay together under the stars that Midsummer, I knew that what we had done was not so much lovemaking as a magical act of passionate power, that his hand, the touch of his body, were reconsecrating me priestess, and that it was her will" (*MA*, 588).

Her sexual relationship with Raven also heals, but like Tayo's relationship with Ts'eh and Lorde's with Afrekete, it becomes something much larger than themselves—part of the glory and the power of the Goddess, the ultimate mirroring:

> It seemed that the real world and Avalon had both slipped away, and again she was in the shadows of the fairy country, held close in the arms of the lady. . . . Morgaine heard in her mind the words of the ancient blessing of Avalon, as Raven touched her slowly, with ritual silence and significance, and the sound seemed to shiver around her in the silence. . . . And then the world began to flow and change and move around her and for a moment it was not Raven in the silence, but a form edged in light, whom she had seen once, years before, at the time when she crossed the great silence . . . and Morgaine knew that she too was glowing in light . . . still the deep flowing silence. (*MA*, 639)

Morgaine feels that she is "received simply in love" for the first time and "that she lay in the lap of her mother . . . no, not Igraine, but welcomed back into the arms of the Great Mother" (*MA*, 640). Marilyn Farwell argues that this scene is pivotal, "undercut[ting] the heterosexuality which informs the rest of the narrative. . . . The space of movement in this novel is at its center defined by female desire, the desire of one woman for another, for Morgaine is at home only when she is in the arms of another woman."[95]

In her personal life, Grahn also illustrates the sacred power of sexuality, particularly for lesbians. With her partner Paula Gunn Allen, she says she experienced "psychic" sex, an altered state of consciousness in which "the experience is that of taking a journey to sources of power and creativity, of 'making' something, and of being made. Of going somewhere and coming back different."[96] Grahn continues: "In the sexual creative trance, metaphors, . . . spirit-guides of every description from earth and sky and parts unknown arrive with messages and meanings, as the lovers pass through level upon level of sexual and psychic feeling in a state that may go on for hours, at or near the level of intensity immediately preceding orgasm."[97]

Grahn describes the power of lesbians visualizing together in this "creative trance" to "bring back the power of any 'goddess' force" that is wanted, "to strengthen any elements of nature and human society" one chooses, and to bring forth "any ideas or altered understandings" in themselves and others selected.[98] This is the power of "ceremonial Lesbians and ceremonial Dykes,"[99] as Grahn sees it. Grahn, who gives intensive workshops on "Goddess and Mythology" at women's events, illustrates how a contemporary lesbian might take elements of the Celtic tradition of which Starhawk speaks, blending and shaping them to incorporate them into her own life.

This power is not only manifested in sexual rituals and relationships, but it can be part of many other kinds of rituals, part of everything one does. As a practicing witch, teacher, and therapist, Starhawk sees as one of her purposes "to create a context that evokes power-from-within each" participant in her rituals or workshops (*DD*, 145).

In her more recent work, *Truth or Dare (TD)*, Starhawk adds a third kind of power—power-with, or "the power not to command, but to suggest and be listened to, to begin something and see it happen" (p. 10). According to Starhawk, this power "bridges the value systems of power-from-within and power-over" (p. 15). Power-over is based on a worldview in which humans are inherently evil and must be saved by grace—they "have no inherent worth; worth must be earned or granted" (p. 14). In the value system of power-from-within, "the world itself is a living being, made up of dynamic aspects, a world where one thing shapeshifts into another, where there are no solid separations and no simple causes and effects" (p. 15).

Power-with sees the world in relationships, as does power-from-within, but it is interested in how to direct, mold, and shape those relationships according to how each affects the other. This is the power to be used creatively, dynamically in group situations to change reality by collective action. But, as Starhawk explains, everyone is trained in power-over dynamics and must work to learn new patterns. An illustration of power-with and the magic of bringing that power forth is an incident that occurred in a gym that held six hundred women who were arrested for blockading the Livermore Weapons Lab in California, known for the design and development of nuclear weapons. On her second day of incarceration, a woman chased by six guards ran into the gym and dived into the center of a meeting the other women were having. The women drew around her, shielding her, while the guards grabbed her arms and legs to pull her out. Tension rose as tempers flared. Starhawk expected nightsticks to "descend on kidneys and heads" (*TD*, 5), but instead someone began to chant, and the women followed in a "low hum that swells and grows with open vowels as if we had become the collective voice of some ancient beast that growls and sings . . . but knows nothing of guns . . . [or] nightsticks yet gives protection" (p. 5).

Another woman said, "Sit down," and the women complied. Now isolated, the standing guards pulled back and finally left. For Starhawk, the power of domination, power-over, had met the power-from-within, another alternative, and the act that evoked it was magic—power-with. Starhawk also defines magic as "the art of liberation, the act that releases the mysteries, that ruptures the fabric of our beliefs and lets us look into the heart of deep space where dwell the immeasurable, life-generating powers" (*TD*, 6).

It is this rupturing, restructuring of society's power-over mentality that is Starhawk's goal. It is the restructuring that results in the healing of the spirit/mind/body split and that eventually would result in the healing of the earth, the reconnecting of all. In this sense, rituals serve to evoke the power-from-within, to create the power-with of action, to help bring the individual to balance, and to remind each person of his or her inherent worth and connectedness to all.

The rituals in Starhawk's tradition usually begin with evoking "the magic circle where all forces come together equally" (*TD*, 25). The four directions and four elements, "which each correspond to qualities within a human being" (p. 23)—East "to air and mind, South to fire and energy, West to water, emotion, and sexuality, North to earth and body" (p. 23)—are called. According to Starhawk, an awareness of all the aspects of ourselves will allow us to "move freely around the wheel, and in and out of the center—to evoke the aspect of ourselves that we need to become whole" (p. 24).

Ritual and the power of the erotic can also extend even to such things as picking up trash along a riverfront because for a witch, as for the Lagunas, everything is connected and therefore all life is sacred—everything pertains to religion. The only thing needed to make a space sacred is the recognition that it is a sacred space.[100] Starhawk sees political acts such as demonstrations and blockades as rituals, and if they involve the use of symbols, they can become magical—a "magicopolitical event" (*DD*, 171). They become "a symbolic act done in a deepened state of consciousness" (p. 169).

Starhawk has been involved in numerous "magicopolitical events" in which she has conducted rituals for change and for healing. In *Dreaming the Dark,* she describes an equinox ritual in which she took part to stop a nuclear power plant from being opened at Diablo Canyon in California. She and others had been involved in a blockade to stop the workers from entering the plant, but she knew that this would not be enough to keep the plant from opening. So she and others conducted rituals on a ridge above the plant and sent the power raised "down to find the plant's weakest spots, the fault lines within its structure-of-being" (*DD*, 179). Later, when the plant's license to conduct low-level testing was revoked because of multiple problems found in the plans of the plant and because of safety violations, Starhawk felt the ritual and the blockade had been a success because they had changed "the reality, the consciousness, of the society in which the plant exists" (p. 180). The magic caused the violations to be found.

Starhawk sees all such actions as "dreaming the dark," as trying to move back to each person's connections and respect for the earth and all living things by reintegrating the female principle—acting on the deepest, innermost knowledge of each. If society does not, it faces the "holocaust" of destroying itself and the earth. She acknowledges that changing society will take many generations, but urges each of us to "plant its seeds . . . dream its shape in our vision" so that "our ritual can feed its growing power" (*DD*, 180). She, like Grahn and the others we have studied, work for the restoration of the female principle and the healing this implies. In this sense, curing society becomes first a curing of the individual—a restoration and acknowledgment of the spiritual power of women—leading to a way of life in harmony with all, leading to a curing of the earth.

FIVE

From the Euro-American Mainstream: Sonia Johnson and Mary Daly

In this chapter we will consider another thread of the Goddess or the female principle, this time as manifested in mainstream American politics and religion by white lesbian feminists Sonia Johnson and Mary Daly, respectively. Johnson and Daly advocate the return of the female principle as a major part of American culture. Johnson brings her Church of Jesus Christ of Latter-day Saints (LDS or Mormon) background to her politics, while Daly brings her Catholic and theological training to her teaching, writing, and activism. Like Starhawk, Johnson is not primarily a writer but an activist, and her work for change comes primarily from her involvement with people. Central to both, however, is the female principle or its symbol, the Goddess.

In order to understand Johnson's perspective on the Goddess, which comes from her experience of being a lifelong Mormon, it is necessary to use her life as "document." She has recorded much of it in her books, *From Housewife to Heretic (HH), Going Out of Our Minds: The Metaphysics of Liberation (GOM),* and *Wildfire: Igniting the She/Volution (WIS).* Like the Laguna and

African-American cultures, Mormonism is a "culture" unto itself within American culture. Born into an LDS family in Malad, Idaho, in 1936, Sonia Johnson grew up in Logan, Utah—Mormon country. The Mormon mother of four children, Johnson's involvement in national politics grew out of her work in 1978 for the passage of the Equal Rights Amendment (ERA). Before that time, she had devoted her life to being a wife, mother, part-time teacher, and "saint" in the LDS church. She has a Bachelor's degree from Utah State University and a Master's and doctorate in education from Rutgers University. Johnson's life, like Lorde's portrayed in *Zami,* is an example of a healing journey.

To Johnson, the Mormon culture in which she was raised has some commonalities with traditional tribal cultures. It elicits some of the same confusions in present-day Mormons with which present-day tribal peoples have to contend. She says that in the "Mormon world . . . all natural phenomena" are interpreted "in a personal or supernatural way," so that being a faithful Mormon in the twentieth century is like living in the dualism of once-colonized peoples like the Africans or Native Americans: "[O]n the one hand, [was] their ancient unfragmented world in which the lines between the living and the dead were blurred and where mystery and the supernatural were natural, and on the other, [was] European rationalism. . . . I, too, had lived with a split consciousness for much of my life" (*HH,* 66).

Another similarity between Mormonism and the traditional religions of Africans or Native Americans is the concept of history or time. As Mark Leone explains, Mormonism

> has reorganized the distinctions between past, present, and future so that these are no longer separate from each other but are considered equally understandable because they are equally accessible. As a result, the normal way of giving meaning to the present, by comparing it with a time assumed to be different, is gone. To a novel degree Mormonism made all events equally understandable and thus the same. Mormonism

> did so by holding that life has neither beginning nor end but is a continuous existence which always was and ever will be. This continuum, which embraces the whole of time, is known as salvation history. The past represents attempts to found and refound God's Kingdom on earth. The future contains the millennium and then existence, not in heaven, but in worlds governed by processes like those we know now.[1]

Of course, the similarity here is not the concept of Salvation History, but the ideas of the continuum—the cyclical recurrence of events in which all time becomes one in the presence of the ever-living spirits. As Jan Shipps explains the Mormon concept of time: the Saints "moved out of the primordial present into the future by replicating the past . . . [which] was not conscious ritual re-creation of events, but rather experiential 'living through' of sacred events in a new age."[2] Silko's *Ceremony* illustrates this same principle. Tayo is " 'living through' . . . sacred events," the propitiation of the Mother to bring back harmony and life to the community. As in the Mormon perspective, his life becomes one with the old sacred stories enacting their importance for a contemporary body of worshipers and readers. The difficulty of his situation is that of his people. Catapulted out of "sacred into profane, linear historical time"[3] by his involvement in the war, Tayo represents the disorientation that has occurred among his people as the veterans return from the war, denying what they had once seen as sacred. Shipps suggests that this occurred to the Mormons when they were forced to give up polygamy. In addition, nineteenth-century Mormons and traditional African and Native cultures were similar in another way. As Leone notes, "Power from the supernatural was used to govern economic and political processes."[4] In other words, for Mormons religious rituals regulated the whole of daily life. It could be argued that much of this continues today and that this is the worldview from which Johnson comes.

As is true of the authors in the previous chapters, words and stories are important to Johnson and have been important in her

Mormon upbringing. She recalls that her family's idea of a good time "was to sit around after supper . . . and tell 'faith-promoting stories.' " She says: "Everyone had stories to tell of miraculous healings. Everyone had seen, expected to see, or knew someone who had seen spirits, or had had glimpses beyond the veil" (*HH*, 63). Johnson herself was a teller of stories. For instance, she told a continuous story to a group of friends every day for years as she walked home from school: "A wandering minstrel, I, beginning my lifelong love affair with words" (p. 67). These stories were testimonies to faith and involved dreams, visions, and perils faced through the goodness of God.

The world in which Johnson grew up was a world "in which the living and dead were on speaking terms, and where heaven and its powerful inhabitants were intimately involved in human affairs and perpetually on call" (*HH*, 64). Shipps reminds us "that within Mormonism, divinity is still as real as all the other realities of every day existence."[5] This worldview in which there is little separation between spirit and matter is similar to that which we have seen in the work of Silko and the others, but Mormon theology is also distinctly different.

Mormonism asserts that in it, the prophecies have been fulfilled—Mormons are the chosen people, inheritors of the true church of Jesus Christ through revelations buried by extinct peoples, descendants of the tribes of Israel, who had immigrated to the area now known as America before 587 B.C.E. It is their task to take up the priesthood of the extinct tribes of Aaron and Melchizedek to preach "the reestablishment of the kingdom of God, not in the future but in the present"[6] in preparation for the millennium when God would restore the world to its Edenic state. As Shipps points out, "The Mormon restoration can best be comprehended if it is placed in the larger context of radical restoration movements which from time to time across the ages have so reordered experience that humanity has been able to see anew the hand of God in history."[7] Today it is the wearing of special undergarments, eating or not eating specific foods, worship activity, participation in community activities such as the priesthood or women's relief society, tithing and adhering to special behavior codes that reminds each Latter-day Saint that he or she is special—of the chosen people.

The Mormon epigram, "As man is, God once was; as God is, man may become,"[8] postulates the belief that people are part of a continuum of spiritual and physical evolution into divinity. As Brigham Young, Utah successor to founder and prophet Joseph Smith, said, "The Lord created us for the purpose of our becoming Gods like Himself when we have been proved in our present capacity—growing up from the low estate of manhood to become Gods until we can create worlds on worlds."[9] Those saints who are married in the Mormon temple are "sealed" together for eternity so that they can continue their relationship in the next stage. Hence, great emphasis is placed on marriage and the basis of the Mormon church is not the individual but the family. While every man can become a priest, women can only succeed in their journey if they are married to a Mormon priest.[10] Because of this doctrine of heavenly husbands and wives, there is, therefore, in Mormon theology, a "Heavenly Mother"—"a glorified goddess, spouse to an actual Heavenly Father, therefore the eternal mother of mortal spirits."[11] This concept has been of great importance to Johnson, as we shall see later.

Eliza R. Snow, who wrote Mormon poems and hymns and who was first one of Joseph Smith's plural wives and then one of Brigham Young's, wrote a hymn expressing Smith's concept of the Heavenly Mother. It was originally entitled "Invocation; or, the Eternal Father and Mother," but is now called, "O! My Father." The relevant stanzas are:

In the heavens are parents single?
No; the thought makes reason stare.
Truth is reason; truth eternal
Tells me I've a mother there.

When I leave this frail existence—
When I lay this mortal by,
Father, mother may I meet you
In your court on high?[12]

When Johnson discusses the idea of a Mother in Heaven, she refers to this hymn as do many scholars and theologians. Johnson says: "Eliza R. Snow first proclaimed her nearly a century and a half ago, and she was legitimized in the middle of this century by Bruce McConkie, an official of the church who asserts that she is equal in 'glory, perfection and holiness to Father' " (*HH*, 241). The idea of Mother in Heaven became crucially important to Johnson in 1978 when she had what she calls "an epiphany."

Johnson was attending a sacrament meeting in the spring of 1978 at which a visiting dignitary of the LDS church was giving an anti-ERA sermon. She says that she had "a profoundly enlightening and spiritual experience" (*HH*, 105), quite contrary to what the visiting dignitary expected; "feminism with all its implications and reverberations . . . struck my soul" (p. 108). The impact of the teaching of her church that women cannot evolve spiritually unless they are "sealed in eternal marriage" to a priest—the impact of her understanding of the place and status of women in a patriarchal culture—changed her life. She "came together, heart and mind"; she "began to be born—not a woman, but a human being" (p. 108).

Later, after her family went to bed, she confronted God with her anger about her discoveries. She calls this night the night she "fought God."[13] She raged and wrestled with the concept of God that she had been taught. She realized that she had always believed in "God as the Old Testament tyrant" (*HH*, 113). Like Celie in Walker's *Color Purple* when she understands that this image of God no longer works for her, Johnson rejects this "villainous and treacherous" (p. 113) patriarchal God and searches for an image of God with which she can identify: "Gradually, stroke by stroke I redrew deity, piece by piece I reorganized heaven, because I wanted neither to give them up nor to fight against them" (p. 116).

What she finds is the image she has known all along—the female principle or "Mother in Heaven." She remembers that "Mormon doctrine attests" to such a deity, and she says, "I gradually reinstated her in her rightful position in my new heaven as equal in power and glory to Father—not in subordination" (*HH*, 119). So empowered, Johnson felt whole and "wonderful." At last she had an understanding "that femaleness is as divine, as desirable, as powerful as maleness" (p. 119). Like the others we have studied, she took certain elements of her tradition and created new combinations.

From this experience, Johnson seems to have adopted the religious mission of telling the truth of what she had discovered —to "really be," with "Mother and Father in Heaven" cheering her on. Of this mission, she says: "I am a warrior in the time of women warriors; the longing for justice is the sword I carry, the love of womankind my shield" (*HH*, 119). She believes that she is on earth at this time so that she can help people do something about sexism, the "very deep, very ancient, and increasingly painful disease in society and religion" (p. 229).

Johnson was pushed into national political prominence when she was asked to testify on August 4, 1978, before the Senate Subcommittee on Constitutional Rights about extending the time allowed to ratify the ERA. Because of her belief in the church and in her understanding of Mother in Heaven, Johnson accepted. Then living in Virginia, she was chosen because of her work in the organization "Mormons for the ERA" and because she was "the only full-time wife and mother" in the group and therefore was available (*HH*, 122). A public Mormon stand against the ERA and "militant feminist tactics" had been taken by Relief Society general president Belle S. Spafford in an address printed in the July 13, 1974, *Church News*. Spafford saw the traditional roles of mother and homemaker as the most important, although she had spoken "in favor of equal pay for equal work, nondiscrimination in hiring practices, and the need for women to develop their full potential."[14] The debate on the ERA within the Mormon church continued, however, because a definitive stand was not taken by the male hierarchy until October 1976, when the church's First Presidency announced its opposition to the ERA. The result was to end discussion and bring to question "the faithfulness" of Mormon women who continued to support the ERA and believed, like Johnson, "that their support of women's rights had precedents in Mormon doctrine and history."[15] Johnson's decision to speak even after the First Presidency had come out against the ERA changed her life and was the beginning of her involvement in national politics, eventually leading to her bid for the presidency of the United States as the Citizens Party candidate in 1984.

Even in her political activities, Johnson did not feel separate from her religion. She says Mormons believe in miracles because they live "in harmony with God's laws" (*HH*, 123). Johnson prayed for the prophet and president of the Mormon church to receive the miracle of a revelation about the situation of women within the church. There was a precedence for such a "miracle" in Johnson's lifetime: the church had had such a revelation about allowing black men into the priesthood a few years earlier. Before she testified in front of the Senate subcommittee, Johnson prepared her speech, drawing on the testimony of her suffragist Mormon foremothers, Emmeline B. Wells, editor of the *Woman's Exponent* and fifth general president of the Relief Society,[16] and Lucinda Lee Dalton, "poet . . . from Beaver, Utah."[17] She says she "wanted to remind the church of the humanitarian and liberal roots it was repudiating by opposing women's rights in this century. I wanted to remind Mormon women, my sisters, of what strength and courage and conviction our mothers had about the necessity of the liberation of women" (*HH*, 126).[18]

As she finished writing her testimony, she prayed to her heavenly parents to help her. Like Starhawk, Johnson is able to use her heightened awareness, developed over many years of fasting and praying, to go from one realm to another. When she opened her eyes, she had a vision of her foremothers whose words she had been reading while writing: "Hearing a rustling, I opened my eyes, and there around the three sides of the room, with their heads about six inches from the ceiling, stood a throng of women in old-fashioned dress. Not like a photograph or a tableau, but moving slightly" (*HH*, 126).

They spoke to her in her mind and told her not "to be afraid. This work has to be done. It is hard, but it is our work too, and we are helping you all we can. Have courage. Know we are with you" (p. 126). According to scholar Mark Leone, Johnson's vision would be in good Mormon tradition in which Mormons attempt "to understand all events as part of God's plan. . . . Each Mormon may search his or her life for illustrations of divine intention . . . [and] the meanings given to the religion are flexible and varied."[19]

As a result of her testimony, Johnson clashed with Utah's Mormon senator, Orrin Hatch, at the subcommittee meeting. Her testimony supported the ERA in opposition to the position held by Mormon church leaders, of whom Hatch was one. She began to get a national reputation as a political activist, but her use of spirituality in politics did not end there.

On vacation with her family in Utah shortly after the subcommittee hearing, she got word that a filibuster was being threatened by Utah's Senator Jake Garn, also a Mormon, to keep the ERA extension bill from a final vote. Angry with her church's involvement in politics, she vowed to use a religious technique common to her religion to stop them, "a genuine Mormon fast, without food or liquid . . . until you stop talking or I die" (*HH*, 147). Johnson's use of fasting may be seen as similar to Starhawk's "magicopolitical" (*DD*, 171) event in that it is "a symbolic act done in a deepened state of consciousness" to cause "change in accordance with will" (p. 169). She obtained a permit to stand on the steps of the Capitol for twenty-three hours a day (she would sleep one hour in a nearby church), but she never had to make good on her vow. Garn did not filibuster. Johnson believes that her plan changed Garn's mind, and one could say, that like Starhawk's blockade, her plan, prepared with prayer and deliberation, caused a change in the "consciousness" of society and allowed the ERA extension to go through.

Johnson used her belief in Mother in Heaven to bring spirituality into her political work. Shortly after she testified before the Senate subcommittee, Johnson became president of the national organization, Mormons for the ERA, a group which numbered five hundred in 1979 but had doubled by 1981 (*HH*, 389). Her political activities on behalf of the ERA and the female principle (Mother in Heaven) sharply increased at this time. She was much in demand as a speaker and was invited to speak to ERA organizations around the country. Mormons for ERA hired a plane to fly the banner, "Mormons for ERA are everywhere!" over the international assembly of Mormon "patriarchs" in Salt Lake City in 1979, to remind the church fathers of their failure to grant women equality. Over other such conferences, they flew banners that said: "Mother in Heaven Loves Mormons for ERA."[20]

When Johnson saw the press release of a picture of the banner, she felt that "the proclamation of Mother in Heaven is an historic act, the beginning of something momentous. It will permanently change the course not just of churches, but of religion." Later she commented that she did not know enough about the women's movement at that time to realize that "this was not a prediction but a statement of fact. The concept of a female deity was revolutionizing world religion right under our very noses at that moment" (*HH*, 247).

It was this very use of spirituality in politics, however, specifically the idea of Mother in Heaven, which led to Johnson's excommunication. Johnson says that the church leaders' actions were against "Mother" as much as they were against her: "As long as Mother remained a shadow appendage of the *real*—i.e., *male*—God, as long as she knew her place and kept it, she was tolerated. But when she began to get uppity, drastic steps had to be taken to return her to anonymity and powerlessness" (*HH*, 246).

The church leaders tried to accuse her of starting "a Mother in Heaven cult" (*HH*, 239). As a teacher of the Relief Society, the Mormon organization for women, Johnson says she never spoke of Mother to her classes, but some of the women in her group were questioned by a Mormon bishop about whether Johnson had led them in prayer to Mother in Heaven or tried to persuade them to pray to her.

After a long ordeal, Johnson was excommunicated from the Church of Jesus Christ of Latter-day Saints in December 1979. Ironically, it was because she cared for her church that she had plunged into political activities in the first place. Johnson had believed that "Mormonism . . . is not just another church, another voluntary organization. . . . It is the Kingdom of God. It is the mortal system, the Earth, the Universe, and the world beyond. It encompasses all that exists" (*HH*, 392). Johnson's religion encompassed all and was all to her. Therefore, she says that true Mormons would not consider leaving the church, but would "stay and fight for change" because of their "love" for the church (p. 392). The traumatic experience of being excommunicated, however, allowed her to take what she felt was good from her tradition and combine it with feminism to create something new—a spiritual-political perspective—in a way similar to Walker's creation of a "womanist" perspective.[21]

She also continued staging magicopolitical or spiritual-political events. In 1980 she was arrested with twenty other women for chaining herself to the gates of the new Mormon temple in Bellevue, Washington, to protest the church's policies (*HH*, 389). In 1982 she fasted for thirty-seven days in Springfield, Illinois, "to underscore the seriousness of women's commitment to the Equal Rights Amendment."[22] As she wrote in her journal, "The fast is like the sun. It's an attempt to focus spiritual attention and energy upon the problem. It gathers all our passion and love together and sends it forth with authority into the hearts of even the most intractable" (*GOM*, 80).

By 1982, when she made her unsuccessful bid for president of the National Organization for Women (NOW), she had been a NOW member for four-and-a-half years and was a member of the Northern Virginia NOW Board. She had made no secret of her view that the struggle for women's rights was a spiritual and religious battle as well as a political one ever since the night she "fought God": "I began to feel a wholeness and a personal power that transcended any happiness I had ever known. With Mother on her throne as a model for me in heaven, I felt wonderful. . . . I felt like the ancient Boadicea, deeply and contentedly strong. Nothing seemed impossible. I was eager for experience, open to everything. . . . I look forward with calm and cheerful anticipation to all the battles that lie ahead" (*HH*, 119). However, many NOW members felt uncomfortable with what was seen as Johnson's "mysticism" and rejected her extension of the spiritual into the political. They argued that she had not "come up through the ranks" of holding office in NOW and did not have enough experience in the NOW leadership to be president. Her civil disobedience, particularly the fasting, was seen as extreme, and many NOW members wanted to have nothing to do with her.[23] These members gave their support to Judy Goldsmith, who was seen as a more moderate candidate—one who would continue NOW's tactics of fighting for the ERA and other goals through the established legal and political system.

Johnson's spiritual and political battle for women's rights can be seen as belonging to a religious tradition, particularly associated with some branches of Protestantism[24] in which a believer's "justification" is by faith alone and not through good works. This is a faith that does not need to be mediated through the clergy or some other middle person. As others have pointed out, Mormonism is the most democratic of religions in which every man can be a priest and beyond that a god.[25] However, its democratic impulse goes only so far when it comes to women, because women are not allowed to become priests; therefore this concept of following one's conscience has been particularly important to women in such religions where they do not have equality within the institutional church. When the Reverend Harvey Egan introduced Johnson at the St. Joan of Arc Catholic Church in Minneapolis, Minnesota, he concurred with Johnson's perspective, saying that "conscience is the supreme moral authority."[26]

This tenet has been particularly important to some women throughout history who have acted "from a deep radical commitment to their own faiths."[27] "Radical obedience" to faith has allowed women to free themselves from the restrictions often placed on them within patriarchal religions and envision new ways of relating to the spiritual aspects of life.[28] It has also enabled women to reclaim their bodies and feelings, an act that can lead to an integration of mind and body. The prominence of women in the religious revivals and in the founding of utopian religious communities in the nineteenth century is a testimony to the use women made of radical obedience to their faiths.[29]

This phenomenon was also prominent in Puritan America and can be seen in such women as Anne Bradstreet and Sarah Edwards. Edwards, like Johnson, had a religious ecstatic experience in which she realized that her personal experience of God came before her loyalty to community and her minister husband. As scholar Amanda Porterfield says of Edwards, she saw "that she was not obliged to meet other people's standards for a wife of a minister of God. Her only responsibility was to God. And her joyful obedience to God would now put her even beyond reach of her husband's criticism."[30]

Put in other words, radical obedience to faith, which in Johnson's case is obedience to the will of the Mother and Father in Heaven—that she spread word of women's equality and of the Mother's existence—and following her own heart and voice, is similar to Starhawk's "magic, the art of evoking power-from-within and using it to transform ourselves, our community, our culture, using it to resist the destruction that those who wield power-over are bringing the world" (*DD*, xi). By Starhawk's definition, power-from-within is the Goddess or "immanence—the awareness of the world and everything in it as alive, dynamic, interdependent, interacting and infused with moving energies: a living being, a weaving dance" (p. 9). Johnson's radical obedience to Mother can also be seen as the creative intelligence of Silko and Allen's Thought Woman, and as Lorde's Black mother or the power of the erotic—"a resource within each of us that lies in a deeply female and spiritual plane, firmly rooted in the power of our unexpressed or unrecognized feeling."[31]

Recent Mormon women writers have voiced the concern that women's role in the Mormon church has changed from the roles that nineteenth-century Mormon women had expected to play in the church's future. As Jan Shipps says in her foreword to *Sisters in the Spirit: Mormon Women in Historical and Cultural Perspective*, it was "expected . . . that Eve's curse would be lifted from women when the kingdom was restored and the millennium ushered in. But in this age of preservation, priesthood and motherhood seem forever balanced, leaving the curse of Eve intact."[32] As Carol Cornwall Madsen explains: "It is by the atoning power of Christ that mortal beings can progress beyond the telestial condition imposed on them by the Edenic transgression. It is logical to assume that this atoning power will ultimately restore the equitable relationship between Adam and Eve that existed before the fall."[33]

It could also be argued that the role of women in the Mormon church has become less important since the nineteenth century. As noted earlier, women's only claim to the priesthood came from their "sharing" or "holding" the priesthood in connection with their husbands. The interpretation of what powers a woman had through this union has been controversial at least since the time Joseph Smith organized the Female Relief Society in Nauvoo, Illinois, in 1842, when he seemed to give them some powers of their own. He installed the early presidents of this organization, who also presided over the female temple ordinance workers. Some, like Eliza Snow, received direct "instruction from the Prophet himself."[34] Carol Cornwall Madsen has said:

> In the early days, women who officiated in the temple were frequently called priestesses. . . . "Sister Eliza [Snow] . . . ministered in the Temple in the holy rites that pertain to the house of the Lord as priestess and Mother in Israel to hundreds of her sex." Frequently she was referred to as "high priestess" of the temple, as were the others who served, like her, as head of the women temple workers.[35]

Linda King Newell claims that the chain of authority that "had existed from Eliza R. Snow's day between the women in the ward and the presiding women of the church" was "severed"[36] in 1914 when the First Presidency issued a statement that "in all sacred functions performed by our sisters there should be perfect harmony between them and the Bishop, who has the direction of all matters pertaining to the Church in his ward."[37] Thus, some of the authority that women had enjoyed in carrying out sacred functions in the areas of healing and ministering to the sick without direct surveillance by the presiding male church officials was switched to the men who came to be seen as the sole arbitrators of sacred functions. As Newell says, "From the 1950s to the early 1980s, at least in official pronouncements, equal citizenship for women in the kingdom seems to have been replaced with the glorification of motherhood,"[38] and motherhood came to be equated with the priesthood. "For contemporary Latter-day Saint women, the pendulum has made its arc from Joseph Smith's prophetic vision of women as queens and priestesses, holders of keys of blessings and spiritual gifts, to Rodney Turner's [1966] metaphor of women as doormats"[39] to "keep . . . men from going . . . with muddy feet to God."[40]

It is with this lost promise and atmosphere of inequality that Johnson began her work to change the Mormon church. Like

Starhawk, Lorde, and the others, Johnson believes that changing the commonly held notion of deity to include the female is important so that all can begin "to value and love women," and so that men can see there is "no divine sanction for men" to "rule over women, because your Heavenly Father does not rule over Mother" (*HH*, 377). She adds that "equality in heaven" needs to be "translated into equality on earth" (p. 380). Johnson professes that women are the ones who must make this happen:

> Women are the ones whose lives are poured into others' lives to make them possible and, sometimes and ideally, full and rich. Women therefore have a tremendous stake in human life. . . . Life has been our career, almost our total responsibility. . . . That is why we must soon sit in the positions to say *no* to war and death—and have that *no* become policy, in the same way men's sole *no* to life has been policy for so long.
>
> For the sake of preservation of the human race, women must establish equality on this planet. (*HH*, 402–3)

Because Johnson believes in the importance of women in making policy—in working to restore the *yes* to life and the *no* to war and death—she ran for president of the United States in 1984 as a candidate of the Citizens Party. Johnson maintains that the political system "doesn't work for women" and that women have to find other ways to work for change.[41] Accordingly, while Johnson used the electoral process to communicate her message, she ran outside the established two-party system as a small alternative party's candidate.[42] Her bid for president can be seen as a series of spiritual-political events meant to change the consciousness of the public, like Starhawk's rituals.

In terms of her goals to bring her message to the public and thus change the consciousness of the public about women, violence, and war, Johnson would have to be judged at least partly successful. In her 1984 bid for president, she was the first third-party candidate to be made eligible for matching campaign funds by the Federal Elections Commission.[43] She raised at least five thousand dollars in each of twenty states from donations under two hundred and fifty dollars to be eligible. She did not, however, win her petition with the Federal Communications Commission to be able to debate with the Democratic and Republican candidates.

As in her campaign for NOW president, Johnson made her spiritually based feminism a major plank in her campaign. She says she "agreed to run for president because someone must say that only in a massive global revolution in the status of women is there hope for the survival of the planet and the human species."[44] She relates the violence toward women, and domination of them, directly to the issue of peace in the world: "If we cannot stop rape in the microcosm of the streets of one U.S. city, we cannot expect to stop violence in the macrocosm of other nations and the planet."[45]

Johnson feels her campaign was important. Even though she did not win, she was able to bring people her message: "I see this campaign as a nine-month direct action, a short-term, massive consciousness-raiser that will have repercussions for alternative power systems. If people can vote for a women for President in 40 states for the first time in the history of this country, feelings about women will change in a central, symbolic way."[46]

Originally, Johnson did not believe in the superiority of women, but as her "thealogy" has evolved one cannot be so sure. It is clear, however, that she does believe in the superiority of many of the values—human values—which have been entrusted to women. She suggests that male (patriarchal) culture and female culture have different values, and that men "need to internalize the values that are now in women's culture and in women's keeping and act out of them consciously, daily."[47] She, like the others we have studied, would make values such as nurturing and caring, which are now ascribed to women, the human norm.

In Johnson's more recent work, *Going Out of Our Minds: The Metaphysics of Liberation* (*GOM*, 1987), she unveils her revised position toward civil disobedience—the very position that made her unacceptable as a presidential candidate to mainstream feminist organizations such as NOW. In a reversal of her position, she now feels that civil disobedience is not worth the effort—that it feeds the very institution she wishes to change. She says that "when we identify ourselves in opposition to something we become its unwitting accomplices. By bestowing the energy of our belief upon it, by acquiescing to it, we reinforce it as reality" (*GOM*, 26–27). Instead she believes that today women's: "destiny . . . is to crowd patriarchy off the stage of history with our own rich, vital reality; in the midst of the rubble of the androcentric, gynocidal world, to create within ourselves right now a post-patriarchal paradise. As we do this, that ugly sick old world—. . . unsupported by our belief and attention and energy—will collapse of the weight of its own misery and evil" (p. 347).

Because of her Mormon background, particularly what Thomas O'Dea calls an "elaborated . . . American theology of self-deification through effort, an active transcendentalism of achievement,"[48] it is not surprising that Johnson continues to rework her "thealogy." It appears that she has identified building a lesbian/feminist community as replacing the old idea of rebuilding the Mormon community or reestablishing the kingdom in the millennium.[49] In the changes following her excommunication, Johnson went from feminism to lesbian/feminism, now proposing that the restoration of Eden will take place in the separatist space created only by Eves—open, of course, to any woman who wishes to join. Presumably, after the collapse of the patriarchy, men would see the error of their ways and, following the model of the women, also be able to enter this Edenic state, but Johnson does not really elaborate on what happens after the collapse of patriarchy. For now her focus is on women creating this model world together.

Johnson still believes passionately that "the Goddess is a metaphor for our own and all women's creative, healing, transformative powers, a representation of our inner selves" (*GOM*, 6), but she fears that women can become too preoccupied with that symbol. Instead, what she actually seems to say is that women need to look to themselves—they are the Goddess or have achieved the Edenic state if they pay attention to their inner thoughts and feelings. Women already have "perfect guides to behavior"—"their desires."[50] When women trust their feelings, they know "that they spring directly from their values."[51] Thus, as a guide to creating theses model lesbian/feminist communities, each woman already has what it takes. The trick is learning to listen, to trust the self. This seems much like Lorde's power of the erotic and Starhawk's power-from-within.

Johnson's rejection of civil disobedience has left some of her followers bewildered, especially those who stood with her through fasts and endured criticism from other feminists. Johnson had succeeded in persuading them about the merits of civil disobedience; they were not prepared for the shift into the millennium. Others, such as Mary Daly, believe her new perspective "can challenge thinking, release volcanic passions, and effect radical change."[52]

Although Johnson and Daly started from very different backgrounds, they have arrived at very similar perspectives. In 1968 Daly published her very influential work, *The Church and the Second Sex (CSS).* Daly had written part of the book in Freiburg, Germany, where she studied for and received two doctorates, one in philosophy and "the 'canonical' Doctorate in Sacred Theology [Catholic]" (*CSS*, 8). Although this opportunity was not open to women in the United States, the theological school in Freiburg was "state-controlled and therefore could not legally exclude women." Equipped with these two degrees, Daly believed she was ready for "the life of a philosopher-theologian, the life of a woman who could think, write and teach about the most fascinating of all questions and earn her living by doing just this" (p. 8).

As she says, she was "naive," but "it was a tough innocence" (*GOM*, 8), and seemed to carry her through the coming storm.

Like Johnson, Daly had an important revelation during a church event, but not the kind she expected. She attended a session of the Second Vatican Council of the Roman Catholic church in the fall of 1965. Borrowing a journalist's pass, she entered St. Peter's being euphoric in her belief that women's position in the church might change. Instead, "watching the veiled nuns shuffle to the altar rail to receive Holy Communion from the hands of a priest" seemed to burn "its multileveled message . . . deep into . . . [her] consciousness" (p. 10), even though at the time she did not grasp its full importance. This experience led her to work diligently on her book.

Like Johnson, Daly looked for a model in women who had gone before. For instance, she relates that a critical piece written by Catholic philosopher Rosemary Laurer in 1963 "legitimated the possibility of my own feminist writing" in ways that more radical writings could not (*CSS*, 11).

Daly finished the book in Boston, and soon after it was published, she was "given a terminal contract" for her teaching position at Jesuit-run Boston College. She became the focus of the question of academic freedom for about fifteen hundred students who demonstrated, signed petitions, and conducted a seven-hour teach-in on her behalf. As her case received national and international press, the administration relented and she was reinstated. However, as a result of this experience, "the interconnections among the structures of oppression in a patriarchal society and the destructive dynamics which these structures generate in their victims became more and more visible" (*CSS*, 13). Like Johnson when she testified for the ERA, Daly had been pushed into politics and national fame, and like Johnson, she became involved in exposing the "misogyny" of an institutional church—this time the Catholic church. Like Johnson, she started from a position as "champion of women's 'equality' within the Church" (p. 14). And like Johnson, she debated powerful men such as William F. Buckley on national television, but this was in the late 1960s—early in the current feminist movement

—not the late 1970s, so that instead of bringing the message of feminism to a group that might have been seen as lagging behind, Daly was one of the originators of that message.

In *The Church and the Second Sex,* Daly analyzes how the Catholic church has oppressed women through time. She explores past changes in the church and expresses hope for change in its treatment of women. Her language is that of a scholar, writing as an insider. Like Johnson, she calls for a "revelation, which will help to create the atmosphere needed for honest reexamination of contemporary issues, such as the Church's attitude concerning women" (*CSS,* 184). Foretelling her own flight from the church, she warns that "as long as Catholic doctrine keeps women in a state of bondage to biological fertility and paralyzes them by a degrading doctrine of exclusive male headship, there is little hope of their achieving adulthood without separating themselves from the Church in some way—if not completely and openly, then partially and clandestinely" (p. 187).

Daly calls for the church to make a "commitment of radical transformation of the negative, life-destroying elements of the Church as it exists today" (*CSS,* 187). Women are to be accepted into the priesthood; the church should stop supporting ideologies that see women as less human than men and that categorize women by their sexual function.

Throughout *The Church and the Second Sex,* Daly's argument is well researched, reasoned, and restrained. Only in the titles is there a hint of some of the playfulness with language and passion that would become more evident in her later work: for example, "An Exercise in Exorcism" (*CSS,* 166) and "The Second Sex and the Seeds of Transcendence" (p. 220). Her personal journey and her shifting perspective can be traced by following her works. When *The Church and the Second Sex* was reprinted in 1975, Daly wrote a "Feminist Postchristian Introduction." For the 1985 edition, she added a "New Archaic Afterwords: Wicked Afterthoughts concerning *The Church and the Second Sex* and its 1975 a.f. (Anno Feminarum) 'Feminist Postchristian Introduction,' understood from the perspectives of 1985 a.f. . . . and Afterwards."

By the time Daly published her second book in 1973, *Beyond God the Father: Toward a Philosophy of Women's Liberation (BGF)*, she had, as she says, greatly "radicalized" her perspective (p. x). Instead of arguing for change within the institutionalized Catholic church as she had in *The Church and the Second Sex*, she abandoned that idea, noting that "the entire conceptual systems of theology and ethics, developed under the conditions of patriarchy, have been the products of males and tend to serve the interests of sexist society" (p. 4). Instead of working to change women's roles within the institutionalized church, she calls for women to join the women's revolution and its "potential . . . to transform human consciousness and its externalizations, that is, to generate human becoming" (p. 6). This work "involves a *castrating* of language and images that reflect and perpetuate the structures of a sexist world" (p. 9).

Daly focuses on the fact that women and others less powerful than men have been robbed of the "the power to name ourselves, the world, or God" (*BGF*, 8). Like the other women we have studied, she is much concerned with language and believes that women must create their own language—not, as she says, "an entirely different set of words coming into being full blown in a *material* sense—that is different sounds or combinations of letters on paper. Rather, words which, materially speaking, are identical with the old become new in a semantic context that arises from qualitatively new experience" (p. 8). This concept is similar to the one noted by the scholar Janheinz Jahn when discussing the Africanizing of the language of former slaves.[53] Like those who study Native American and African cultures, Daly notes that "women still have a primarily oral tradition" because they have "been denied equal access to the realm of the printed word" (*BGF*, xi).

Daly sees the "new creation" of women as arising from "a

becoming process of 'the Other'—women—in which we hear and speak our own words. The development of this hearing faculty and power of speech involves the dislodging of images that reflect and reinforce the prevailing social arrangements" (*BGF*, 10).

Nelle Morton, a longtime friend of Daly's[54] and a theologian of the Protestant tradition, discusses a process that develops women's speech and dislodges the patriarchal images. She calls it "hearing to speech." For women—especially those inculcated by patriarchal constructs who have never taken themselves seriously—support from other women may be necessary to begin the journey to self-knowledge and naming. Morton describes an incident in which a woman felt that the group had heard her into speech: "After a silence, she looked from one woman to another. 'You heard me. You heard me all the way.' Her eyes narrowed. She looked directly at each woman in turn and then said slowly: 'I have a strange feeling you heard me before I started. You heard me to my own story.' "[55]

This is a function of storytelling that is akin to that which is part of the Laguna storytelling tradition. The woman seems to be saying that she told the story of her life, which is part of the collective experience of women, and, like the Laguna storyteller who draws the story from the listeners, she drew on that collective experience "to hear" herself into speech. In this way the telling of one's story becomes a communal ceremony of naming one's own experience, a necessary step to "human becoming."

When women began to realize their own "Elemental/Spiritual Powers" (*CSS*, ix)—that they do not have to depend on the church fathers to bestow spiritual power on them or to mediate for them—then they are ready to leave the church and what Daly sees as "spiritual death—a death of the Wild, Independent Self" (p. xiv). Johnson's discovery of the Mother in Heaven and her power to communicate directly with her—without the help of the church fathers—is an example of this.

Daly's "Wild Independent Self" can be identified as the lesbian within women—the part that is not under the control of any man. Daly says that leaving the patriarchal church "involves Leap after Leap of Living Faith" (*CSS*, xii) in order to go through the terror of separation from the church and the fear of spiritual death to "self-affirming transcendent experiences" (p. xiv). This seems to parallel the Native American story about the pregnant Sky Woman, which Allen uses in *The Woman Who Owned the Shadows*. Sky Woman's sorcerer husband, who is jealous of her powers, uproots the tree of life associated with Sky Woman, leaving a huge hole with no bottom in sight. She is coaxed and shoved into the hole and to what is assumed to be her death. Instead, aided by a number of animals or spiritual guides, she lands on Grandmother Turtle's back. There she gives birth and creates a new world. Thus, what appears to lead to death, in fact, leads to new life, independent of the control attempted by the patriarchy. While the terror of falling, of leaving, is tremendous, once women have taken this leap they discover that they are the source of their own spiritual power; it does not come from without. They also discover these "women-identified powers of being" (*CSS*, xv) within other women as they hear each other into speech, creating community. In *Beyond God the Father*, Daly says that "the emerging feminist ethic has as its primary emphasis not self-abnegation but self-affirmation in community with others" (*BGF*, 110).

In her critique of society, Daly notes that traditional morality seems to be "reactions on the part of men . . . to the behavioral excesses of the stereotypic male." The emphasis has been on "charity, meekness, obedience, humility, self-abnegation, sacrifice, service." Subordinate males act these out whenever superior males are present, but these qualities are seen as more appropriately belonging to females and as "feminine" (*BGF*, 100). Daly calls this "the morality of victimization" (p. 105). She sees the women's revolution pointing toward a becoming that "transcends the most basic role stereotypes, those of masculine/feminine." In a culture such as the Laguna that embraced "a wholeness of personhood," Silko's character Tayo "would be seen to have been masculinized, that is, to have lost half of himself" (*BGF*, 105) at the beginning of the novel. Indeed, as we attempt to analyze Tayo's situation from a traditional Laguna perspective, that is the conclusion to which we come—that the Euro-American war and influences have masculinized him, cutting him off from the qualities that connect him to the land, to the Mother, to his people. To heal, he must take the journey back to the "wholeness of personhood" which his traditional culture values.

Like Johnson, Daly links Euro-American society's assignment of certain qualities as masculine or feminine to violence against women, to war, and to eventual destruction of the earth. Because men learn that to be male, for instance, they must be aggressive without the tempering quality of nurturing that is ascribed to females, Euro-American society has no vision of what a whole person is. Since men have the power to make war, for instance, and the qualities that might give them pause are ascribed to women, there is nothing to hold them back from their destructive course. She believes that women hold the key to break out of this cycle to preserve the earth:

> The Most Unholy Trinity of Rape, Genocide, and War is a logical expression of phallocentric power. These are structures of alienation that are self-perpetuating, eternally breeding further estrangement. The circle of destruction generated by the Most Unholy Trinity and reflected in the Unwhole Trinitarian symbol of Christianity will be broken when women, who are by patriarchal definition objects of rape, externalize and internalize a new self-definition whose compelling power is rooted in the power of being. The casting out of the demonic Trinities *is* female becoming. (*BGF*, 122)

This idea is contrary to the vision particularly of Allen, Silko, Starhawk, and Walker, who do not see women as "the answer," but seek a redefinition of what it means to be male and female—

a balancing into a whole person. Silko and Allen see it as a return to an earlier concept of women's power which was balanced with men's power. Because their vision is connected to one within memory, the task is a bit simpler than the Euro-American vision which has no recent models. Starhawk's reclaiming and inventing such a perspective on the power of women is admirable in this respect. It is possibly this lack of connection to any viable models for Johnson and Daly that contributes to the lack of inclusiveness of their visions, which seem to grow narrower rather than more encompassing. It is difficult to imagine how their professed separateness of women can in itself change the world, although it might be a step. The women who see themselves in a hopeless battle with the patriarchy and who need a space for personal and spiritual growth may find Johnson's and Daly's visions quite compelling. However, those who are a part of groups that are also discriminated against because of their race seem to trust less that women—even white lesbian women—know the right ways well enough to create this model world.[56]

Daly sees women's striving for becoming—the casting out of patriarchal nonbeing—as the role of sisterhood, a kind of "war" to "surround nonbeing, forcing it to shrink back into itself" to preserve the planet. She cautions, however, that this is not "the war to end all wars" because "the power of sisterhood is not warpower." It is rather "the creative drawing power of the Good Who is self-communicating Being, Who is the Verb from whom, in whom, and with whom all true movements move" (*BGF*, 198)—a sort of struggle to free oneself from "destructive social forces" (p. 138) and to have a " 'right' relationship with the sacred cosmos" (p. 141). This concept describes the journey or process that all of the primary characters in this study—real or imaginary—are taking.

Sisterhood, "the unique bonding of women against our reduction to low caste" has as its function "undercut[ting] the credibility of sexist religion [and society] to the degree that it undermines sexism itself" (*BGF*, 133). Writing almost a decade before Johnson's admission of the futility of civil disobedience and of working within the structures of the patriarchy, Daly says:

> In fighting "within" such space, we should allow it only the minimal degree of power over our expenditure of energies that will serve our own purposes. . . . Our war . . . is . . . with the prevailing sense of reality, according to which we must be relegated to nonbeing. Our self-recovery, in part, depends upon our refusal to take *this* "reality" too seriously. . . . We have to live *now* the future we are fighting for, rather than compromising in vain hope of a future . . . always deferred, always unreal. (*BGF*, 138)

For Daly, the "'withdrawal' into boundary space and time constitutes the most radical involvement/participation in the cosmic community" (*BGF*, 191). This is in particular contrast to the positions taken by Allen, Silko, Starhawk, and Walker. For instance, Walker's Celie in *The Color Purple* is able to free herself from the patriarchal God, find her own power and love of herself with Shug's help, and come to terms with her husband, Mister, who has also grown, discovering qualities within himself that he would earlier have described as feminine. Both he and Celie become whole persons. For Celie, however, there is a period of withdrawal, of discovery, of economic independence, fueled by Shug. It is this "passage" that Daly describes in her companion journey books.

In *Gyn/Ecology (GE)*, Daly becomes even more adamant about language. She says that "there is some old semantic baggage to be discarded so that Journeyers will be unencumbered by malfunctioning (male-functioning) equipment" (*GE*, xi). Further, she says, "This book is primarily concerned with the mind/spirit/body pollution inflicted through patriarchal myth and language on all levels" (p. 9). She notes that she will be using "irregular" capitalization for emphasis on her meaning (p. 25). Her language sometimes breaks "into incantations, chants, alliterative lyrics" and "the words themselves seem to have a life of their own" (p. 24). Thus the journeyer/reader of Daly's work must be particularly attentive to Daly's "deconstruction" of words, her play with them, her hyphenation of them to bring out hidden meanings, her return to archaic definitions, her attempt to break through the patriarchal images and meanings embedded in the mind. These "incantations" fuel the perspective that Daly is conducting a ceremony of exorcism and of new possibilities through her writing.

Gyn/Ecology is a journey through patriarchal myths, through atrocities carried out around the world: the widow-burning of India, the Chinese ritual of foot binding of female feet into three-inch "lotus hooks," African genital mutilation, European witch burnings, and the "sado-rituals"[57] of American gynecologists and Nazi doctors. These Daly connects to the reenactment of the murder of the Goddess, the getting rid of the "Self-affirming be-ing of women" (*GE*, 111). Daly says, "Our refusal to collaborate in this killing and dismembering of our own Selves is the beginning of re-membering of the Goddess—the deep Source of creative integrity in women" (p. 111).

Gyn/Ecology details the journey and process a woman must take or enact to move "deeper into the Otherworld—which is her own time/space" (*GE*, 32). In *Gyn/Ecology*, Daly plays with the concepts of time and hierarchy, saying that "all women who define our own living, defining the deception of patriarchal history . . . belong to the same time and . . . are foresisters to each other" (p. 33). She collapses time in the way that Silko does by referring to Thought Woman who holds in her mind the story that Silko is telling—Goddess time.

The concept of the Goddess informs this journey because Daly sees the Goddess as affirming "the life-loving be-ing of women and nature" in contrast to God as "the necrophilia of patriarchy" (*GE*, xi). However, like Johnson, Daly cautions that "Goddess images are truthful and encouraging, but reified/objectified images of 'The Goddess' can be mere substitutes for 'God,' failing to convey that Be-ing is a Verb, and the She is many verbs" (p. xii). In this respect what Daly calls Be-ing, "the verb that says the dimensions of depth in all verbs, such as intuiting, reasoning, loving, imaging, making, acting, as well as the couraging, hoping, and playing that are always there when one is really living" (pp. 23–24), is reminiscent of Audre Lorde's power of the erotic or the Black Mother.

The journey into which Daly draws the reader goes through the barriers erected by the patriarchy against the process of woman naming her experience and discovering her woman self. In *Gyn/Ecology*, Daly's analysis shifts from the church fathers to the patriarchal fathers worldwide and institutionwide, but she focuses on how women can free themselves of these patriarchal fathers. She says that *Gyn/Ecology*

> is about dis-covering, de-veloping the complex web of living/loving relationships *of our own kind.* It is about women living, loving, creating our Selves, our cosmos. It *is* dis-possessing our Selves, enspiriting our Selves, hearing the call of the wild, naming our wisdom, spinning and weaving world tapestries out of genesis and demise. In contrast to gynecology, which depends upon fixation and dismemberment [the concept of] Gyn/Ecology affirms that everything is connected. (*GE*, 10–11)

Unlike most of the others in this study except Johnson, Daly gives up all pretext of concern over men—over "humanity"—in *Gyn/Ecology*, choosing instead to focus on women "who choose to be present to each other" (*GE*, xii). She says, "The Spinsters, Lesbians, Hags, Harpies, Crones, Furies who are the Voyagers of *Gyn/Ecology* know that we choose to accept this invitation for our Selves" (p. xii). Daly notes that this self-acceptance is in spite of the real fear of male revenge and the fear of the loss of male approval.

In a manner similar to Silko's and Allen's, Daly invites the reader/voyager to participate in this "journey" of the book to rid themselves/women of the things that keep them from being present to the self and to each other. For the reader who chooses to participate, the book becomes a sort of healing ceremony, an exorcism of patriarchal ritual "embedded" (*GE*, 108) in the mind, a movement deeper into that space on the boundary of patriarchy. Like the protagonists in Silko's and Allen's novels, readers are supposed to become aware of the lies told them by Euro-American patriarchal culture so that they can see how everything is connected and what their part is, in this case, in the story of sisterhood.

She calls on the journeyer/reader to govern herself "by the Witch within—the Hag within" (*GE*, 15). She continues: "For women who are on the journey of radical be-ing, the lives of the witches, of the Great Hags of our hidden history are deeply intertwined with our own process. As we write/live our own story, we are uncovering their history" (p. 15). With these words, Daly echoes the circularity and connectedness found in Allen's work as her main character walks in the footsteps of the ancient medicine woman, and Silko's belief that all these stories have been heard before, only the names have changed. It is the outlaw woman, the witch, the lesbian within who guides these stories, connecting them to one another. This process is "discovering our deep sources, our spring . . . finding our native resiliency, springing into life, speech, action" (p. 21).

As the journeyer/reader moves through this book, she is to sense "a growing integrity of vision and purpose," to "find the focus of her anger, so that it no longer blocks her passion and her creativity" (*GE*, 112). Thus she is prepared to enter into the Otherworld. The last part of the book attends to exorcising the more sophisticated forms of patriarchal oppression, as Daly sees them, especially of sexist language and of grammatical constructions such as the passive that obscure the agent of action. She also points out the deadening effects of tokenism—women who "have been allowed into pieces of patriarchal territory as a *show of female presence*" (p. 334).

Once women have understood these oppressive "rituals," it is time to recover the self: "The dis-covered Self washes her hands/mind of the anti-septic anti-Self; the internalized Possessor. At first her handwashing/mindwashing may seem itself to be a ritual. If so, it is the right rite, the suitable ceremony of the one who has been named 'unclean.' She dispossesses her Self of the purifiers who muddy her mind, who try to master her mind" (*GE*, 339). However, like the others in this study, Daly does not see the journey to recovery as a one-time event. She admits that because women have "been damaged in a variety of ways, our yes-saying [to the self] assumes different forms and *is* in different degrees. In some cases it is clear and intense; in other instances it is sporadic, diffused, fragmented" (p. xiii). In all cases, it is a process, and although she defines a possible process in her books for women's journeys to the self, it is the task of each woman to "dis-cover the mystery of her own history, and find how it is interwoven with the lives of other women" (p. xiii).

Daly refers again to the creative power of language that she calls "enspiriting": "As she becomes dispossessed, enspirited, she moves out of range of the passive voices and begins to hear her own Active Voice, speaking her Self in successive acts of creation. As she creates her Self she creates new space: semantic, cognitive, symbolic, psychic, physical spaces. She moves into these spaces and finds room to breathe, to breathe forth further space" (*GE*, 340). In the enspirited state, women can recall "the fundamental lost bonding . . . between mothers and daughters" (p. 346), which Daly calls "Daughter-Right." This is "the right to reclaim our original movement, to re-call our Selves. It is this Self-centering identity that makes female bonding possible" (p. 347). It is the discovering of the Daughter, the Goddess within ourselves and others that makes radical friendship possible. As Daly notes, radical friendship "means loving our own freedom, loving/encouraging the freedom of the other, the friend and therefore *loving freely*" (p. 367). This is the relationship in Walker's *The Color Purple*, which Celie illustrates as she supports Shug's relationship with a young man. Celie realizes that Shug's freedom to love whom she wishes is of much importance to their relationship.

Daly points out that

> female-identified erotic love is not dichotomized from radical female friendship, but rather is one important expression/manifestation of friendship. . . . The Presence of Enspiriting Female Selves to each other is a creative gynergetic flow that may assume different shapes and colors. The sparking of ideas and the flaming of physical passion emerge from the same source. The bonding of women-loving women survives its transformations because its source is the Sister-Self. (*GE*, 373)

It is this community of women, "spinning threads of connectedness" (*GE*, 389), which aid each other in building the enspiriting atmosphere in which each woman can create her self, her "spirit spiraling, whirling"—a "labyrinth" inward journey (*GE*, 391). Daly says that this "movement inward is not crawling into an alien being and/or space, nor is it toward a 'dead center.' Spider Woman who is Isis/Ishtar/Daughter/Self is Be-ing. When we find her we have not merely reached The End but The Beginning, who spins and spirals outward, inward, in all directions" (p. 403).

In the manner of Silko and Allen, Daly dedicates her fourth book, *Pure Lust: Elemental Feminist Philosophy* (1984), to spirit itself; to images of the spirit, the Goddess; and to the spirit within. She writes:

> To the Spirit
> who lives and breaths
> in all Elemental be-ing
>
> To the Lady of Words of Power
> who communicates herSelf
> through the inadequate images—
> from Isis and Ishtar
> to Our Lady of Bourgillon

> To the Muse
> in Metamorphosing women
> whose Presence inspires the Realizing
> of our *own* powers of creation
> finally, now, and always.

In *Pure Lust (PL),* Daly further delineates the journey that she began in *Gyn/Ecology,* laying out the possibilities, spinning a web of words/images, incantations which her readers might find helpful. Like Starhawk in her *Dreaming the Dark,* Daly attempts to lead readers on a journey through personal perils to a reunion with themselves.[58] However, instead of Starhawk's Celtic dagger as a spiritual/symbolic tool, Daly exhorts readers to use their "Labryses/double axes of our own Wild wisdom and wit" to "cut through the mazes of man-made mystification to intensify our sense of genuine and organic complexity" (*PL,* xii).

Daly says that *Pure Lust* is a "conjuring of the Elemental Spirits of women and all Wild natures. Such conjuring conjoins women with our Selves and our Sisters, and with earth, air, fire, and water. It connects us with the rhythms of the farthest stars and of our own sun and moon. It mends our broken ties with the Witch within ourSelves, who spins and weaves the tapestries of Elemental creation" (*PL,* xii). *Pure Lust,* then, can be seen as a ritual, a ceremony for its readers. Imaginative readers could use its imaging to pattern their own journeys.

In *Pure Lust,* Daly goes even further in inventing/creating a past for women as a group. She speaks of women as tribes in a race of women who are recovering their lost "country," that is, into "the Realms of Elemental Reality, of ontological depth" (*PL,* 6). Daly notes that because women "belong to different tribes and have great individual diversity" (p. 25), no symbol can be right for all women, hence the many names of the Goddess and also the recognition of those who do not ascribe to such metaphors. Like the Triple Goddess whose image "signifies unity and harmony in Diversity" (p. 187), so the idea of tribes of women can signify unity and harmony in the race of women. However, Daly says that women need to follow their "intuitions about which symbols ring true, listening to the sounds of their names and the rhythms of the contexts in which the Naming occurs" (p. 25). Daly likes to avoid metaphors that become static; for her, the Goddess points "Metaphorically to the Powers of Be-ing, the Active Verb in whose potency all biophilic [living] reality participates" (p. 26). If she ceases to do this, then the Goddess will no longer be a useful image.

Also in *Pure Lust,* Daly describes patriarchal institutions, the patriarchy, and those who adhere to it in language reminiscent of Silko's description of the witchery. Daly delineates "the tawdry tactics of the Fix-Masters who continually aim to freeze life, making Ele-mental be-ing stationary, implanted with fixes, nonvolatile, solid/stolid killed, hardened, preserved, selectively bred, fastened, captured, castrated, made defenseless, bribed, tampered with. . . . This is the State of the Grateful Dead" (*PL,* 23). In the center of her book, *Ceremony,* Silko has a passage describing the witchery carried out by the white people, ending with: "Set in motion now/ set in motion/ To destroy/ To kill/ Objects to work for us/ objects to act for us/ Performing the witchery/ for suffering/ for torment/ for the still-born/ the deformed/ the sterile/ the dead" (p. 144).

Daly believes that the energies of women are "trapped/snapped are limited . . . by a massive social conspiracy" (*PL,* 45) and the energies of minority women, poor women, and Third World women even more so. Daly sees the "rape of all matter as well as all women" as "a project which has been the goal of patriarchal civilization for millennia" (p. 75). The result is "activities that are socially approved by males" such as "nuclearism, chemical contamination of the earth, famine, torture of political prisoners, torture of laboratory animals, obscene medical experimentation" (p. 75).

As to how women who support the phallocentric culture fit

in, Daly points out that because women have not been allowed to "become fully Self-actualizing" in phallocentric culture, they "reproduce their altered—that is patriarchally identified—selves in an endless circle of Self-destruction" (*PL*, 365). However, women who "act with obvious corruption and cooptation" (p. 378) against women struggling to battle the phallocentric culture cannot be excused. Daly points out that the "Nags, Shrews, and Scolds learn not to expend inordinate amounts of energy berating such women [women who cannot move beyond patriarchy], although we grieve for them" (p. 398).

For those women who are battling the patriarchy, part of the answer may be the rage that leads to separatism. Daly believes that rage "is a transformative, focusing Force" (*PL*, 376). Separatism from the patriarchy is a necessary step in the journey to woman-self, the Otherworld, because patriarchy has caused woman to dissociate "from her original identity as a woman—not as the sadosociety defines 'woman,' but as an Archaic, Elemental woman. . . . [S]eparatism is an essential aspect of gynophilic communication, for it separates a woman from the causes of fragmentation —the obstacles, internal and external—which separate her from the flow of integrity within her Self" (p. 370). This separatism may lead to lesbianism, as it did for Sonia Johnson, who says:

> The decision to throw in my lot with women completely, to give them my whole allegiance—the ultimate subversion in patriarchy—was deliberate and of the highest seriousness. . . . It gives me the incredible hope for the world that I was able to give my love and trust openly to another woman, despite the most consummate brainwashing with the twin patriarchal doctrines of revolution for women and eternal damnation for refusing to worship men, and despite the fear of public outrage. It persuades me that other women also have the great good sense and the courage to do whatever is demanded by our planet's peril. (*GOM*, 123)

For Johnson, lesbianism seems to be a political and erotic choice to give her energy to women in spite of the patriarchy.

Her third book, *Wildfire: Igniting the She/Volution* (*WIS*, 1989), explores the idea of an entire women's community much like the separatist world envisioned by Daly.[59] However, Johnson does not accept the label "separatist" because that label defines her as "in relation to men" (*WIS*, 267). The most important thing to her is not women's relationship to the patriarchy, is not fighting the patriarchy, but women's coming together, "myself and other like-minded women now as the goddess, creating a new pattern, creating the world afresh" (p. 46). Johnson believes that if enough women get together to "make the necessary shifts . . . then the ideas, perceptions, and feelings of the whole society will shift rapidly, almost all at once, in the direction we have been pioneering" (p. 253). This idea seems very much akin to Starhawk's magic or changing consciousness. Thus Johnson's world of women, while separate from the patriarchal world, might forever change humanity, an emphasis Daly does not seem to make.

These worlds of women are quite different, however, from Allen's concept of the sisterhood of medicine women. As she shows in her novel, *The Woman Who Owned the Shadows*, the medicine women would have been following a spiritual calling to serve the Mother for the good of the people. These women would have been sacred people, chosen by the spirits to fulfill their roles. They would have served not only the women of the group, but also the men, because they were believed to have double vision—an ability to see with the perspective of both male and female—and an ability to mediate between the spiritual and the physical.[60] Thus, in contrast to Daly whose community of women becomes a narrowing focus, cut off from the rest of society, Allen's community of medicine women is an integral part of society and helps the whole to function better.

Even though these fundamental differences exist between Daly's vision and the vision of others, storytelling/naming plays an integral part in both. The process of restoring/healing women is accomplished through the recovery of the deep memory of women's basic potential. Daly believes that the recovery or naming of any part "makes the hope of Memory more accessible to other women, for . . . memories are connected. A woman who re-members actualizes her own potency, and . . . [the] re-membering is the most radical, the most necessary activism" (*PL*, 178). Memory can be activated/triggered by the strong emotion generated by women telling their stories, by writing, by listening to other women's stories, and by "seeing/hearing the words come forth on the page" (p. 173). Remembering is also the act of creation—"re-membering the lore of our foremothers and through Spinning Original tales" (p. 279). Again it is the words, the naming, the "images [which] stir the atmosphere E-motionally, awakening ancient connections not only with each other, but with the winds, waters, rocks, trees, birds, butterflies, bats, cats, stars" (p. 405).

Thus, for Daly and Johnson the world created by the patriarchy can be left behind and created anew as women move toward its boundaries, creating new spaces and reconnecting with the spirit that infuses all. As Johnson says,

> [t]rust[ing] mightily that having let go of our belief in patriarchy's judgments and lies and methods, believing in women's voices and world, the rope will appear in our hands and out of our sure, strong feeling of ourselves, we will swing free and joyous out of the violent planetary mind into our own reality, into a new mind—or into a very, very ancient, truly archaic [from Daly: "Original, Primal, Primordial"] mind. (*GOM*, 340)[61]

SIX

Conclusion: The Female Principle and a Lesbian-Feminist Ethics

THIS study has now followed four threads of contemporary spiritual traditions in which the Goddess or female principle is central. All of these threads radiate from a female center that is often identified with the Goddess as symbol, using one of her many names and aspects—Thought Woman, Mother in Heaven, the Black Mother, or Ceridwen, the Celtic Goddess. Although Walker's *The Color Purple* is an exception to this, her *Temple of My Familiar* is not. Although *The Color Purple* does not use the Goddess as symbol, both stories center on the female or "womanist" principle as Walker identifies it. Another commonality is the emergence of a lesbian-feminist ethic that allows for a broad range of ways of be-ing for women.

Women who claim identity as lesbian-feminist, womanist, the woman-unto-herself, the outrageous woman, the dyke, the medicine-woman, or the witch have already set themselves apart from the Euro-American homophobic, heterosexist, patriarchal norm. As such the ethics emerging from these threads of spirituality are less a set of rules than they are principles of a process of survival and of moving farther away from the patriarchal norm. For these groups, patriarchal oppression in the form of racism, sexism, and homophobia is a given, as is the harm that has been done to the individual. One never knows when internalized oppression and the resulting hurt and anger will surface to cause harm in the community. By the very nature of identities chosen and choices made to seek community with other women who go against the grain of Euro-American society, lesbian-feminists are a feisty lot with whom to be in community.

Nevertheless, a lesbian-feminist ethics arising out of these threads has as its components the creation and maintenance of a woman-centered community, and for the participants in the community a strong sense of self in relationship to and within the context of the community—a sense of self as powerful, creative, and important. Traditional Euro-American attributes for women such as nurturing and caring are part of this sense of self, but they are not seen as the whole; the model for the lesbian-feminist woman is the Goddess in her many guises—Thought Woman who creates the stories upon which life is patterned and told by the storyteller, Celtic goddesses and warrior queens, Yellow Woman who follows a strange spirit man away from friends and family but is no passive victim, or Afrekete through whom the Goddess speaks.

Basic to this ethics is not a focus on original sin or being born sinful and needing redemption, but a respect for the individual, the choice she has made to be part of the community, and to create together lesbian space, Native American women's space, ritual space, womanist space, and so forth. Because of the varied attributes of individuals from different cultures as well as the varied hurts, angers, and internalized oppressions, a high tolerance and respect for difference is part of a lesbian-feminist ethics. One need not try to impose outside rules on women who are already more self-directed than most. Coming from a multitude of cultures, no perfectly correct lesbian woman can exist, since all must deal with oppression and difference. Rather than focusing on rules or correctness, there is a commitment to survive and aid one another in the effort to move away from patriarchal ways. This commitment provides a sense of mission even if one cannot visualize the result. It is a kind of courage to create.

Along with the concepts of respect and tolerance for each other, one needs a sense of humor, playfulness, creativity, and clowning to cope with differences and with the ways in which the patriarchy has harmed us all. Daly calls this "spinning and sparking," and a version of this playfulness is exhibited in all her writings, especially in her *Websters' First New Intergalactic Wickedary of the English Language.* In the Native American thread, examples of trickster figures appear frequently, one of whose functions is to bring people back to balance when some personality characteristic, such as pride, has gotten out of whack. For instance, coyote is a traditional Native American trickster figure who teaches by example, often of coyote's own foolishness. Beth Brant, a Native American lesbian, uses coyote to teach that lesbianism is an ordinary way of being. In "Coyote Learns a New Trick,"[1] Coyote, who thought to trick Fox by pretending to be a male and having sexual relations with her, is herself tricked when she discovers that Fox knew her identity all along and *still* wants to have sexual relations. In addition, Coyote discovers that she *likes* having sexual relations with a female.

Within the Native American, African-American, and Goddess Religion threads lies a strong sense of the connectedness of the individual to the planet and an understanding, particularly by women of color, that all peoples are connected. These threads also display a sense of delight in the natural world and a connection to it, often bordering on the magical. A personal sense of responsibility and reciprocity with the surrounding world played out in creativity and giving attention to small things in daily life is also a strong part of a lesbian-feminist ethics. For instance, in "In Search of Our Mother's Gardens," Walker discusses her mother's garden as the only creative work she was allowed, but which, in response to her mother's loving care, nurtured her mother and herself. Walker's mother could also be seen as creating women's space in an otherwise hostile world. In the world created by a lesbian-feminist ethics, a carefully stitched and patterned quilt or lovely garden would be as much an accomplishment as a poem or a novel, and domestic joys would help participants feel more connected to and sustained by the environment around them. When Lorde speaks of knowing the erotic and allowing ourselves to live in accordance with this deepest knowledge, it is to this she refers—the joy of feeling fully, a celebration of life: "For once we begin to feel deeply all the aspects of our lives, we begin to demand from ourselves and from our life-pursuits that they feel in accordance with that joy which we know ourselves to be capable of."[2] Lorde speaks of the joy of being self-connected in everyday activities—"in the way my body stretches to music and opens into response, harkening to its deepest rhythms," in "building a bookcase, in writing a poem, examining an idea."[3]

Examples of this self-connection celebrated in ordinary daily things appear in *The Color Purple,* for instance. Celie's pants business exemplifies this, and it becomes a way for her to share her joy. Celie glories in the pants she will make for her sister Nettie and imagines love going into every stitch. One of the consistent messages in *The Color Purple* is that once people begin to be self-connected—allow themselves to feel joy as well as pain—that they can also take pleasure and nurturance in domestic things. Indeed, that is to what the title refers—the joy that can be found in the color of ordinary wildflowers.

The Color Purple also celebrates relationships in an unconventional way. Lorde points out that once she has shared the erotic in daily life—in fighting, playing, or working—she knows or connects to those with whom she has shared the erotic differently. A kind of bonding occurs. This bonding allows even difference to be accepted and cuts across gender, race, and other differences. In *The Color Purple,* as the characters connect from their self-knowing to each other, they discover ways to live more freely, to be more fully who they are and to contribute to the well-being of the group. As they practice an ethics based on the female principle, they see each other less often as "other." For instance, Eleanor Jane, the daughter of Sofia's white employers, begins to understand Sofia's distrust of her because of what her parents had done. However, she genuinely cares about Sofia and her family, so rather than abandon her relationship, she does what she can. She uses her kitchen gadgets to make special yam dishes for Sofia's ailing daughter, Henrietta, who needs yams to recover from her illness, but who does not like them. Of course, a relationship or community requires reciprocity, and Sofia begins to show an acceptance of Eleanor Jane by changing her attitude toward Eleanor Jane's son, Reynolds Stanley, whom she previously had rejected as just another future racist.

Toward the end of the novel, the characters' evolving lives illustrate balance between community and personal needs and a rejection of judgments of "the right way" prescribed by patriarchal societies—African or African-American. For instance, even though Celie does not approve of Tashi's scarification, she understands and cares for Tashi. One of the differences in the ways which Walker and Lorde seem to handle the West-African and related Caribbean traditions is that Lorde concentrates on the mythic and on the parts she can accept and weaves them into her personal culture, while Walker addresses the patriarchy in both African and Afro-American cultures and comes out on the side of neither. However, in both cases, the result of the use of their West-African heritage is transformative. Lorde creates a "biomythography" and Walker creates a "womanist" culture, but both are based on a female principle.

In a lesbian-feminist vision, sexuality and the expression of sexuality in ways sanctioned by the state is unimportant—there are no illegitimate children. The woman-unto-herself owns her body, and a strong sense that sexual activity can be part of the sacred, the magical, is displayed in the work of Silko, Lorde, and Grahn. It is often a way of bonding and connection in a spiritual/

physical sense with the female principle for participants, as it is for Tayo in *Ceremony*, Celie in *The Color Purple*, and Morgaine in *The Mists of Avalon*.

Another component of a lesbian-feminist ethics is the alternative ways of viewing family. From a spiritual perspective, family or kin are those with whom one has a spiritual/ritual connection. For Lorde, these are the women who aid her in her journey. For Johnson and Daly, these are the women who take the leap beyond the patriarchy. In the Native American and African-American threads, connection to one's mother and mother's family, especially the women, is important. This is what tells the woman who she is. As white lesbian-feminists move farther from the patriarchal norm, matrilineage also becomes increasingly important. For each of these, family does not conform to a traditional Euro-American definition.

In a lesbian-feminist or womanist community made up of strong, independent women from different cultures, many differences are bound to arise. Here Lorde's sharing of the joy that comes from self-connectedness in mutual activity might work to bridge these gaps. For instance, Allen's character, Ephanie, is able to share the joy that comes from self-connectedness in mutual activity with other women, bridging the gaps in world-view between them. She experiences this joy with the Chicana, Elena, with the nuns, and partly with the Euro-American, Teresa. It is because this type of bonding transcends differences of race that she can be willing at the end of the novel to teach Teresa, one who "is ready to know" (*WOS*, 20), about her tribal world—Ephanie's self-connected world of the medicine women. In *The Color Purple*, Celie's experience of stitching pants with Albert shows that this type of bonding can even bridge gender differences if only in a limited way.

As Silko, Johnson, Starhawk, and Walker particularly note, the personal responsibility in a lesbian-feminist ethics is not limited to those individuals with whom one has a close relationship; it extends to one's community at large and to the world.

For example, nuclear holocaust is greatly feared by Silko and the others; it is the ultimate act of disconnection, of lack of respect.

When the inevitable conflict arises within the community, individual withdrawal for a time may be the only way for the individual to survive. Withdrawal can be seen as an individual choice—a taking into account of one's particular boundaries. Lesbian philosopher Sarah Hoagland suggests withdrawal as a strategy for dealing with conflict rather than the often-used community ostracism that pretends that a clear right and wrong can be discerned and sets up members in judgment against one another.[4] She suggests that it is not judgment which is unworkable, but the fact that many members of a community do not decide for themselves and simply go along with the ostracism as an act of loyalty, thus giving up the individual's sense of responsibility and agency.

Lorde's essay "The Uses of Anger" seems particularly applicable here. Although she was writing about responses to racism, her ideas seem to apply to conflicts between women in a women's community. She says: "The strength of women lies in recognizing differences between us as creative, and in standing to those distortions which we inherited without blame, but which are now ours to alter. The angers of women can transform difference through insight into power. For anger between peers births change, not destruction, and the discomfort and sense of loss it often causes is not fatal, but a sign of growth."[5] Along with this is the attempt to use power-from-within and power-with instead of power-over, which is seen as patriarchal.

The creation of lesbian-feminist space/culture abounds in examples in the literature. Celie withdraws from her husband and goes to form a community with Shug. In Walker's work, men are allowed to join the womanist community when they can demonstrate they are operating more on a female principle. Thus, in *Temple of My Familiar*, Suwelo, the rather arrogant black history professor, is allowed to come back into the womanist community after he learns from the elders, Miss Lissie and Hal.

Johnson proposes whole experimental communities of women, creating culture, each doing what she likes to do best. If no one wants to do particular tasks, she suggests that perhaps those tasks contribute to "anti-life and anti-freedom" and should be rethought as women redesign the world.[6] She says: "In believing in our own internal voices we reinvent human nature, we create another, more interesting, more playful and at the same time more serious myth of humanness. Guided by our desires, we live moment by moment in richest chaos—that is, at the summit of creativity, where every possibility is alive at the same time."[7]

Perhaps one of the differences between the white activists, Johnson and Daly, and Silko, Allen, Lorde, and Starhawk is that the former two could be seen as having fewer practical models on which to pattern their ideas. Consequently, they appear to operate from an abstract, idealistic, and noninclusive perspective. However, Daly and Johnson attempt to counter this. For instance, in a recent essay, Daly says: "Uh, oh! I am hearing voices. 'Who does she think she is, with her impossible questions and grandiose schemes.' . . . They're coming from the old brotherhood of doubt demons who are always trying to undermine women's Self-confidence."[8] Johnson claims that women's not being able to trust their own desires has to do with patriarchal conditioning—that as women work through this conditioning, her plans for a community where each woman follows her own desires is workable. However, perhaps because whatever power white women have had has always been so intertwined with the patriarchal power of white men, Johnson and Daly do not envision a world inclusive of men. Rather, they envision an exclusively female world that might serve as a model for the outside world.

Because Silko, Allen, Lorde, and Starhawk claim connection to women-centered traditions, they envision a world in which men who adhere to these traditions can participate, as does Tayo, Josiah, Ku'oosh, Betonie, and Robert in *Ceremony*. Women of color often also have a closer connection to men of their group because of common racist oppression, and because the men are often not seen as having the kind of investment in the patriarchy as do white men.

Another difference is an acceptance of the cyclical patterns of life and death by Silko, Allen, Lorde, Walker, and Starhawk. As Allen says, "Walking in balance, in harmony, and in a sacred manner requires staying in your body, accepting its discomforts, decayings, witherings, and blossomings and respecting them."[9] However, all the threads display a sense of creating and evolving into an unknown woman-centered future.

Inherent in a lesbian-feminist ethics is the power of words, of communication, which is available to anyone, male or female, operating out of a female principle. Silko's passage about choosing the words carefully so that the story might be told properly with the right connections, so that the community can respond and become part of the story, is a beautiful expression of the power of words. Implicit is the power of words to heal, to bring together, if the listeners can participate and respond. This, of course, can be the power of literature, of ritual. The storyteller, healer, priestess, or medicine woman bonds with the listeners so that the story or ritual can evolve to fit the needs of both the teller and listener—together they make the story, and in this possibility lies the promise of healing, of connection—feminist curing ceremonies. As the spirit women say to Ephanie:

> The story of the people and the spirits, the story of the earth, is the story of what moves, what moves on, what patterns, what dances, what sings, what balances, so life can be felt and known. The story of life is the story of moving. Of moving on.
>
> Your place in the great circling spiral is to help in that story, in that work. To pass on to those who can understand what you have learned, what you know. (*WOS*, 210)

For there are those who wait, who are ready to know.

Notes

1. Introduction

1. See, for instance, the coyote stories in Richard Erdoes and Alfonzo Ortiz, eds., *American Indian Myths and Legends* (New York: Pantheon, 1984); in Margot Astrov, ed., *American Indian Prose and Poetry* (New York: Capricorn, 1962); and in Alice Marriott and Carol K. Rachlin, eds., *American Indian Mythology* (New York: New American, 1972).
2. See Audre Lorde, *Sister Outsider, Essays and Speeches* (Trumansburg: Crossing Press, 1984), 110–13.
3. Alice Walker, *In Search of Our Mothers' Gardens, Womanist Prose* (New York: Harcourt Brace Jovanovich, 1973), xii.
4. Annette Kolodny, *The Land Before Her: Fantasy and Experience of the American Frontiers, 1630–1860* (Chapel Hill: University of North Carolina Press, 1984), 10.
5. Ibid., 10.
6. See Leslie Silko, *Ceremony* (New York: New American, 1978), 36–37.
7. Paula Gunn Allen, *The Sacred Hoop: Recovering the Feminine in American Indian Traditions* (Boston: Beacon Press, 1986), 11.
8. Luisah Teish, *Jambalaya: The Natural Woman's Book of Personal*

Charms and Practical Rituals (San Francisco: Harper and Row, 1985), 113.

9. Ibid., 104.
10. See ibid., 111–29, for a discussion of the similarities of the gods and goddesses of African-diasporic religions.
11. See Myriam Diaz-Diocaretz, "Black North-American Women Poets in the Semiotics of Culture." In *Women, Feminist Identity and Society in the 1980's: Selected Papers*, ed. Diaz-Diocaretz and Iris M. Zavala (Philadelphia: John Benjamins, 1985), 49–51.
12. See, for example, Ruether's discussion of Catholicism's absorption of the Goddess symbol in the worship of Mary in *New Woman/New Earth*, 36–62. See also Teish's correspondence charts of African deities and European Catholic Saints in *Jambalaya*, 107.

2. *Curing Ceremonies*

Note: Portions of this chapter appeared in my "The Journey Back to Female Roots: A Laguna Pueblo Model," in *Lesbian Texts and Contexts: Radical Revisions*, ed. Karla Jay and Joanne Glasgow (New York: New York University Press, 1990), 339–54.

1. I follow Bronislow Malinowski's definition of mythology as "the sacred tradition of a society . . . a body of narratives woven into their culture, dictating their belief, defining their ritual, acting as [the] chart of their social order and the pattern of their moral behavior"; see *Sex, Culture, and Myth* (New York: Harcourt, Brace and World, 1962), 249.
2. See Alan R. Velie, *Four American Indian Literary Masters: N. Scott Momaday, James Welch, Leslie Silko, and Gerald Vizenor* (Norman, Oklahoma: University of Oklahoma Press, 1982), for instance, who writes that she is one of "four American Indian literary masters."
3. See *American Indian Quarterly: A Journal of Anthropology, History, and Literature* 5, no. 1 (February 1979).
4. Paula Gunn Allen, "Symbol and Structure in Native American Literature: Some Basic Considerations," *College Composition and Communication* 24, no. 3 (October 1973): 267–70.
5. Elsie Clews Parsons, *Pueblo Indian Religion*, 2 vols. (Chicago: University of Chicago Press, 1939), xi.

6. See N. Scott Momaday, "I Am Alive," in *The World of the American Indian,* ed. Jules B. Billard (Washington, D.C.: National Geographic, 1979), 54–60, and Edward P. Dosier, *The Pueblo Indians of North America* (New York: Holt, Rinehart and Winston, 1970), 31–34, for general information about the Pueblos and their ancestors. The actual dates for the founding of Laguna are controversial. Many scholars say that it was founded after the Pueblo rebellion against the Spanish in 1680. This time period seems to be selected because Governor Don Pedro Rodriquez Cubero visited the pueblo and named it San Jose de la Laguna in 1669. For instance, see Parsons, *Pueblo Indian Religion,* 888, and Fred Eggan, *Social Organization of the Western Pueblos* (1950; reprint, Chicago: University of Chicago Press, 1963), 253, for discussions of Laguna's founding. However, Florence Hawley Ellis makes a good argument that it was founded in the thirteenth century. See Ellis, "Anthropology of Laguna Pueblo Land Claims," in *Pueblo Indians,* vol. 3, ed. David Agree Horr (New York: Garland, 1974), 45–46.
7. Reyes Garcia, "Senses of Place in *Ceremony,*" *MELUS* 10, no. 4 (Winter 1983): 46.
8. Allen in Mary Dougherty Bartlett, *The New American Novel: Works in Progress* (Albuquerque: University of New Mexico Press, 1986), 58.
9. Simon J. Ortiz, "Towards a National Indian Literature: Cultural Authenticity in Nationalism," *MELUS* 8, no. 2 (Summer 1981): 11.
10. Silko quoted in "Stories and Their Tellers—A Conversation with Leslie Marmon Silko," in *The Third Woman: Minority Women Writers of the United States,* ed. Dexter Fisher (Boston: Houghton Mifflin, 1980), 20.
11. Allen, "The Sacred Hoop: A Contemporary Indian Perspective on American Indian Literature," in *Literature of the American Indians: Views and Interpretations,* ed. Abraham Chapman (New York: New American, 1975), 117.
12. Allen, *The Sacred Hoop: Recovering,* 45.
13. Ibid., 50.
14. Allen, interview with author, June 20, 1985.
15. See Norma Wilson, "Outlook for Survival," *Denver Quarterly,* 14, no. 4 (Winter 1980): 23.
16. Silko quoted in Lawrence Evers and Dennis Carr, "A Conversation

with Leslie Silko," *Sun Tracks* 3 (Fall 1976): 30. Elsie Clews Parsons was an early anthropologist trained by Franz Boas who worked with the Southwest Indian tribes in the early 1900s. Her two-volume *Pueblo Indian Religion* was an important work in the field.

17. See especially Silko's renditions in *Ceremony*, 74, 110, 118, 159, 187, and compare to Franz Boas, *Keresan Texts*, vol. 8, part 1 (New York: The American Ethnological Society, 1928), 11–13. One can assume that some of the ethnographer's versions were fairly accurate or have become the accepted versions.
18. Silko, "Language and Literature from a Pueblo Perspective," in *English Literature: Opening Up the Canon*, ed. Leslie A. Fiedler and Houston A. Baker, Jr., Selected Papers from the English Institute, New Series, no. 4 (Baltimore: Johns Hopkins University Press, 1981), 55–64.
19. See Eggan, *Social Organization*, for a discussion of Laguna clans.
20. See Silko, "Language," 57.
21. Ibid., 56.
22. Allen says that "the goddess who appeared to the Indian Juan Diego in 1659 and who is known as Our Lady of Guadalupe" is represented as appearing much like the Laguna concept of the Goddess, Iyatiku (Corn Woman or Earth Woman). See Allen, *The Sacred Hoop: Recovering*, 26. I believe she is using Guadalupe as symbolically equivalent to Laguna, and in this context, the use also puts more emphasis on the Goddess or female principle.
23. In a note to her poem "Grandmother," Allen also identifies herself as a member of Oak Clan. See Fisher, *The Third Woman*, 126.
24. In his book, *The Spirit and the Flesh: Sexual Diversity in American Indian Culture* (Boston: Beacon Press, 1986), 11, Walter Williams describes the Native American women who take on an essentially male social role in their respective cultures as "amazons," for lack of a better term.
25. Allen, *Sacred Hoop: Recovering*, 48. Keres is a language cluster spoken by many of the Pueblo peoples, but because some Pueblo peoples belong to other language groups, people from different villages often have difficulty understanding one another. See Dosier, *Pueblo Indians*, 37, and Parsons, *Pueblo Indian Religion*, 10–11. Allen is making the point that only the Keres-speaking group is considered to be a "mother-right" people.

26. Parsons, *Pueblo Indian Religion,* 182, 192–93, 888–89.
27. Allen, "Where I Come From God Is a Grandmother," *Sojourner: The Women's Forum,* August 1988, 17.
28. Because Ephanie is essentially without community, there is also some reference in the novel to her being a "witch," a designation given to those who were seen as causing harm, often someone outside the group.
29. Silko, "Language," 57.
30. See Allen, *Woman,* 123–28, for a version of this myth. This also points out some of the problems encountered in looking at the different mythological accounts in the ethnographies where the names have different spellings and change frequently. There are even differences between the versions that Silko and Allen use in their novels. Silko uses Nau'ts'ity'i and I'tcts'ity'i as the names of the two sisters, with the former as the mother of the Indians and the latter as the mother of the others. Allen uses Uretsete (Iyatiku) as mother of the Indians and Naotsete as the mother of the others. See also Allen's discussion in *The Sacred Hoop: Recovering,* 20.
31. Allen, "Grandmother," in Fisher, *The Third Woman,* 26. See also Susan J. Scarberry, "Grandmother Spider's Lifeline," in *Studies in American Indian Literature: Critical Essays and Course Designs,* ed. Paula Allen (New York: Modern Language Association of America, 1983), 106–7, for a discussion of the poem.
32. Allen, "The Sacred Hoop," 113.
33. For instance, Allen comments that women were so important to the Iroquoi that "the penalty for killing a woman of the tribe" was "double that for killing a man . . . given the high regard in which the tribes held women and given that in killing a woman one killed the children she might have borne" (*Sacred Hoop: Recovering,* 32).
34. Ibid., 49–50.
35. Silko refers to several of these spirit-people who are said to be Ck'o'yo magicians or medicine men in poems that retell some of the myths. These spirit-people appear to work a kind of evil magic and seem to be trickster figures. See, for instance, Silko's *Storyteller* (New York: Seaver, 1981), 161–69, and *Ceremony,* 178–84.
36. See Carol Mitchell, "*Ceremony* as Ritual," in *American Indian Quarterly,* 32–34, for a discussion of the function of Ts'eh in *Ceremony,* and Allen, "The Feminine Landscape of Leslie Marmon

Silko's *Ceremony*," in *Studies*, 127–33, for a discussion of both Night Swan and Ts'eh.

37. Allen, "The Feminine," 130.
38. Ibid., 130–31.
39. Ibid., 133. See also her discussion in "Where I Come From God is a Grandmother," 16–18.
40. See Allen, "How the West Was Really Won," in *The Sacred Hoop: Recovering*, 194–208.
41. Allen, *The Sacred Hoop: Recovering*, 256.
42. Ibid., 257.
43. Will Roscoe, ed., "Double Woman," in *The Living Spirit: A Gay American Indian Anthology* (New York: St. Martin's Press, 1988), 88.
44. Allen, *The Sacred Hoop: Recovering*, 258.
45. Ibid., 257.
46. Ibid.
47. Walter L. Williams, *The Spirit and the Flesh: Sexual Diversity in American Indian Culture* (Boston: Beacon Press, 1986), 29.
48. Ibid.
49. Allen, excerpt from *Raven's Road*, in Roscoe, *The Living Spirit*, 143–44.
50. Williams, *Spirit*, 30.
51. Ibid., 2.
52. Allen, *The Sacred Hoop: Recovering*, 124.
53. Williams, *Spirit*, 41–42.
54. Ibid., 34.
55. Allen quoted in ibid., 251.
56. Allen, "Where I Come From," 17.
57. Ibid.
58. A recent controversy within the academic community has been over whether literature can be therapeutic and, if so, how that happens. See, for instance, Marshall W. Alcorn, Jr., and Mark Bracher, "Literature, Psychoanalysis, and the Re-Formation of the Self: A New Direction for Reader-Response Theory," *PMLA* 100, no. 3 (May 1985): 322–54, and responses to Alcorn and Bracher in "Forum," *PMLA* 100, no. 5 (October 1985): 818–20. See also James Hillman, *Healing Fiction* (Barrytown, N.Y.: Station Hill, 1983).

59. Allen, "Who Is Your Mother? Red Roots of White Feminism," *Sinister Wisdom* 25 (Winter 1984): 39.

3. *The West African Tradition and the Female Principle*

1. See, for instance, John Blassingame, *The Slave Community: Plantation Life in the Antebellum South*, rev. ed. (New York: Oxford University Press, 1979), 20–48; Eugene D. Genovese, *Roll, Jordan, Roll: The World the Slaves Made* (New York: Vintage, 1976), 209–32; Melville J. Herskovits, *Dahomey: An Ancient West African Kingdom*, vol. 1 (Evanston, Ill.: Northwestern University Press, 1967); Herskovits, *The Myth of the Negro Past* (New York: Harper and Brothers, 1941); Lawrence W. Levine, *Black Culture and Black Consciousness: Afro-American Folk Thought from Slavery to Freedom* (New York: Oxford University Press, 1977); August Meier and Elliott Rudwick, *From Plantation to Ghetto*, 3d ed. (New York: Hill and Wang, 1976), 21–26; and Robert Farris Thompson, *Flash of the Spirit: African and Afro-American Art and Philosophy* (New York: Vintage, 1984).
2. Meir and Rudwick, *From Plantation*, 25–26.
3. See Walker, *In Search*, xii.
4. Walker, "Writing *The Color Purple*," in her *In Search*, 355–56. Walker says her "'history' starts not with the taking of lands, or the births, battles and deaths of Great Men, but with one woman asking another for her underwear."
5. Audre Lorde, "Poetry Is Not a Luxury," in her *Sister Outsider*, 38.
6. John Mbiti, *African Religions and Philosophy* (New York: Praeger, 1969), 2.
7. Ibid., 197.
8. See Teish, *Jambalaya*, for a discussion of the African-diasporic tradition. In a further blending, for instance, Alice Walker acknowledges that her great-grandmother on her mother's side was "mostly" Cherokee; see *Living by the Word* (San Diego: Harcourt Brace Jovanovich, 1988), 43. Literary critics have begun to develop what some call an Afracentric theory of literary criticism which unfortunately has not often been applied to the work of African-American women writers. These writers are gaining attention but are still

often left out of major theoretical work, especially by male critics. See, for instance, Houston A. Baker, Jr.'s *The Journey Back: Issues in Black Literature and Criticism* (Chicago: University of Chicago Press, 1980), in which Phillis Wheatley is the only black woman writer mentioned.

9. Janheinz Jahn, *Muntu: An Outline of Neo-African Culture*, trans. Marjorie Grene (London: Faber and Faber, 1958), 123.
10. Ibid., 124.
11. Ibid., 127.
12. Ibid., 133.
13. Ibid., 133–34.
14. Ibid., 134.
15. Ibid., 135.
16. Ibid., 138.
17. Lorde, "Poetry," in *Sister Outsider*, 38–39.
18. Ibid., 39.
19. Lorde, "Uses of the Erotic: The Erotic as Power," in *Sister Outsider*, 53.
20. Ibid., 55.
21. "Severed" here also refers to Lorde's mastectomy.
22. Allen, "Grandmother," in Fisher, *The Third Woman*, 126.
23. The kings of Dahomey, a West African kingdom, had battalions of women who, as Lorde says in *The Black Unicorn*, "were highly prized, well-trained, and ferocious women-warriors" (p. 119). The cover of her poetry book, *Our Dead Behind Us (ODBU)* (New York: W. W. Norton, 1986), has a picture of "the last Dahomean Amazons/taken the year I was born/three old Black women in draped cloths/holding hands" ("Beams," 71). See also Herskovits, *Dahomey* 1: 46, 84, for a discussion of the Amazons.
24. See also Lorde in *Zami*, in which Lorde says, "The casing of this place [Seventh Street, New York City] had been my home for seven years, the amount of time it takes for a human body to completely renew itself, cell by cell" (p. 255).
25. Lorde, "Eye to Eye: Black Women, Hatred, and Anger," in *Sister Outsider*, 151.
26. Lorde, "An Interview: Audre Lorde and Adrienne Rich," in *Sister Outsider*, 101.
27. Susan Gubar, " 'The Blank Page' and the Issues of Female Crea-

tivity," in *The New Feminist Criticism: Essays on Women, Literature, and Theory*, ed. Elaine Showalter (New York: Pantheon, 1985), 303.

28. Marjorie Pryse, "Zora Neale Hurston, Alice Walker, and the 'Ancient Power' of Black Women," in *Conjuring: Black Women, Fiction, and Literary Tradition*, ed. Pryse and Hortense J. Spillers (Bloomington: Indiana University Press, 1985), 5. See also Walker's comments about writing *The Color Purple* in *In Search*, 356, in which she says that her characters were "trying to contact me, to speak *through* me."
29. Lorde, *A Burst of Light, Essays* (Ithaca, N.Y.: Firebrand, 1988), 20.
30. Ibid., 18.
31. Ibid., 42.
32. Lorde, "On My Way Out I Passed Over You and the Verrazano Bridge," in *ODBU*, 54.
33. Lorde, "Call," in *ODBU*, 73–74. Lorde's note (p. 75) says that Aido Hwedo is "the Rainbow Serpent; also a representation of all ancient divinities who must be worshipped but whose names and faces have been lost in time." See also Mary Deshazer's discussion of Lorde's use of African goddesses in her work, "Sisters in Pain: The Warrior Muse of Audre Lorde," in *Inspiring Women: Reimagining the Muse* (New York: Pergamon Press, 1986), 170–95.
34. Walker, *In Search*, 289. Reacting to the criticism of the portrayal of lesbianism in *The Color Purple*, Walker clearly connects lesbianism to the freedom of women. She says: "Women loving women, and expressing it 'publicly,' if they so choose, is part and parcel of what freedom for women means just as this is what it means for anyone else. If you are not free to express your love, you are a slave; anyone who would demand that you enslave yourself by not freely expressing your love is a person with a slaveholder's mentality" (*Living*, 91).
35. See Walker's discussion, "All the Bearded Irises of Life: Confessions of a Homospiritual," in *Living by the Word* (San Diego: Harcourt Brace Jovanovich, 1988), 163–69.
36. Barbara Christian, *Black Women Novelists: The Development of a Tradition, 1892–1976* (Westport, Conn.: Greenwood, 1980), 61.
37. Ibid., 60.

38. Mary Helen Washington, Introduction to *I Love Myself When I Am Laughing . . . And Then Again When I am Looking Mean and Impressive: A Zora Neale Hurston Reader* (Old Westbury, N.Y.: The Feminist Press, 1979), 8.
39. Allen, interview with the author, June 20, 1985.
40. Walker, *In Search*, xii. See also Elliot Butler-Evans's discussion of Walker's use of lesbianism in *The Color Purple* in his *Race, Gender, and Desire: Narrative Strategies in the Fiction of Toni Cade Bambara, Toni Morrison, and Alice Walker* (Philadelphia: Temple University Press, 1989), 168–69.
41. Walker, *In Search*, xi–xii.
42. Zora Neal Hurston, *Their Eyes Were Watching God* (Urbana: University of Illinois Press, 1978), 29.
43. Walker, *In Search*, xi.
44. Ibid., xii.
45. Gloria Naylor shows this idea again in "The Two," in her *Women of Brewster Place* (New York: Penguin, 1983), 129–73, when a black lesbian is killed because the black community does not support her. See Barbara Christian, "No More Buried Lives: The Theme of Lesbianism in Audre Lorde's *Zami*, Gloria Naylor's *The Women of Brewster Place*, Ntozake Shange's *Sassafras, Cypress and Indigo*, and Alice Walker's *The Color Purple*," in her Black *Feminist Criticism: Perspectives on Black Women Writers* (New York: Pergamon, 1985), 191 and 201, for a discussion of Naylor's work. Christian also points out that Celie's mother is destroyed because of her isolation from other womenfolk" (p. 201).
46. Christian, "No More Buried," 194.
47. Lorde, "Uses," in *Sister Outsider*, 53.
48. Ibid., 58.
49. Christian, "No More Buried," in her *Black Feminist Criticism*, 191.
50. Lorde, "Uses," in *Sister Outsider*, 57.
51. See the back cover of Lorde's *Zami*.
52. Compare to Silko's passage in *Ceremony* about Tayo and Night Swan: "He . . . wondered what she kept behind the curtains. He could feel something back there, something of her life which he could not explain. The room pulsed with feeling, the feeling flowing with the music and the breeze from the curtains, feeling colored by the blue flowers painted in a border around the walls. He could

feel it everywhere, even in the blue sheets that were stretched tightly across the bed. Somewhere, from another room, he heard a clock ticking slowly and distinctly, as if the years, the centuries, were lost in that sound. . . . He dreamed it again and again, sinking and rolling with the light blue sheets twisted around his thighs and ankles, and the excitement of wet smells of rain, and their sweat. He wanted to lie like that forever" (p. 103).

53. The reference to the goddess "riding" Lorde is from the voodoo religion in which a person is taken over by the god and in some cases behaves as if he or she is a horse, "ridden" by the god. See Zora Neale Hurston, *Tell My Horse* (1938; reprint, Berkeley, Calif.: Turtle Island, 1983), 232–50, for the Caribbean tradition. See Serge Bramly, *Macumba: The Teaching of Maria-Jose, Mother of the Gods,* trans. Meg Bogun (New York: St. Martin's Press, 1977), 37, for a discussion of the Brazilian tradition. Reginald Martin, in *Ishmael Reed and the New Black Aesthetic Critics* (London: Macmillan, 1988), says that a "human may 'carry' a fetish [icon or trance] attributed to a god; the human carrier is then labelled a 'horse,' and may show a quality attributed to a god; or it [the fetish] may be the god itself in control of the horse" (p. 69).

54. Lorde, *A Burst of Light,* 128. Lorde also reveals her holistic approach to life in her 1980 account of her struggle with breast cancer in *The Cancer Journals* (New York: Spinsters, Ink)—one of the earliest such accounts to be written.

55. Lorde, *Burst,* 133.

56. See Allen, *The Sacred Hoop,* 51–52.

57. Lorde, *Burst,* 130.

58. Lorde, "Uses," in *Sister Outsider,* 58.

59. Jahn, *Mintu,* 130.

60. See also "The Revenge of Hannah Kemhuff" in her *In Love & Trouble: Stories of Black Women* (New York: Harcourt Brace Jovanovich, 1973), 60–80, and "Nuclear Exorcism: Beyond Cursing the Day We Were Born," in *Mother Jones,* September–October 1982, 20–21, for other examples of the use of curses in Walker's work.

61. Walker, "Nuclear," 21.

62. See also Herskovits, *Dahomey* 1: 291–95, for a discussion of cicatrization. In a similar way, Maxine Hong Kingston, *The Woman War-*

rior: Memoirs of a Girlhood among Ghosts (New York: Alfred A. Knopf, 1977), records a passage in which the parents "carve revenge on" the protagonist's back so that "wherever you go, whatever happens to you, people will know our sacrifice. . . . And you'll never forget either" (p. 34). Clitoridectomy is the removal of the clitoris, an African practice that has aroused much controversy in the feminist community, especially in the United States. For instance, see Mary Daly's discussion in *Gynecology: The Metaethics of Radical Feminism* (Boston: Beacon Press, 1978), 153–77, and Audre Lorde's response to her in "An Open Letter to Mary Daly" in *This Bridge Called My Back: Writings by Radical Women of Color*, ed. Cherrie Moraga and Gloria Anzaldua (Watertown, Mass.: Persephone Press, 1981), 94–97.

63. Herskovits, *Dahomey* 1: 319–20.
64. Ibid., 320. He says: "It now becomes clear why this type of marriage is given the name it bears. The native statement is: 'When the goat becomes big, one does not ask which buck caused her to conceive.' "
65. See Walker, *The Temple of My Familiar* (San Diego: Harcourt Brace Jovanovich, 1989), in which Walker not only explores the roles of African goddesses, but in which Celie and Shug appear again. Celie and Shug form their own church, "a tradition of long standing among black women" (p. 209) because "spirituality was, above all, too precious to be left to the perverted interpretations of men" (p. 300).
66. Doris Davenport, "Afracentric Visions," review of *The Temple of My Familiar*, in *The Women's Review of Books* 6, no. 12 (September 1989): 13–14.
67. Walker, *In Search*, xi.
68. Walker's novel does seem to have some flaws, however; one of the characters who is also an artist (a flute player) seems to use his "art"—a kind of following of his spirit guardian—to justify sleeping with his wife's mother. Walker really never resolves the situation satisfactorily. The character says: "He knew . . . why he was capable of falling in love so easily, even with his own wife's mother. It was because he was a musician, and an artist. Artists . . . were simply messengers. On them fell the responsibility for uniting the world" (ibid., 125).

69. Walker, *Living*, 66.
70. Ibid., 64.
71. Jahn, *Mintu*, 135.

4. Revisioning Celtic Traditions

Note: The epigraph is from Judy Grahn, *The Queen of Wands* (Trumansburg, N.Y.: The Crossing Press, 1982), 78.

1. Not all witches are feminists, nor would all of them identify themselves as lesbian. There are many traditions of witchcraft, and the witchcraft movement predates witches identifying themselves as feminist. For instance, see Charles Leland, *The Gospel of Witches* (1900; reprint, London: The C. W. Daniel Company, 1974), who discusses the Dianic tradition of Italy. This book has since been called a hoax, but has influenced a number of anthropologists, including Margaret Murray. It later influenced Gerald Gardner, who is responsible for starting "a small religious movement in its own right" (Jeffrey Burton Russell, "Concepts of Witchcraft," in *The Encyclopedia of Religion*, ed. Mircea Elaide [New York: Macmillan, 1987], 421). For other witchcraft traditions, see Leo Martello, *Witchcraft: The Old Religion* (Secaucus, N.J.: University, [1973]), who discusses a number of traditions; Gerald Gardner, *Witchcraft Today* (London: Rider, 1954), who heads a tradition using his name; and Z. Budapest, *The Holy Book of Women's Mysteries*, 2 vols. (Oakland, Calif.: Susan B. Coven No. 1, 1982), who is from the Dianic tradition passed on to her through her Hungarian mother, in which generally only women participate.
2. *Dreaming the Dark* is Starhawk's Master's thesis in the Feminist Therapy Program. See her *The Spiral Dance: A Rebirth of the Ancient Religion of the Great Goddess* (San Francisco: Harper and Row, 1979), 40–41, for a discussion of her training. See also Norma Lorre Goodrich, *Priestesses* (New York: Franklin Watts, 1989), for an extensive discussion of priestesses in antiquity.
3. Misti Schumacher, "Witch Born in St. Paul Casts Spell That Demolishes Stereotypes," *Minneapolis Star and Tribune*, March 21, 1985, C2.
4. I use the word "empowerment" here because witches believe in a reciprocity between human beings and the divine and the creations

of the divine. See Starhawk, *Spiral,* 11–12, and further discussion in this chapter.

5. See Norman Cohn, *Europe's Inner Demons: An Enquiry Inspired by the Great-Witch Hunt* (New York: New American Library, 1977).
6. See Schumacher, "Witch Born," for Starhawk's discussion of this topic.
7. Jeffrey B. Russell, *A History of Witchcraft: Sorcerers, Heretics, and Pagans* (London: Thames and Hudson, 1980), 8.
8. Murray, *The Witch-Cult in Western Europe* (1921; reprint, Oxford: Clarendon Press, 1963), 11–12.
9. Mircea Eliade, *Occultism, Witchcraft, and Cultural Fashions* (Chicago: University of Chicago Press, 1976), 73.
10. Ibid., 78–85.
11. Jean Markale, *Women of the Celts,* trans. A. Mygind, C. Hauch, and P. Henry (Rochester, Vt.: Inner Traditions International, Ltd., 1986), 243.
12. For a good discussion of the reliability of classical sources, see Proinsias MacCana, *Celtic Mythology* (London: Hamlyn, 1973), 16–18.
13. See Starhawk's Appendix A, "The Burning Times: Notes on a Crucial Period of History," in *Dreaming the Dark: Magic, Sex & Politics* (Boston: Beacon Press, 1982), for a discussion of witch persecutions.
14. Russell, *A History,* 92.
15. MacCana, *Celtic Mythology,* 19.
16. Ibid., 19.
17. Ibid., 20.
18. Ibid., 20.
19. Z. Budapest is one of the original founders of the feminist witchcraft movement.
20. Adler, *Drawing Down the Moon: Witches, Druids, Goddess-Worshippers, and Other Pagans in America Today* (Boston: Beacon Press, 1979), 178.
21. Starhawk, *Spiral,* 5. See also Doreen Valiente, *An ABC of Witchcraft Past & Present* (New York: St. Martin's Press, 1973), who says that witchcraft means "the craft of the wise" (p. 12). Russell, however, disagrees with this interpretation, saying that the Old English

wicca meant "male witch," *wicce* meant "female witch," both from the verb *wiccan*, meaning "to cast a spell" *(A History*, 12).

22. See Adler, *Drawing Down*, 56–59.
23. From "The Charge of the Goddess" recorded in Starhawk, *Spiral*, 76, which Starhawk says "is traditional to almost all branches of Witchcraft" (pp. 91–92, n. 1). For another recording, see Lady Sheba, *The Book of Shadows* (St. Paul, Minn.: Llewellyn, 1973), 65.
24. For instance, see Sibylle von Cles-Reden, *The Realm of the Great Goddess: The Story of the Megalith Builders* (London: Thames and Hudson, 1961), for archaeological information; and Joseph Campbell, *The Power of Myth*, ed. Betty Sue Flowers (New York: Doubleday, 1988), chap. 6, for a discussion of the role of the Goddess in Mediterranean cultures.
25. MacCana, *Celtic Mythology*, 86.
26. See Gardner's *Witchcraft Today* for more information on the movement attributed to him.
27. Adler, *Drawing Down*, 343.
28. Both Martello, *Witchcraft*, and Valiente, *An ABC*, discuss similar tenets.
29. See Starhawk, "Witchcraft as the Basis for Goddess-Religion of the Future," in *Book to the Goddess*, ed. Ann Forfreedom and Julie Ann (Sacramento, Calif.: The Temple of the Goddess Within, 1980), 174.
30. Jahn, *Mintu*, 123.
31. Russell, *A History*, 13.
32. See also Martello, *Witchcraft*, 31.
33. Adler, *Drawing Down*, 340–4l.
34. Allen, *Sacred Hoop: Remembering*, 5.
35. For instance, see Budapest, *Holy Book* 2: 19, and Justine Glass, *Witchcraft, the Sixth Sense* (No. Hollywood, Calif.: Wilshire, 1965), 57–58, for a discussion of this concept.
36. Lorde, "Uses," in *Sister Outsider*, 53.
37. Allen, "The Feminine," 130–31.
38. See Susan Griffin, *Pornography and Silence: Culture's Revenge Against Nature* (New York: Harper and Row, 1981).
39. Sjoestedt, *Gods and Heroes of the Celts*, trans. Myles Dillion (London: Methuen and Co., Ltd., 1949), 24–37.

40. See Starhawk, *Dreaming*, chap. 4, for an example of one of these healing journeys.
41. Markale, *Women of Celts*, 253.
42. MacCana, *Celtic Mythology*, 94.
43. Judy Grahn, *Another Mother Tongue: Gay Words, Gay Worlds* (Boston: Beacon Press, 1984), 139.
44. Ibid., 137.
45. Ibid., 47.
46. See Allen, *The Sacred Hoop: Recovering*, 257.
47. Grahn, *Mother Tongue*, 35.
48. Ibid., 35.
49. Ibid., 34.
50. See Adler, *Drawing Down*, 196, for instance, and pp. 201, 423, 440 in her 1986 revised and expanded edition.
51. See also Gareth Knight, *A History of White Magic* (London and Oxford: Mowbrays, 1978), 217, for another discussion of the use of poetry to convey esoteric truths.
52. Hartley, *The Western Mystery Tradition* (London: Aquarian Press, 1968), 169.
53. See also Knight, *History*, 77, and W. Y. Evans-Wentz, *The Fairy-Faith in Celtic Countries* (1911; reprint, [Secaucus, N.J.]: University Books, 1966), 330–31, for more discussion of the Arthurian legends and their history.
54. See Evelyn Blackwood, "Sexuality and Gender in Certain Native American Tribes: The Case of Cross-Gender Females," in *Feminist Frontiers II: Rethinking Sex, Gender, and Society*, ed. Laurel Richardson and Verta Taylor (New York: Random House, 1989), 146, for a more thorough discussion of this point.
55. Russell, *A History*, reminds us that if a belief is part of a "coherent world view" (p. 12), it is not a superstition, so that conquering traditions try to win validity by attempting to destroy the coherency of the worldviews of the conquered. While discussing the Celtic tradition, Jean Markale identifies the witch with opposition to Christianity and patriarchal society. Further, she says that "the magical powers of the true witch . . . in popular traditions are often a debased form of the powers attributed to divinities" such as the "ancient Breton goddess honoured in the region of the Pointe du

Raz and invariably remembered as the 'good witch' " (*Women of Celts*, 46).

56. See also Russell, *A History*, who says that contemporary witches "emphasize the threefold nature of the goddess: she is warrior maid; she is mother; she is hag of darkness and rebirth" (p. 158).
57. Compare this idea with Lorde's idea of woman becoming Afrekete in *Zami*, 255. For a discussion of "the triplication of a single personage," see Russell, *A History*, 48–50.
58. Silko in Fisher, *The Third Woman*, 18.
59. Russell, however, says that although some contemporary witches believe in "reincarnation, which, they claim, derives from the 'Celtic/Druid/witch tradition,' " it "is not an important doctrine of Western religions and has little place in Celtic or Teutonic beliefs" *(A History*, 161). See also Alfred Nutt's analysis of the Celtic doctrine of rebirth in which he says that rebirth applies only to a "favored few" —those connected with or of the gods such as the Tuatha De Danann—and that "Irish doctrine, if doctrine it may be called, has no apparent connection with any belief in a soul as distinct from the body, or in a life led by the soul after the death of the body" (*The Celtic Doctrine of Rebirth*, ed. and trans. Kuno Meyer [London: David Nutt, 1897], 96). However, as J. A. MacCulloch, in *Celtic and Scandinavian Religions* (London: Hutchinson's University Library, 1948), says, referring to Caesar's comment that "the Druids teach that souls do not die, but pass from one to another after death," this "doesn't refer to a transmigration belief . . . but to the soul's being clad . . . with a new body in the other world" (p. 81).
60. Markale, *Women of Celts*, 81. See also her quotation from Strabo, in *Women of Celts*, 81, and MacCulloch, *Celtic*, 76.
61. Valiente, *An ABC*, 56.
62. Evans-Wentz, *Fairy-Faith*, 62. The seer also says, "There are 'three great worlds which we can see while we are still in the body: the earth-world, mid-world, and heaven world.' "
63. Ibid., 59. See also Charles Squire, *The Mythology of the British Islands: An Introduction to Celtic, Myth, Legend, Poetry, and Romance* (New York: Charles Scribner's Sons, [1905]), 65, for another discussion of the Celtic gods arriving in Ireland as recorded in the legends.

64. Markale, *Women of Celts*, 51.
65. Glass, *Witchcraft*, 52. See also Dion Fortune's novel, *Moon Magic, Being the Memoirs of a Mistress of That Art*, in which the main character is also Morgan Le Fay, who is reborn into modern England.
66. Hartley, *Western Mystery*, 49.
67. Ibid., 57. Markale (*Women of Celts*, 113) confirms that Morgan comes from old Celtic *morigenos* ("born of the sea").
68. Markale, *Women of Celts*, 82.
69. Ibid., 48.
70. Ibid., 47.
71. Ibid., 48. Also discussed in MacCulloch, *Celtic*, 91.
72. Markale, *Women of Celts*, 47–48.
73. Glass, *Witchcraft*, 27. See also von Cles-Reden, *The Realm*, for a discussion of the Great Goddess and Stonehenge.
74. Glass, *Witchcraft*, 28. See also Gardner, *Witchcraft*, 28, for a discussion of Druidesses or witches.
75. MacCana, *Celtic Mythology*, 35.
76. Ibid.
77. See, for instance, Pennethorne Hughes, *Witchcraft* (London and New York: Longmans, Green and Company, 1952), 72, on women's roles in maintaining the mystery traditions.
78. Markale, *Women of Celts*, 174.
79. Concerning the grail, Bradley, *MA*, says: "In the cup of the Goddess, O Mother, is the cauldron of Ceridwen, wherein all men are nourished and from which all men have all the good things of this world" (p. 770).
80. See also Bradley, *MA*, 398–99, on Christianity's relationship to the Old Religion.
81. Markale, *Women of Celts*, 199.
82. Ibid., 200.
83. See John Sharkley, *Celtic Mysteries: The Ancient Religion* (London: Thames and Hudson, 1975), 19, and Markale, *Women of Celts*, 251, for information on fosterage by Celtic tribes.
84. Glass, *Witchcraft*, 57.
85. See also Martello, *Witchcraft*, 101, for a discussion of the place of the fertility rites in witchcraft today.
86. See Valiente, *An ABC*, 164.

87. Ibid., 166.
88. Lorde, "Uses," in *Sister Outsider,* 53.
89. Linda Hogan, interview with author, October 3, 1985.
90. See, for instance, Hartley, *Western Mystery,* 162.
91. Spivack, *Merlin's Daughters: Contemporary Women Writers of Fantasy* (New York: Greenwood Press, 1987), 161.
92. See, for instance, Margaret Murray, *The God of the Witches* (London: Sampson, Law, Marston, [1933]), 157–58. This is one of Murray's most controversial books, and recently her work on witchcraft has been widely criticized, even though "the *Encyclopaedia Britannica* used her article on 'witchcraft' for decades; and a number of historians and folklorists followed her lead" (Russell, *A History,* 41). See also Alwyn Ress and Brinley Ress, *Celtic Heritage: Ancient Tradition in Ireland and Wales* (London: Thames and Hudson, 1961), 146, and Valiente, *An ABC,* 25. Bradley, *MA,* 835, also summarizes the legend of the Divine Victim and connects it to the death of Jesus.
93. MacCana, *Celtic Mythology,* 120.
94. Ibid., 120.
95. Marilyn Farwell, "Heterosexual Plots and Lesbian Subtexts: Toward a Theory of Lesbian Narrative Space," in *Lesbian Texts and Subtexts: Radical Revisions,* ed. Karla Jay and Joanne Glasgow (New York: New York University Press, 1990), 102.
96. Grahn, *Another Mother Tongue,* 256.
97. Ibid.
98. Ibid, 258.
99. Ibid.
100. Starhawk, in a lecture given in Minneapolis, Minnesota, March 3, 1985.

5. *From the Euro-American Mainstream*

1. Mark Leone, *Roots of Modern Mormonism* (Cambridge, Mass.: Harvard University Press, 1979), 119.
2. Jan Shipps, *Mormonism: The Story of a New Religious Tradition* (Urbana and Chicago: University of Illinois Press, 1985), 52.
3. Ibid., 126.
4. Leone, *Roots,* 9.

5. Shipps, *Mormonism*, 39.
6. Ibid., 120
7. Ibid., 69.
8. Ray B. West, Jr., *Kingdom of the Saints* (New York: Viking, 1957), 118. According to William J. Whalen in *The Latter-day Saints in the Modern Day World*, rev. ed. (Notre Dame, Ind.: University of Notre Dame Press, 1967), 91, this epigram was first written down by Lorenzo Snow, president and prophet of the LDS church from 1898 to 1901.
9. Brigham Young as quoted in Whalen, *Latter-day Saints*, 91. It should be noted that the information given here relates to the Utah Mormons, of which Johnson was a member, and not to the reorganized church of the Latter Day Saints based in Missouri.
10. See ibid., 88–107, and Thomas O'Dea, *The Mormons* (Chicago: University of Chicago Press, 1957), 119–54, for a discussion of Mormon theology.
11. Linda Wilcox, "The Mormon Concept of a Mother in Heaven," in *Sisters in Spirit: Mormon Women in Historical and Cultural Perspective*, ed. Maureen Ursenback Beecher and Lavina Fielding Anderson (Urbana and Chicago: University of Illinois Press, 1987), 65.
12. Quoted in West, *Kingdom*, 118, and Whalen, *Latter-day Saints*, 92.
13. See Johnson, "The Woman Who Talked Back to God," *Ms.*, November 1981, 52–53.
14. Jill Mulvay Derr, " 'Strength in Our Union': The Making of a Mormon Sisterhood," in Beecher and Anderson, *Sisters*, 125.
15. Ibid., 196.
16. See Carol Cornwall Madsen, "Mormon Women and the Temple: Toward a New Understanding," 98, and Derr, "Strength," 182, both in Beecher and Anderson, *Sisters*, for a mention of Wells.
17. Derr in ibid., 179.
18. Marilyn Warenski points out in *Patriarches and Politics: The Plight of Mormon Women* (New York: McGraw-Hill, 1978), 1–20, that although many contemporary Mormon women believe the church's current stand on women's rights is inconsistent with the church's support of women's right to vote in the nineteenth century, she feels it is not. Warenski claims that the church supported women's voting rights so that Mormon women could defend polygamy, and that the church's convenience has always come first.

19. Leone, *Roots,* 8.
20. See Johnson, *From Housewife,* 156–58, for a discussion of the Mormons for ERA activities.
21. See Walker, *In Search,* xii.
22. Johnson, "Candidate Information Sheet," National NOW Conference, Indianapolis, Indiana, October 8–10, 1982.
23. From comments made at the National NOW Conference, Indianapolis, Indiana, October 8–10, 1982. See also Johnson, *From Housewife,* 397–402, for a discussion of other reactions to Johnson's views. In the NOW election, Johnson received the vote of about 40 percent of the delegates.
24. There is some argument whether Mormonism can be seen in the Protestant tradition. For instance, Whalen argues that Mormonism is not Protestant, nor does he see it as Christian *(Latter-day Saints),* 108–17. See also Shipps, *Mormonism,* in which she argues that "Mormonism is a separate religious tradition [from Christianity] and that it must be understood and respected on its own terms" (p. x). However, Johnson seems to be acting in the Protestant tradition, in that she is following her own conscience.
25. R. Laurence Moore, *Religious Outsiders and the Making of Americans* (New York: Oxford University Press, 1986), 31.
26. Reverend Harvey Egan, "Introduction to Sonia Johnson," Citizens Party of Minnesota, Minneapolis, Minnesota, March 15, 1984. Egan was pastor at Joan of Arc until May 30, 1986, when he retired.
27. Georgis Elaine Fuller, "In Celebration of Women," in her *Waving the Star Spangled Cross: Fundamentalism and the New Right* (Washington, D.C.: National Organization for Women, 1982), 36.
28. Ibid., 38.
29. See Rosemary Radford Ruether and Rosemary Skinner Keller, eds., *Women and Religion in America,* vol. 1 (San Francisco: Harper and Row, 1981).
30. Amanda Porterfield, *Feminine Spirituality in America, from Sarah Edwards to Martha Graham* (Philadelphia: Temple University Press, 1980), 47.
31. Audre Lorde, "Uses," in her *Sister Outsider,* 53.
32. Shipps in Beecher and Anderson, *Sisters,* xii. Leonard J. Arrington and Davis Bitton also discuss this in their chapter, "Mormon Sisterhood: Charting the Changes," in *The Mormon Experience: A His-*

tory of the Latter-day Saints (New York: Alfred A. Knopf, 1979), 221–40.

33. Madsen in Beecher and Anderson, *Sisters*, 93.
34. Newell in ibid., 86
35. Madsen in ibid., 90.
36. Newell in ibid., 135.
37. Ibid., 136.
38. Ibid., 140.
39. Ibid., 142.
40. Ibid., 141.
41. Johnson, "Independent Conscience . . . in a Christian Community?" Citizens Party of Minnesota, Minneapolis, Minnesota, March 5, 1984. See also Drude Daherup, "Overcoming the Barriers: An Approach to the Study of How Women's Issues Are Kept from the Political Agenda," in *Women's Views of the Political World of Men*, ed. Judith Hicks Stiehm (Dobbs Ferry, N.Y.: Transnational, 1984), 33–66, for a discussion of how women's issues get excluded from the political process.
42. Johnson was the Citizens Party candidate for president; she received 72,153 votes in the 1984 election. See "Third Parties Posted Lowest Total in Years," *Minneapolis Star and Tribune*, December 22, 1984, A3.
43. Aron Kahn, "Citizens Party Candidate Sonia Johnson Begins Bid," *St. Paul Pioneer Press*, August 12, 1984, A1.
44. Johnson, "War Is the Only Word for Women's Lives," *Sojourner* [Cambridge, Mass.], June 1984, 10.
45. Ibid., 11.
46. Barbara Beckwith, "Sonia Johnson: 'Why Women Should Support Me,'" *Sojourner* [Cambridge, Mass.], April 1984, 10.
47. Johnson, "Independent."
48. O'Dea, *The Mormons*, 154.
49. In a 1991 letter, Johnson indicates that "the first of the group [has] moved . . . [to land near Albuquerque, New Mexico] to begin the experiment of living in women's way as fully as possible."
50. Johnson quoted in Joan Gossel, "Ex-Mormon Wants Own Community," *The Columbus Dispatch*, September 21, 1990, F3.
51. Ibid.
52. Daly on the back cover of Johnson's *Going Out*.

53. Jahn, *Mintu*, 123–38.
54. See Daly, *Gyn/Ecology: The Metaethics of Radical Feminism* (Boston: Beacon Press, 1978): "Nelle Morton has been a guiding spirit, reminding me always of the unutterable importance of images. She hears me forth to new speech, and because of her I can never forget that 'in the beginning is the hearing' " (p. xvii).
55. Nellie Morton, *The Journey Is Home* (Boston: Beacon Press, 1985), 127.
56. For example, see Lorde's "An Open Letter to Mary Daly," in *This Bridge Called My Back: Writings by Radical Women of Color*, ed. Cherrie Moraga and Gloria Anzaldua (Watertown, Mass.: Persephone Press, 1981), 94–97.
57. See Daly, *Gyn/Ecology*, chap. 7.
58. See especially Starhawk, *Dreaming the Dark*, 45–71.
59. See "Part III: Women's Abundant Universe."
60. See Walter Williams, *The Spirit and the Flesh: Sexual Diversity in American Indian Culture* (Boston: Beacon Press, 1989), 41–42.
61. See also Daly's *Websters' First New Intergalactic Wickedary of the English Language*, conjured in cahoots with Jane Caputi (Boston: Beacon Press, 1987), 62, for her definition/discussion of "archaic."

6. *Conclusion*

1. See Beth Brant, *Mohawk Trail* (Ithaca, N.Y.: Firebrand Books, 1985), 31–36.
2. Lorde, *Sister Outsider*, 59.
3. Ibid., 57.
4. Hoagland, *Lesbian Ethics: Toward New Value* (Palo Alto, Calif.: Institute of Lesbian Studies, 1988), 267–71.
5. Lorde, *Sister Outsider*, 31.
6. See Sonia Johnson, "Women, Desire and History," *Woman of Power* 16 (Spring 1990): 73–77.
7. Johnson, "Women, Desire and History," 77.
8. Daly, "Spiraling into the Nineties," *Woman of Power* 17 (Summer 1990): 6.
9. Allen, "The Woman I Love Is a Planet; The Planet I Love Is a Tree," *Woman of Power* 18 (Fall 1990): 5.

Bibliographical Essay

2. *Curing Ceremonies*

Paula Gunn Allen's works include books of poetry: *A Cannon Between My Knees* (New York: Strawberry, 1981); *Coyote's Daylight Trip* (Albuquerque, N.M.: La Confluencia, 1978); *Shadow Country* (Los Angeles: University of California American Indian Studies Center, 1982); *Skin and Bones* (Cambridge, Mass.: West End, 1988); *Star Child* (Marvin, S.D.: Blue Cloud Quarterly, 1981); and *Wyrds* (San Francisco: Taurean Horn, 1987). Her poem, "Grandmother," is included in *The Third Woman: Minority Women Writers of the United States*, ed. Dexter Fisher (Boston: Houghton Mifflin, 1980), 126; and in *That's What She Said: Contemporary Poetry and Fiction by Native American Women*, ed. Rayna Green (Bloomington: Indiana University Press, 1984), 15. She has written a novel, *The Woman Who Owned the Shadows* (San Francisco: Spinsters, Ink, 1983), and excerpts of another, *Raven's Road*, are published in *The Living Spirit: A Gay American Indian Anthology*, ed. Will Roscoe (New York: St. Martin's Press, 1988), 134–52; and in *The New Native American Novel, Works in Progress*, ed. Mary Dougherty Bartlett (Albuquerque: University of New Mexico Press, 1986), 51–63. Her poetry and fictional excerpts have also been widely anthologized.

Her essays and literary criticism include: "Answering the Deer,"

American Indian Culture and Research Journal, 6, no. 3 (1982): 35–45; "Beloved Woman: The Lesbians in American Cultures," *Conditions* 7 (1981): 65–87; and "The Feminine Landscape of Leslie Marmon Silko's *Ceremony*," in her *Studies in American Indian Literature: Critical Essays and Course Designs* (New York: Modern Language Association of America, 1984), 127–33. This last book is extremely helpful for those wishing to prepare course materials for teaching Native American literature; it contains essays on approaches to the literature and an extensive bibliography on works by and about Native Americans.

Her critical works also include: "Foreword to 'Song of the Sky,'" *The Greenfield Review:* American Indian Writings 9, nos. 3 & 4 (1981): 116–21; "The Grace that Remains—American Indian Women's Literature," *Book Forum*, ed. Elaine Jahner, 5, no. 3 (1981): 376–88; "Iyani: It Goes This Way," in *The Remembered Earth: An Anthology of Contemporary Native American Literature*, ed. Gary Hobson (Albuquerque, N.M.: Red Earth, 1979); Guest Editorial, *A, A Journal of Contemporary Literature*, Special Issue: Native Women of New Mexico, 3, no. 2 (Fall 1978): 1; "Judy Grahn: 'Gathering the Tribe,'" *Contact II*, Special Issue on Women Poets, 5, nos. 27–29 (1982–83): 7–9; "The Mythopoetic Vision in Native American Literature," *American Indian Culture and Research Journal* 1, no. 1 (1974): 3–13; review of *What Moon Drove Me to This?* by Joy Harjo, *The Greenfield Review*, American Indian Writings, 9, nos. 3 & 4 (1981): 12–14; and "The Sacred Hoop: A Contemporary Indian Perspective on American Indian Literature," in *Literature of the American Indians: Views and Interpretations*, ed. Abraham Chapman (New York: New American, 1975). Versions of much of Allen's critical work has been put together in her book, *The Sacred Hoop: Recovering the Feminine in American Indian Traditions* (Boston: Beacon Press, 1986).

Other materials include "A *MELUS* Interview: Paula Gunn Allen," by Franchot Ballinger and Brian Swann, *MELUS* 10, no. 2 (Summer 1983): 3–25; a letter to the author, December 31, 1984, and a personal interview, June 20, 1985; "Sipapu: A Cultural Perspective," Ph.D. diss., University of New Mexico, 1975; "A Stranger in My Own Life: Alienation in American Indian Prose and Poetry," *MELUS* 7, no. 2 (Summer 1980): 3–19; "Symbol and Structure in Native American Literature: Some Basic Considerations," *College Composition and Communication* 24, no. 3 (October 1973): 267–70; "Where I Come From

God Is a Grandmother," *Sojourner: The Women's Forum,* August 1988, 16–18; "Who Is Your Mother? Red Roots of White Feminism," *Sinister Wisdom* 25 (Winter 1984): 34–46; and "The Woman I Love Is A Planet; The Planet I Love Is a Tree," *Woman of Power* 18 (Fall 1990): 5–7.

Reviews of Allen's novel, *The Woman Who Owned the Shadows,* include Michelle Cliff, "Journey of the Spirit," *The Women's Review of Books* 1, no. 6 (March 1984): 8; Alice Hoffman, "Ephanie's Ghosts," *New York Times Book Review* 89 (June 3, 1984), sec. 7: 18; Jean Swallow, *New Women's Times Feminist Review* 9, no. 35 (September–October 1984): 7; and Annette Van Dyke's reviews—"Balancing," *Hurricane Alice* 1, no. 4 (Spring–Summer 1984): 9; and in *Exploration in Sights and Sounds* 5 (Summer 1985): 3–4. Some of the material on Paula Gunn Allen in this chapter previously appeared in Van Dyke's "The Journey Back to Female Roots: A Laguna Pueblo Model," in *Lesbian Texts and Contexts: Radical Revisions,* ed. Karla Jay and Joanne Glasgow (New York: New York University Press, 1990): 339–54.

Allen's poetry is discussed in the following: Helen Bannon, "Spider Woman's Web: Mothers and Daughters in Southwestern Native American Literature," in *The Lost Tradition: Mothers and Daughters in Literature,* ed. Cathy N. Davidson and E. M. Broner (New York: Frederick Ungar, 1980); Elaine Jahner's "An Laddered, Rain-bearing Rug: Paula Gunn Allen's Poetry," in *Women and Western American Literature,* ed. Helen Winter Stauffer and Susan Rasowski (Troy, N.Y.: Whitson, 1982); and her review of *Shadow Country,* by Paula Gunn Allen, *American Indian Quarterly: A Journal of Anthropology, History, and Literature* (Summer 1983): 84–86; John R. Milton, ed. "Paula Allen (Laguna-Sioux-Lebanese)," in his *Four Indian Poets* (Vermillion, S.D.: Dakota, 1974); James Ruppert, "Paula Gunn Allen and Joy Harjo: Closing the Distance between Personal and Mythic Space," *American Indian Quarterly* 7, no. 1 (1983): 27–40; and Susan J. Scarberry, "Grandmother Spider's Lifeline," in *Studies in American Indian Literature: Critical Essays and Course Design,* ed. Paula Gunn Allen (New York: The Modern Language Association, 1983).

Leslie Marmon Silko's primary works include: *Ceremony* (New York: New American, 1978); and *Storyteller* (New York: Seaver, 1981). Interviews with Silko and her essays include: "A Conversation with Leslie Silko" by Lawrence Evers and Dennis Carr, *Sun Tracks* 3 (Fall 1976): 28–33; "Language and Literature from a Pueblo Indian Perspective," in

English Literature: Opening Up the Canon, ed. Leslie A. Fiedler and Houston A. Baker, Jr., Selected Papers from the English Institute, New Series, 4 (Baltimore: Johns Hopkins University Press, 1981); "An Old-Time Indian Attack Conducted in Two Parts: Part One—Imitation 'Indian' Poems; Part Two—Gary Snyder's Turtle Island," in *The Remembered Earth: An Anthology of Contemporary Native American Literature*, ed. Geary Hobson (Albuquerque, N.M.: Red Earth, 1979); "Stories and Their Tellers—A Conversation with Leslie Marmon Silko," by Dexter Fisher, ed., in *The Third Woman: Minority Women Writers of the United States* (Boston: Houghton Mifflin, 1980); and "Teller of Stories: An Interview with Leslie Marmon Silko," by James C. Work and Pattie Cowell, *Colorado State Review*, New Series, 8, no. 2 (Spring–Summer 1981): 68–79.

Literary criticism of Silko's work includes Robert Bell, "Circular Design in *Ceremony*," *American Indian Quarterly* 5, no. 1 (February 1979): 47–61; Peter G. Beidler, "Animals and Theme in *Ceremony*," *American Indian Quarterly* 5, no. 1 (February 1979): 13–17; Edith Blicksilver, "Tradition vs. Modernity: Leslie Silko on American Indian Women," *Southwest Review* 64, no. 2 (Spring 1979): 149–60; Galen Butler, "New Interpretations of Native American Literature: A Survival Technique," *American Indian Culture and Research Journal* 4, nos. 1 & 2 (1980): 165–77; Jan Garden Castro, "The Threads of Life," review of *Storyteller*, *The Greenfield Review*, American Indian Writings, 9, nos. 3 & 4 (1981): 100–105; Lorelei Cederstrom, "Myth and Ceremony in Contemporary North American Native Fiction," *The Canadian Journal of Native Studies* 2, no. 2 (1982): 285–301; Elizabeth N. Evasdaughter, "Silko's *Ceremony:* Healing Ethnic Hatred through Mixed Breed Laughter," *MELUS* 15, no. 1 (Spring 1988): 83–95; and Larry Evers, "A Response: Going Along with the Story," *American Indian Quarterly* 5, no. 1 (February 1979): 71–75.

Further criticism includes Reyes Garcia, "Senses of Place in *Ceremony*," *MELUS* 10, no. 4 (Winter 1983): 37–48; Kristin Herzog, "Thinking Woman and Feeling Man: Gender in Silko's *Ceremony*," *MELUS* 12, no. 1 (Spring 1985): 25–36; Elaine Jahner, "An Act of Attention: Event Structure in *Ceremony*," *American Indian Quarterly* 5, no. 1 (February 1979): 37–46; Mick McAllister, "The Color of Meat, The Color of Bone," *Denver Quarterly* 14, no. 4 (Winter 1980): 10–18; Ronald E. McFarland, "Leslie Silko's Story of Stories," *A, A Journal of Contem-*

porary Literature, Special Education Issue: Contemporary Native American Literature, 4, no. 2 (Fall 1979): 18–23; Carol Mitchell, "*Ceremony* as Ritual," *American Indian Quarterly* 5, no. 1 (February 1979): 27–35; Rebecca A. Pereyra, review of *Ceremony* in *American Indian Culture and Research Journal* 4, no. 4 (1980): 140–47; A. LaVonne Brown Ruoff, "Ritual and Renewal: Keres Traditions in the Short Fiction of Leslie Silko," *MELUS* 5, no. 4 (Winter 1978): 2–17; Kathleen M. Sands and A. LaVonne Ruoff, eds., "A Discussion of *Ceremony*," *American Indian Quarterly* 5, no. 1 (February 1979): 63–70; Susan J. Scarberry, "Memory as Medicine: The Power of Recollection in *Ceremony*," *American Indian Quarterly* 5, no. 1 (February 1979): 19–26; Kathleen Teltsch, "Fellowships Ending; Real World Awaits," *Minneapolis Star and Tribune*, July 19, 1986, sec. C, 1–2; Alan R. Velie, *Four American Indian Literary Masters: N. Scott Momaday, James Welch, Leslie Marmon Silko, and Gerald Vizenor* (Norman: University of Oklahoma Press, 1982); and a biography, by Per Seyersted, *Leslie Marmon Silko* (Boise, Idaho: Boise State University Press, 1980).

General material on Native American literature can be found in Gretchen Bataille, "American Indian Literature: Traditions and Translations," *MELUS* 6, no. 4 (Winter 1979): 17–26; Abraham Chapman, ed., *Literature of the American Indians: Views and Interpretations* (New York: New American Library, 1975); Elizabeth Cook, "Propulsives in Native American Literature," *College Composition and Communication* 24, no. 3 (October 1973): 271–75; Leslie A. Fiedler, *The Return of the Vanishing American* (New York: Steen and Day, 1968); Arlene B. Hirschfelfer, comp., *American Indian Authors: A Representative Bibliography* (New York: Association of American Indian Affairs, 1979); Linda Hogan, interview with the author, October 3, 1985; and "Who Puts Together," *Denver Quarterly*, American Indian Literature Issue, 14, no. 4 (Winter 1980): 103–12; Maurice Kenny, "Special Focus: Strawberry Press, Origins," *The Greenfield Review*, American Indian Writings, 9, nos. 3 & 4 (1981): 199–203; Tom King, "A *MELUS* Interview: N. Scott Momaday—Literature and the Native Writer," *MELUS* 10, no. 4 (Winter 1983): 66–72; Karl Kroeber, "Deconstructionist Criticism and American Indian Literature," *Boundary 2*, 7, no. 3 (Spring 1979): 66–72; idem, ed. and comp., *Traditional Literatures of the American Indian: Texts and Interpretations* (Lincoln: University of Nebraska Press, 1981); Arnold Krupat, "An Approach to Native American

Texts," *Critical Inquiry* 9, no. 2 (December 1982): 323–38; Kenneth Lincoln, *Native American Renaissance* (Berkeley: University of California Press, 1983); and idem, "Native Literatures," *American Indian Culture and Research Journal* 4, no. 4 (1980): 1–4.

More general material includes: Peter Nobokov, "American Indian Literature: A Tradition of Renewal," *Association for the Study of American Literature (ASAIL) Newsletter* 2, no. 3 (Autumn 1978): 31–40; William Oandasan, "Simon Ortiz: The Poet and His Landscape," *A, A Journal of Contemporary Literature*, Special Education Issue: Contemporary Native American Literature, 4, no. 2 (Fall 1979): 29–34; Walter J. Ong, "Oral Culture and the Literate Mind," in *Minority Language and Literature: Retrospective and Perspective*, ed. Dexter Fisher (New York: Modern Language Association of America, 1977); Elizabeth J. Ordonez, "Narrative Texts by Ethnic Women: Rereading the Past, Reshaping the Future," *MELUS* 9, no. 3 (Winter 1982): 19–28; Simon Ortiz, "Song, Poetry and Language—Expression and Perception," *Sun Tracks* 3 (Spring 1977): 9–12; reprint in *A, A Journal of Contemporary Literature*, Special Education Issue: Contemporary Native American Literature, 4, no. 2 (Fall 1979): 2–9; and Ortiz's "Towards a National Indian Literature: Cultural Authenticity in Nationalism," *MELUS* 8, no. 2 (Summer 1981): 8–12.

Further general literature can be found in Jarold Ramsey, *Reading the Fire: Essays in the Traditional Indian Literatures of the Far West* (Lincoln: University of Nebraska Press, 1983); Kenneth M. Roemer, "Native American Oral Narratives: Context and Continuity," in *Smoothing the Ground: Essays on Native American Oral Literature* (Berkeley: University of California Press, 1983); Kenneth Rosen, ed., *The Man to Send Rain Clouds* (New York: Vintage, 1975); Jerome Rothenberg, ed., *Techniques of the Sacred: A Range of Poetries from Africa, America, Asia and Oceania* (Garden City, N.Y.: Doubleday, 1968); A. LaVonne Brown Ruoff, "American Indian Oral Literatures," *American Quarterly*, Bibliography Issue, 33 (1981): 327–38; James Ruppert, "Literature on the Reservation—Source for the Future of Native American Literature," *MELUS* 8, no. 2 (Summer 1981): 86–88; idem, "The Uses of Oral Tradition in Six Contemporary Native American Poets," *American Culture and Research Journal* 4, no. 4 (1980): 87–110; Thomas Sanders, *Literature of the American Indian* (New York: Glencoe, 1973); idem, "Tribal Literature: Individual Identity and the Collective Unconscious,"

College Composition and Communication 24, no. 3 (October 1973): 256–74; Brian Swann, ed., *Smoothing the Ground: Essays on Native American Oral Literature* (Berkeley: University of California Press, 1983); Barre Toeklen and Tachenni Scott, "Poetic Retranslation and the 'Pretty Languages' of Yellowman," in *Traditional Literatures of the American Indian: Texts and Interpretations*, comp. and ed. Karl Kroeber (Lincoln: University of Nebraska Press, 1981); and Andrew Wiget, "Sending a Voice: The Emergence of Contemporary Native American Poetry," *College English* 46, no. 6 (October 1984): 598–609.

Material relating specifically to Native American women can be found in Gretchen M. Bataille and Kathleen Mullen Sands, *American Indian Women, Telling Their Lives* (Lincoln: University of Nebraska Press, 1984); Rayna Green, "Honoring the Vision of 'Changing Woman,' " in *Sisterhood Is Global: The International Women's Movement Anthology*, ed. Robin Morgan (Garden City, N.Y.: Anchor/Doubleday, 1984); idem, *Native American Woman: A Biography* (Wichita Falls, Tex.: Ohoyo Resource Center, 1981); idem, *Native American Women: A Contextual Bibliography* (Bloomington: Indiana University Press, 1983); Jane B. Katz, *I am the Fire of Time: The Voices of Native American Women* (New York: E. P. Dutton, 1977); Carolyn Neithammer, *Daughters of the Earth: The Lives and Legends of American Indian Women* (New York: Collier, 1977); Clara Sue Kidwell, "American Indian Women: Problems of Communicating a Cultural/Sexual Identity," *The Creative Woman* 2, no. 3 (1979): 33–38; *New America: A Journal of American and Southwestern Culture*, Women Artists and Writers of the Southwest issue, ed. Vera Norwood, 4, no. 3 (Albuquerque, N.M.: 1982); Nancy Oestreich Lurie, "Indian Women: A Legacy of Freedom," in *Look to the Mountain Top*, ed. Robert L. Iacopi (San Jose, Calif.: Gousha, 1972); Vera Norwood and Janice Monk, eds., *The Desert Is No Lady: Southwestern Landscapes in Women's Writing and Art* (New Haven: Yale University Press, 1987); Roxanne Dunbar Ortiz, "Colonialism and the Role of Women: The Pueblos of New Mexico," *Southwest Economy and Society* 4, no. 2 (Winter 1978–79): 28–46; Kate Shanley, "Thoughts on Indian Feminism," in *A Gathering of Spirit: Writing and Art by North American Indian Women*, 2d ed., ed. Beth Brant (Amherst, Mass.: Sinister Wisdom, 1984); John Upton and Donna M. Terrell, *Indian Women of the Western Morning: Their Life in Early America* (New York: Dial Press, 1974); Marta Weigle, *Spiders and Spinsters:*

Women and Mythology (Albuquerque: University of New Mexico Press, 1982); Norma Wilson, "Outlook for Survival," *Denver Quarterly* 14, no. 4 (Winter 1980): 22–30; and Judith Witherow, "Native American Mother," *Quest* 3, no. 4 (Spring 1977): 29–33.

Material on Native American lesbianism and/or the exchanging of male and female roles in addition to that written by Paula Gunn Allen can be found in Evelyn Blackwood, "Sexuality and Gender in Certain American Indian Tribes: The Case of Cross-Gender Females," *Signs: The Journal of Women in Culture and Society* 10, no. 1: 27–42; John D'Emilio and Estelle B. Freedman, *Intimate Matters: A History of Sexuality in America* (New York: Harper and Row, 1988); Judy Grahn, *Another Mother Tongue: Gay Words, Gay Worlds* (Boston: Beacon Press, 1984); Jonathan Katz, *Gay American History: Lesbians and Gay Men in the U.S.A.* (New York: Harper and Row, 1976); Will Roscoe, ed., *The Living Spirit: A Gay American Indian Anthology* (New York: St. Martin's Press, 1988); Beatrice Medicine, "Warrior Women"—Sex Role Alternatives for Plains Indian Women, in *The Hidden Half*, ed. P. Albers and B. Medicine (Landham, Md.: University Press of America, 1983), 267–80; Claude E. Schaeffer, "The Kutenai Female Berdache: Courier, Guide, Prophetess, and Warrior," *Ethnohistory* 12, no. 3 (Summer 1965): 193–236; and Walter Williams, *The Spirit and the Flesh: Sexual Diversity in American Indian Culture* (Boston: Beacon Press, 1986). In addition to Paula Gunn Allen's writing, contemporary Native American lesbian work can be found in Beth Brant, *Mohawk Trail* (Ithaca, N.Y.: Firebrand, 1985); Beth Brant, ed., *A Gathering of Spirit: Writing and Art by North American Indian Women*, 2d ed. (Montpelier, Vt.: Sinister Wisdom, 1984); Chrystos, *Not Vanishing* (Vancouver, B.C.: Press Gang, 1988); Cherrie Moraga and Gloria Anzaldua, eds., *This Bridge Called My Back: Writings by Radical Women of Color* (Watertown, Mass.: Persephone Press, 1981). Although she is not Native American, Anne Cameron has collected her stories from Native Vancouver Islanders, the Salish, and her *Daughters of Copper Woman* (Vancouver, B.C.: Press Gang, 1981) and *Dzelarhons: Myths of the Northwest Coast* (Madeira Park, B.C.: Harbour, 1986) are recommended.

Background information on Native Americans, and particularly the heritage of Allen and Silko, can be found in Hartley Burr Alexander, *The World's Rim: Great Mysteries of the North American Indians* (Lincoln: University of Nebraska Press, 1953); Adolph F. Bandelier, *The Southwestern Journals, 1880–1882,* edited and annotated by Charles H. Lange and Carroll L. Riley (Albuquerque: University of New Mexico Press, 1966); Adolph Bandelier and Edgar L. Hewett, *Indians of the Rio Grande Valley* (1937; reprint, New York: Cooper Square, 1973); Ruth Benedict, "Eight Stories from Acoma," *Journal of American Folklore* 43, no. 37 (January–March 1930): 59–87; Jules B. Billard, ed., *The World of the American Indian* (Washington D.C.: National Geographic Society, 1979); Franz Boas, *Keresan Texts,* vol. 8, part 1 (New York: The American Ethnological Society, 1928); Ruth L. Bunzel, *Zuni Origin Myths* (Washington, D.C.: Smithsonian Institution, Bureau of American Ethnology, Annual Report 47, 1932), 545–610; idem, *Zuni Texts,* ed. Franz Boas, vol. 15, American Ethnological Society (New York: G. E. Stechert, 1933); Cottie Burland, *North American Indian Mythology* (1965; reprint, London: Hamlyn, 1970); Walter Holden Capps, assisted by Ernest F. Tonsings, *Seeing with a Native Eye: Essays on Native Religion* (New York: Harper and Row, 1976); Curtin and Hewitt, "The Woman Who Fell from the Sky," in *Tales of the North American Indians,* selected and annotated by Sith Thompson (Cambridge, Mass.: Harvard University Press, 1929); Edward P. Dozier, *Hano: A Tewa Indian Community in Arizona* (New York: Holt, Rinehart and Winston, 1966); idem, *The Pueblo Indians of North America* (New York: Holt, Rinehart and Winston, 1970); idem, "Rio Grande Pueblos," in *Perspectives in American Indian Culture Change,* ed. Edward H. Spicer (Chicago: University of Chicago Press, 1969).

Further background material includes Harold E. Driver, *Indians of North America,* 2d ed. (1961; reprint, Chicago: University of Chicago Press, 1969); Father Noel Dumarest, *Notes on Cochiti, New Mexico,* Memoirs of the American Anthropological Association, 6 (1919): 137–237; Bertha P. Dutton, *American Indians of the Southwest* (1975; reprint, Albuquerque: University of New Mexico Press, 1986); Fred Eggan, *The American Indian: Perspectives for the Study of Social Change* (Chicago: Aldine, 1966); idem, *Social Organization of the Western Pueblos* (1950; reprint, Chicago: University of Chicago Press, 1963); Carl and Lilian Eickemeyer, *Among the Pueblo Indians* (New York: Merriam, 1895); Florence Hawley Ellis, "An Outline of Laguna Pueblo History and Social Organization," *Southwestern Journal of Anthropology* 15 (1959): 325–47; idem, "Anthropology of Laguna Land Claims," in *Pueblo*

Indians, vol. 3 (New York: Garland, 1974); and Aurelio M. Espinosa, "Pueblo Indian Folk Tales," *Journal of American Folklore* 49, nos. 191–192 (January–June 1936): 69–133.

More background information can be found in Robin Fox, *The Keresan Bridge: A Problem in Pueblo Ethnology* (London: Athlone, 1967); Arrell Morgan Gibson, *The American Indian: Prehistory to the Present* (Lexington, Mass.: D. C. Heath, 1980); John Malcolm Gunn [a relative of Paula Gunn Allen], *Schat-Chem: History, Traditions and Narratives of the Queres Indians of Laguna and Acoma* (Albuquerque, N.M.: Albright and Anderson, 1917); H. K. Haeberlin, *The Idea of Fertilization in the Culture of the Pueblo Indians*, Memoirs of the American Anthropological Association, 3, no. 1 (January–March 1916): 1–55; Edgar L. and Bertha P. Dutton, eds., *The Pueblo Indian World: Studies on the Natural History of the Rio Grande Valley in Relation to Pueblo Indian Culture* (Albuquerque: University of New Mexico and the School of American Research, 1945); Jamake Highwater, *The Primal Mind: Vision and Reality in Indian America* (New York: Harper and Row, 1981); Patrick Hubbard, "Trickster, Renewal and Survival," *American Indian Culture and Research Journal* 4, no. 4 (1980): 113–24; Jane B. Katz, *This Song Remembers: Self-Portraits of Native Americans in the Arts* (Boston: Houghton Mifflin, 1980); Charles H. and Carroll L. Riley Lange, eds., *The Southwestern Journals of Adolph F. Bandelier, 1880–1882* (Albuquerque: University of New Mexico Press, 1966); and Richard and Alfonso Ortiz, eds., *American Indian Myths and Legends* (New York: Pantheon, 1984).

Other Native American materials include: Ekkehart Malotki, *Gullible Coyote, Una'ihu: A Bilingual Collection of Hopi Coyote Stories* (Tucson: University of Arizona Press, 1985); Alice Marriott and Carol K. Rachlin, eds., *American Indian Mythology* (New York: New American, 1972); Michael Edward Melody, "Maka's Story: A Study of a Lakota Cosmology," *Journal of American Folklore* 90, no. 356 (April–June 1977): 149–67; Mamie Ruth Tanquist Miller, *Pueblo Indian Culture as Seen by the Early Spanish Explorers* (University of Southern California School of Research Studies, no. 18, Social Science Series 21 [1941]: 1–30); Ward Alan Minge, *Acoma, Pueblo in the Sky* (Albuquerque: University of New Mexico Press, 1976); G. M. Mullett, selector and trans., *Spider Woman Stories: Legends of the Hopi Indians* (Tucson: University of Arizona Press, 1979); and Walter J. Ong, *New Perspectives on the Pueblos* (Albuquerque: University of New Mexico Press, 1972).

Some of the most comprehensive work on the Pueblo has been done by Elsie Clews Parsons. See her *Hopi and Zuni Ceremonialism*, Memoirs of the American Anthropology Association 39 (1930): 1–108; idem, *Isleta, New Mexico* (Washington, D.C.: 47th Annual Report of the Bureau of American Ethnology), 193–466; idem, *Laguna Genealogies*, Anthropological Papers of the American Museum of Natural History, 19, part 5 (1923): 13–292; idem, "Nativity Myth of Laguna and Zuni," in *The Golden Age of American Anthropology*, ed. Margaret Mead and Ruth L. Bunzel (New York: George Braziler, 1960); idem, "Notes on Acoma and Laguna," *American Anthropologist*, New Series, no. 20 (1918): 162–86; idem, *Notes on Ceremonialism at Laguna*, Anthropological Papers of the American Museum of Natural History, 19, part 4 (1920): 85–132; idem, *Pueblo Indian Journal, 1920–1921*, Memoirs of the American Anthropology Association, no. 32 (1925): 1–123; idem, *Pueblo Indian Religion*, 2 vols. (Chicago: University of Chicago Press, 1939); idem, *The Pueblo of Jemez* (New Haven: Yale University Press, 1925); idem, *Taos Tales* (New York: American Folk-Lore Society, J. J. Augustin, 1940); idem, "Waiyautitsa of Zuni, New Mexico," in her *American Indian Life* (New York: B. W. Huebsch, 1922); and idem, "Zuni Tales," *Journal of American Folklore* 43, no. 167 (March 1930): 1–57. Information on this prominent anthropologist and her relationship to feminism can be found in Rosalind Rosenberg, *Beyond Separate Spheres: Intellectual Roots of Modern Feminism* (New Haven: Yale University Press, 1982).

Other sources of information on Native American culture include: Anthony Purley, "Keres Pueblo Concepts of Deity," *American Indian Culture and Research Journal* 1, no. 1 (1974): 29–32; Gladys A. Reichard, *Spider Woman: A Story of Navajo Weavers and Chanters* (New York: Macmillan, 1934); William J. Robbins, "Some Aspects of Pueblo Indian Religion," *Harvard Theological Review* 34, no. 1 (January 1941): 25–47; Williard H. Rollings, "Indian Land and Water: The Pueblos of New Mexico (1848–1924)," *American Indian Culture and Research Journal* 6, no. 4 (1982): 1–21; Anna Rooth Birgitta, "The Creation Myths of the North American Indians," *Anthropos* 52 (1957): 497–508; Helen Rushmore with Wolf Robe Hunt, *The Dancing Horses of Acoma and Other Acoma Indian Stories* (Cleveland: World, 1963); Mathew W. Stirling, *Origin Myth of Acoma and Other Records* (Washington D.C.: Bureau of American Ethnology/Bulletin 135, 1942); Dennis and Barbara Tedlock, eds., *Teachings from the American Earth: Indian Religion and Philosophy* (New York: Liveright, 1975); Stith Thompson, *The Folktale* (Berkeley: University of California Press, 1977); Hamilton A. Tyler, *Pueblo Animals and Myths* (Norman: University of Oklahoma Press, 1975); Ruth M. Underhill, *First Penthouse Dwellers of America* (New York: J. J. Augustin, 1938); idem, *Red Man's America: A History of Indians in the United States* (Chicago: University of Chicago Press, 1953); idem, *Red Man's Religion: Beliefs and Practices of the Indians North of Mexico* (Chicago: University of Chicago Press, 1965); Wilson D. Wallis, "Folktales from Shumopovi, Second Mesa," *Journal of American Folklore* 49, nos. 191–92 (January–June 1936): 1–68; Frank Waters, *Masked Gods: Navaho and Pueblo Ceremonialism* (Albuquerque: University of New Mexico Press, 1950); idem, *Pumpkin Seed Point* (Chicago: Sage Books, 1969).

Further Native American material can be found in Erminie Wheller-Voegelin and Remedios W. Moore, "The Emergence Myth in Native North America," *Studies in Folklore*, ed. W. Edson Richmond, Indiana University Publications, Folklore Series, no. 9 (1957): 66–91; Leslie A. White, *New Material from Acoma* (Washington, D.C.: Smithsonian Institution), Bureau of American Ethnology Bulletin 136, Anthropological Papers, no. 32 (1943): 301–59; idem, "The Pueblo of San Felipe," *Memoirs of the American Anthropology Association*, no. 38 (1930): 1–69; idem, "The Pueblo of Santa Ana, New Mexico," *American Anthropologist*, New Series, no. 60: 44, no. 4, part 2 (1942): 1–360; idem, "The Pueblo of Santo Domingo, New Mexico," *Memoirs of the American Anthropology Association*, no. 43 (1935): 1–210; idem, *The Acoma Indians* (Washington, D.C.: Smithsonian Institution), Forty-seventh Annual Report for 1929–1930, Bureau of American Ethnology (1932): 17–192; idem, "The World of the Keresan Pueblo Indians," in *Culture in History, Essays in Honor of Paul Radin*, ed. Stanley Diamond (New York: Columbia University Press, 1960); and Karl A. and Esther S. Goldfrank Wittfogel, "Some Aspects of Pueblo Mythology and Society," *Journal of American Folklore* 56 (1943): 17–30.

Anthropological and cultural theory can be found in Bronislaw Malinowski's *Sex, Culture, and Myth* (New York: Harcourt, Brace and

World, 1962); Walter J. Ong, *Orality and Literacy: The Technologizing of the Word* (London: Methuen, 1982); and Michelle Zimbalist Rosaldo, "The Use and Abuse of Anthropology: Reflections on Feminism and Cross-cultural Understanding," *Signs* 5 (1980): 389–417.

Information on "healing fiction" can be found in Marshall W. Alcorn, Jr., and Mark Bracher, "Literature, Psychoanalysis, and the Re-formation of the Self: A New Direction for Reader-Response Theory," *PMLA* 100, no. 3 (May 1985): 342–54; "Forum," *PMLA* 100, no. 5 (October 1985): 818–20; and James Hillman, *Healing Fiction* (Barrytown, N.Y.: Station Hill, 1983).

3. *The West African Tradition and the Female Principle*

Audre Lorde's works consulted for this book include the following. Poetry: *The Black Unicorn* (New York: W. W. Norton, 1978); and *Our Dead Behind Us* (New York: W. W. Norton, 1986). Essays: *The Cancer Journals* (Argyle, N.Y.: Spinsters, Ink, 1980); "My Words Will Be There," in *Black Women Writers (1950–1980), A Critical Evaluation*, ed. Mari Evans (Garden City, N.Y.: Anchor/Doubleday, 1984): 261–68; *A Burst of Light* (Ithaca, N.Y.: Firebrand, 1988); and *Sister Outsider, Essays and Speeches* (Trumansburg, N.Y.: Crossing, 1984). Her "biomythography" is *Zami: A New Spelling of My Name* (Watertown, Mass.: Persephone Press, 1982). Her "An Open Letter to Mary Daly" appeared in *This Bridge Called My Back: Writings by Radical Women of Color*, ed. Cherrie Moraga and Gloria Anzaldua (Watertown, Mass.: Persephone Press, 1981): 94–97.

Interviews with Lorde can be found in "Images of Invisibility," interview by Judith Barrington, *Advocate*, no. 368, May 26, 1983, 39–40; interview by Adrienne Rich, *Woman Poet*, vol. 2 (Reno, Nev.: Woman-In-Literature, 1981); and interview by Claudia Tate, ed., in *Black Women Writers at Work* (New York: Continuum, 1984). Lorde's comments on "What I Do When I Write" are in *The Women's Review of Books* 6, nos. 10–11 (July 1969): 27; and *Feminist Studies* 14, no. 3 (Fall 1988): 440–52, has a response by Lorde, "Against Apartheid." Jennifer Abod has produced *A Radio Profile of Audre Lorde* (Cambridge, Mass.: Profile Productions, 1988).

Literary criticism and articles about Audre Lorde include Pamela Annas, "A Poetry of Survival: Unnaming and Renaming in the Poetry of

Audre Lorde, Pat Parker, Sylvia Plath, and Adrienne Rich," *Colby College Library Quarterly* 23 (March 1982): 9–25; Jerome Brooks, "In the Name of the Father: The Poetry of Audre Lorde," in *Black Women Writers (1950–1980): A Critical Evaluation*, ed. Mari Evans (Garden City, N.Y.: Anchor/Doubleday, 1984); Susan Denelsbeck, "The Power of Lorde's Poetry," *Equal Time*, Special Supplement, no. 3 (June 1988): 1, 6; Mary DeShazer, " 'Sisters in Pain': The Warrior Muse of Audre Lorde," in her *Inspiring Women: Reimagining the Muse* (New York: Pergamon Press, 1986); Joan Martin, "The Unicorn Is Black: Audre Lorde in Retrospect," in *Black Women Writers (1950–1980): A Critical Evaluation*, ed. Mari Evans (Garden City, N.Y.: Anchor/Doubleday, 1984); Judy Simmons, "The Many Faces of Audre Lorde," *Contact II* 5, nos. 27–29 (1982–83): 44–48; and Barbara Smith, "The Truth That Never Hurts: Black Lesbians in the Fiction in the 1980s," in *Wild Women in the Whirlwind: Afra-American Culture and the Contemporary Literary Renaissance*, ed. Joanne Braxton and Andree Nicola McLaughlin (New Brunswick, N.J.: Rutgers University Press, 1990).

Reviews of Lorde's work include Jacqui Alexander, review of *A Radio Profile of Audre Lorde*, in *NWSA Journal* 2, no. 1 (Winter 1990): 29–30; Barbara Christian, "The Dynamics of Difference," review of *Sister Outsider*, in her *Black Feminist Criticism: Perspectives on Black Women Writers* (New York: Pergamon Press, 1985); Rosemary Daniell, "The Poet Who Found Her Own Way," review of *Zami: A New Spelling of My Name* and *Chosen Poems Old and New*, in *New York Times Book Review* 7, December 19, 1982, 12, 29; and Dexter Fisher, "Breaking the Silence of Fear," review of *The Cancer Journals*, in *Contact II*, Special Issue on Women Poets, 5, nos. 27–29 (1982–83): 46.

Alice Walker's works include the following. Novels: *The Color Purple* (New York: Harcourt Brace Jovanovich, 1982); *Meridian* (New York: Washington Square, 1977); *The Temple of My Familiar* (San Diego: Harcourt Brace Jovanovich, 1989); and *The Third Life of Grange Copeland* (New York: Harcourt Brace Jovanovich, 1970). Poetry: *Good Night, Willie Lee, I'll See You in the Morning* (New York: Harcourt Brace Jovanovich, 1979); *Horses Make a Landscape Look More Beautiful* (New York: Harcourt Brace Jovanovich, 1984); *Once* (New York: Harcourt Brace Jovanovich, 1968); *Revolutionary Petunias & Other Poems* (New York: Harcourt Brace Jovanovich, 1973). Short stories: *In Love and In Trouble: Stories of Black Women* (New York: Harcourt Brace Jovanovich, 1973); "Laurel" and "Advancing Luna and Ida B. Wells," in *Midnight Birds: Stories by Contemporary Black Women Writers*, ed. Mary Helene Washington (Garden City, N.Y.: Anchor/Doubleday, 1980); and *You Can't Keep a Good Woman Down* (New York: Harcourt Brace Jovanovich, 1981).

Her interviews include: interview with Eudora Welty, *The Harvard Advocate* 106 (Winter 1973): 68–72; interview by John O'Brien, ed., *Interviews with Black Writers* (New York: Liveright, 1973); interview by Linnea Lannon, "Reactivating Ancient Memory, Search for Her Spiritual Connections Resulted in Novel," *Cincinnati Enquirer*, May 14, 1989, sec. F, 2; interview by Maureen T. Reddy, *Minnesota Daily*, February 22, 1983, 11; interview by Claudia Tate, ed., *Black Women Writers at Work* (New York: Continuum, 1984); and a panel discussion, "Women on Women," in *American Scholar* 41 (Autumn 1972): 599–622.

Her essays and books of essays include *In Search of Our Mothers' Gardens, Womanist Prose* (New York: Harcourt Brace Jovanovich, 1983); *Living by the Word* (San Diego: Harcourt Brace Jovanovich, 1988); "Nuclear Exorcism: Beyond Cursing the Day We Were Born," *Mother Jones*, September–October 1982, 20–21; "Writing *The Color Purple*," in *Black Women Writers (1950–1980): A Critical Evaluation*, ed. Mari Evans (Garden City, N.Y.: Anchor/Doubleday, 1984); and the introduction to *I Love Myself When I Am Laughing and Then Again When I Am Looking Mean and Impressive: A Zora Neale Hurston Reader*, ed. Alice Walker (Old Westbury, N.Y.: The Feminist Press, 1979).

Reviews of Alice Walker's work can be found in Rudolph Byrd, review of *Living by the Word*, in *MELUS* 15, no. 1 (Spring 1988): 109–15; Robert Coles, "To Try Men's Souls," review of *The Third Life of Grange Copeland*, in *New Yorker*, February 27, 1971, 104–6; Betty Collier, review of *In Love and in Trouble: Stories of Black Women*, in *Journal of Social and Behavioral Sciences* 21 (Winter 1975): 136–42; Doris Davenport, "Afracentric Visions," review of *The Temple of My Familiar*, in *The Women's Review of Books* 6, no. 12 (September 1989): 13; Jewelle Gomez, "Before the Ink Dries," review of *The Temple of My Familiar*, in *Belles Letters* 5, no. 1 (Fall 1989): 37; Loyle Hairston, "Works of Rare Beauty and Power," review of *The Third Life of Grange Copeland*, in *Freedomways* 11, no. 2 (Second Quarter 1971): 170–77; Norma Rogers, "Struggle for Humanity," review of *Meridian*, in *Free-*

domways 16, no. 2 (Second Quarter 1976): 120–22; Mark Schorer, "Being and Nothingness," review of *The Third Life of Grange Copeland*, in *American Scholar* 40 (Winter 1970–71): 168–74; Cam Walker, "Essay," review of *The Third Life of Grange Copeland* and *Meridian*, in *Southern Exposure* 5, no. 1 (Spring 1977): 102–3; Jerry W. Ward, review of *Revolutionary Petunias and Other Poems*, in *CLA Journal* 17, no. 1 (September 1973): 127–29.

Literary criticism and articles about Alice Walker are in Elliot Butler-Evans, *Race, Gender, and Desire: Narrative Strategies in the Fiction of Toni Cade Bambara, Toni Morrison, and Alice Walker* (Philadelphia: Temple University Press, 1987); John F. Callahan, "The Higher Ground of Alice Walker," *The New Republic*, September 14, 1974, 21–22; Barbara Christian, "Alice Walker: The Black Woman Artist as Wayward," in *Black Women Writers (1950–1980): A Critical Evaluation*, ed. Mari Evans (Garden City, N.Y.: Anchor/Doubleday, 1984); reprint in her *Black Feminist Criticism: Perspectives on Black Women Writers* (New York: Pergamon Press, 1985); idem, "The Contrary Women of Alice Walker: A Study of Female Protagonists in 'In Love and Trouble'," in her *Black Feminist Criticism* (New York: Pergamon Press, 1985); and idem, "Novels for Everyday Use: The Novels of Alice Walker," in her *Black Women Novelists: The Development of a Tradition, 1892–1976* (Westport, Conn.: Greenwood, 1980).

Additional criticism can be found in Peter Erickson, "Cast out Alone to Heal/and Re-Create/Ourselves: Family-Based Identity in the Work of Alice Walker," *CLA Journal* 23, no. 1 (September 1979): 71–94; Ellen Foley, "Writer Walker Says We Can Learn by 'Listening' to Trees," *Minneapolis Star and Tribune*, March 3, 1983, sec. C, 1; Chester J. Fontenot, "Alice Walker: 'The Diary of an African Nun' and Du Bois' Double Consciousness," in *Sturdy Black Bridges: Visions of Black Women in Literature*, ed. Roseann P. Bell, Bettye J. Parker, and Beverly Guy-Sheftall (Garden City, N.Y.: Doubleday, 1979); Trudier Harris, "Folklore in the Fiction of Alice Walker: A Perpetuation of Historical and Literary Traditions," *Black American Literature Forum* 11, no. 2 (Spring 1977): 3–8; idem, "Violence in the *Third Life of Grange Copeland*," *CLA Journal* 19 (December 1975): 238–47; and W. Lawrence Hogue, "History, the Feminist Discourse, and Alice Walker's *The Third Life of Grange Copeland*," *MELUS* 12, no. 2 (Summer 1985): 45–62.

More comments on Walker's work can be found in Patricia McLaughlin, Comment on Women on Women Panel, *American Scholar* 41 (Fall 1972): 622–27; "Pulitzer Winner Reshapes World with Words," *St. Paul Pioneer Press*, April 24, 1983, sec. A, 12; Bettye Parker-Smith, "Alice Walker's Women: In Search of Some Peace of Mind," in *Black Women Writers (1950–1980): A Critical Evaluation*, ed. Mari Evans (Garden City, N.Y.: Anchor/Doubleday, 1984); Marjorie Pryse, "Zora Neale Hurston, Alice Walker, and the 'Ancient Power' of Black Women," in *Conjuring: Black Women, Fiction and Literary Tradition*, ed. Marjorie Pryse and Hortense J. Spillers (Bloomington: Indiana University Press, 1985); Gloria Steinem, "Do You Know This Woman? She Knows You: A Profile of Alice Waker," *Ms.*, June 1982, 35–37; Mary Helen Washington, "Alice Walker: Her Mother's Gifts," *Ms.*, June 1982, 38; idem, "An Essay on Alice Walker," in *Sturdy Black Bridges: Visions of Black Women in Literature*, ed. Roseann P. Bell, Bettye J. Parker, and Beverly Guy-Sheftall (Garden City, N.Y.: Doubleday, 1979); and Susan Willis, "Alice Walker's Women," in *Specifying: Black Women Writing the American Experience* (Madison: University of Wisconsin Press, 1987).

Background material on West African diasporic tradition can be found in J.F.A. and Michael Crowder, eds., *History of West Africa*, vol. 1 (New York: Columbia University Press, 1976); W. J. Argyle, *The Fon of Dahomey: A History and Ethnography of the Old Kingdom* (Oxford: Clarendon, 1966); William Bascom, *The Yourba of Southwestern Nigeria* (New York: Holt, Rinehart and Winston, 1969); Houston A. Baker, Jr., *The Journey Back: Issues in Black Literature and Criticism* (Chicago: University of Chicago Press, 1980); John W. Blassingame, *The Slave Community: Plantation Life in the Antebellum South*, rev. ed. (London: Oxford University Press, 1979); Serge Bramly, *Macumba: The Teachings of Maria-Jose, Mother of the Gods*, trans. Meg Bogin (New York: St. Martin's Press, 1977); K. A. Busia, "The Ashanti," in *African Worlds: Studies in the Cosmological Ideas and Social Values of African Peoples*, ed. Daryll Forde (London: Oxford University Press, 1954); Michelle Cliff, " 'I Found God in Myself and I Loved Her/I Loved Her Fiercely': More Thoughts on the Work of Black Women Artists," in *Women, Feminist Identity and Society in the 1980's: Selected Papers*, ed. Myriam Diaz-Diocaretz and Iris M. Zavala (Philadelphia: John Benjamins, 1985); and Myriam Diaz-Diocaretz, "Black North-

American Women Poets in the Semiotics of Culture," in ibid.; Daryll Forde, "The Yoruba-Speaking Peoples of Southwestern Nigeria," in his *Ethnographic Survey of Africa: Western Africa*, part 4 (London: International African Institute, 1951); Eugene D. Genovese, *Roll, Jordan, Roll: The World the Slaves Made* (New York: Vintage, 1976); Judith Gleason, *Orisha: The Gods of Yorubaland* (New York: Atheneum, 1971); Melville J. Herskovits, *Dahomey: An Ancient West African Kingdom*, 2 vols. (Evanston, Ill.: Northwestern University Press, 1967); and idem, *The Myth of the Negro Past* (New York: Harper and Brothers, 1941).

Zora Neale Hurston's *Of Mules and Men* (1935; reprint, Bloomington: Indiana University Press, 1978); and idem, *Tell My Horse* (1938; reprint, Berkeley: Turtle Island, 1983), are important studies of the African diasporic tradition. Other studies include: Janheinz Jahn, *Muntu: An Outline of Neo-African Culture*, trans. Marjorie Grene (London: Faber and Faber, 1958); Lawrence W. Levine, *Black Culture and Black Consciousness: Afro-American Folk Thought from Slavery to Freedom* (New York: Oxford University Press, 1977); Reginald Martin, *Ishmael Reed and the New Black Aesthetic Critics*, especially "Hoodoo as Literary Method" (London: Macmillan, 1988); John S. Mbiti, *African Religions and Philosophy* (New York: Praeger, 1969); August and Elliot Rudwick, *From Plantation to Ghetto*, 3d ed. (New York: Hill and Wang, 1976); P. Mercier, "The Fon of Dahomey," in *African Worlds: Studies in the Cosmological Ideas and Social Values of African Peoples*, ed. Daryll Forde (London: Oxford University Press, 1954); Peggy Reeves Sanday, *Female Power and Male Dominance: On the Origins of Sexual Inequality* (New York: Cambridge University Press, 1981); Luisah Teish, *Jambalaya: The Natural Woman's Book of Personal Charms and Practical Rituals* (San Francisco: Harper and Row, 1985); and Robert Farris Thompson, *Flash of the Spirit: African and Afro-American Art and Philosophy* (New York: Vintage, 1984).

Other works related to this chapter include Toni Cade, ed., *The Black Woman: An Anthology* (New York: New American, 1970); Natalie M. Rosinsky, "Mothers and Daughters: Another Minority Group," in *The Lost Tradition: Mothers and Daughters in Literature*, ed. Cathy N. Davidson and E. M. Broner (New York: Frederick Ungar, 1980); Zora Neale Hurston, *Their Eyes Were Watching God* (J. B. Lippincott, 1937; reprint, Urbana: University of Illinois Press, 1978); Maxine Hong Kingston, *The Woman Warrior: Memoirs of a Girlhood among Ghosts*

(New York: Alfred A. Knopf, 1977); and Gloria Naylor, *The Women of Brewster Place* (New York: Penguin, 1983).

General articles on black feminist literary criticism or African-American literary criticism pertinent to this chapter include Lorraine Bethel, "This Infinity of Conscious Pain: Zora Neale Hurston and the Black Female Literary Tradition," in *All the Women Are White, All the Blacks Are Men, But Some of Us Are Brave*, ed. Gloria T. Hull, Patricia Bell Scott, and Barbara Smith (Old Westbury, N.Y.: The Feminist Press, 1982); Nan Bauer Maglin, " 'Don't Never Forget the Bridge That You Crossed Over On': The Literature of Matrilineage," in *The Lost Tradition: Mothers and Daughters in Literature*, ed. Cathy N. Davidson and E. M. Broner (New York: Frederick Ungar, 1980); Deborah E. McDowell, "New Directions for Black Feminist Criticism," *Black American Literature Forum* 14, no. 4 (Winter 1980): 53–59; Dellita L. Martin, "In Our Own Black Images: Afro-American Literature in the 1980's," *MELUS* 8, no. 2 (Summer 1981): 65–71; Valerie Smith, "Gender and Afro-Americanist Literary Theory and Criticism," in *Speaking of Gender*, ed. Elaine Showalter (New York: Routledge, 1989); Gloria Wade-Gayles, *No Crystal Stair: Visions of Race and Sex in Black Women's Fiction* (New York: Pilgrim Press, 1984).

More general articles can be found in Mary Helen Washington, "Introduction," in her *Black-Eyed Susans: Classic Stories by and about Black Women* (Garden City, N.Y.: Anchor/Doubleday, 1975); and her "Teaching Black-Eyed Susans: An Approach to the Study of Black Women Writers," *Black American Literature Forum* 11, no. 1 (Spring 1977): 20–24, reprinted in *All the Women Are White;* Barbara Frey Waxman, "Canonicity and Black American Literature: A Feminist View," *MELUS* 14, no. 2 (Summer 1987); Craig Werner, "New Democratic Vistas: Toward a Pluralistic Genealogy," in *Belief vs. Theory in Black American Literary Criticism*, ed. Joe Weixlmann and Chester J. Fontenot (Greenwood, Fla.: Penkevill, 1986); Delores S. Williams, "Black Women's Literature and the Task of Feminist Theology," in *Immaculate & Powerful: The Female in Sacred Image and Social Reality*, ed. Clarissa W. Atkinson, Constance H. Buchanan, and Margaret R. Miles (Boston: Beacon Press, 1985).

4. *Revisioning Celtic Traditions*

A book on the Celtic religious belief system which is most important to this study is Jean Markale's *Women of the Celts,* trans. A. Mygind, C. Hauch, and P. Henry (Rochester, Vt.: Inner Traditions International, Ltd., 1986), in which she uses a Marxist approach to the Celtic myths and laws recorded in manuscript form to support her thesis that the ancient Celts were a people for which the patriarchal structure was not fully developed.

Other books useful for background on the Celtic belief system include Nora K. Chadwick, *Celtic Britain* (London: Thames and Hudson, 1963); W. Y. Evans-Wentz, *The Fairy-Faith in Celtic Countries* (1911; reprint, Secaucus, N.J.: University Books, 1966); George Henderson, *Survivals in Belief among the Celts* (Glasgow: James Maclehose and Sons, 1911); Alexander MacBain, *Celtic Mythology and Religion* (Inverness: n.p., 1885); J. A. MacCulloch, *Celtic and Scandinavian Religions* (London: Hutchinson's University Library, 1948); Alfred Nutt, *The Celtic Doctrine of Rebirth,* ed. and trans. Kuno Meyer ([London: David Nutt, 1897]); Alwyn Ress and Brinley Ress, *Celtic Heritage: Ancient Tradition in Ireland and Wales* (London: Thames and Hudson, 1961); John Sharkley, *Celtic Mysteries: The Ancient Religion* (London: Thames and Hudson, 1975); and Charles Squire, *The Mythology of the British Islands: An Introduction to Celtic Myth, Legend, Poetry, and Romance* (New York: Charles Scribner's Sons, [1905]). Marie-Louise Sjoestedt's *Gods and Heroes of the Celts,* trans. Myles Dillon (London: Methuen, 1949), has a particularly interesting chapter on the "Mother-Goddesses" of Ireland. Proinsias MacCana's *Celtic Mythology* (London: Hamlyn, 1973) uses both archaeological artifacts and recorded mythology to discuss Celtic beliefs.

Other archeological approaches to questions of Celtic belief include Anne Ross, *Pagan Celtic Britain: Studies in Iconography and Tradition* (New York: Columbia University Press, 1967); Gerald Hawkins, *Beyond Stonehenge* (New York: Harper and Row, 1973); and idem, *Stonehenge Decoded* (Garden City, N.Y.: Doubleday, 1965), in collaboration with John B. White.

Starhawk's major writings include *Dreaming the Dark: Magic, Sex and Politics* (Boston: Beacon Press, 1982); *The Spiral Dance: A Rebirth of the Ancient Religion of the Great Goddess* (San Francisco: Harper and Row, 1979); *Truth or Dare: Encounters with Power, Authority, and Mystery* (San Francisco: Harper and Row, 1987); and "Witchcraft as the Basis for Goddess-Religion of the Future," in *Book of the Goddess* (Sacramento, Calif.: The Temple of the Goddess Within, 1980).

Other primary sources for Starhawk include a lecture she gave in Minneapolis, Minnesota, March 21, 1983; a workshop, "A Rite of Passage for Women," she conducted in Minneapolis, Minnesota, on February 26, 1984; and "An Evening of Ritual and Storytelling," which she conducted in Minneapolis, Minnesota, on August 2, 1986, with Luisah Teish. In addition, bibliographic information can be found in Misti Schumacher's "Witch Born in St. Paul Casts Spell That Demolishes Stereotypes," *Minneapolis Star and Tribune*, March 21, 1985, sec. C, 1–2.

Works discussing the Goddess as she relates to religions past and present include Marsha Lichtenstein, "Radical Feminism and Women's Spirituality: Looking before You Leap," in *Lady-Unique-Inclination-of-the-Night*, Cycle 2 (Autumn 1977), 36–43; Judith Ochshorn, *The Female Experience and the Nature of the Divine* (Bloomington: Indiana University Press, 1981); Raphael Patai, *The Hebrew Goddess* (Philadelphia: KTAV Publishing House, 1967); Anne Kent Rush, *Moon, Moon* (New York and Berkeley: Random House and Moon Books, 1976); Charlene Spretnak, *Lost Goddesses of Early Greece* (Boston: Beacon Press, 1984); idem, *The Politics of Women's Spirituality: Essays on the Rise of Spiritual Power within the Feminist Movement* (Garden City, N.Y.: Anchor, 1982); Grant Showerman's *The Great Mother of the Gods* (1901; reprint, Chicago: Argonaut, 1969); Sibylle von Cles-Reden, *The Realm of the Great Goddess* (London: Thames and Hudson, 1961). James Preston's "Goddess Religion: Theoretical Perspectives," in *The Encyclopedia of Religion*, ed. Mircea Eliade, vol. 6 (New York: Macmillan, 1987), 53–59, gives a good summary of the scholarly perspectives on goddess worship.

See also Merlin Stone's *When God Was a Woman* (New York: Harcourt Brace Jovanovich, 1976), which has been of great influence on feminist beliefs even though it is discounted by some scholars; and Joseph Campbell's *The Power of Myth*, ed. Betty Sue Flowers (New York: Doubleday, 1988), especially the chapter, "The Gift of the Goddess." Sylvia Brinton's *Descent to the Goddess: A Way of Initiation for Women* (Toronto: Inner City, 1981), is a Jungian interpretation of the

Goddess. Marija Gimbutas's *The Language of the Goddess* (San Francisco: Harper and Row, 1989) examines pictoral motifs on artifacts to attempt to document an extensive Goddess religion. Norma Lorre Goodrich's *Priestesses* (New York: Franklin Watts, 1989) connects ancient priestesses with their goddesses and discusses the training or life cycles of priestesses.

Marion Zimmer Bradley's *The Mists of Avalon* (New York: Ballantine, 1984) is helpful in explaining Starhawk's interpretation of Celtic traditions concerning the Goddess. Recent critical studies of *The Mists of Avalon* include Marilyn Farwell, "Heterosexual Plots and Lesbian Subtexts: Toward a Theory of Lesbian Narrative Space," in *Lesbian Texts and Subtexts: Radical Revisons*, ed. Karla Jay and Joanne Glasgow (New York University Press, 1990); Thelma Shinn, *Worlds within Women: Myth and Mythmaking in Fantastic Literature by Women* (New York: Greenwood Press, 1986); and Charlotte Spivack, *Merlin's Daughters: Contemporary Women Writers of Fantasy* (New York: Greenwood Press, 1987).

Questions about where contemporary witchcraft fits into historic accounts of witchcraft are covered in Jeffrey B. Russell, *A History of Witchcraft: Sorcerers, Heretics, and Pagans* (London: Thames and Hudson, 1980), and in his essay, "Concepts of Witchcraft," in *The Encyclopedia of Religion*, ed. Mircea Eliade, vol. 15 (New York: Macmillan, 1987), 415–23; Mircea Eliade, *Occultism, Witchcraft, and Cultural Fashions: Essays in Comparative Religions* (Chicago: University of Chicago Press, 1976); and Norman Cohn, *Europe's Inner Demons: An Enquiry Inspired by the Great Witch-Hunt* (New York: New American Library, 1977).

Overviews of contemporary witchcraft and Goddess worship can be found in Margot Adler, *Drawing Down the Moon: Witches, Druids, Goddess-Worshippers, and Other Pagans in America Today* (Boston: Beacon Press, 1981, and the 1986 revised and expanded edition); and James J. Preston, "Goddess Worship: Theoretical Perspectives," in *The Encyclopedia of Religion*, ed. Mircea Eliade, vol. 6 (New York: Macmillan, 1987), 53–59.

Books that played a major part in fueling contemporary witchcraft traditions, even though they are considered fraudulent or questionable by scholars, include Charles Leland, *Aradia, the Gospel of the Witches* (London: C. W. Daniel, 1899); Margaret Alice Murray, *The God of the*

Witches (1921; reprint, London: Sampson, Law, Marston, [1933]), and idem, *The Witch-Cult in Western Europe* (1921; reprint, Oxford: Clarendon Press, 1963).

Material on feminist witchcraft can be found in Z. Budapest, *The Holy Book of Women's Mysteries*, 2 vols. (Oakland, Calif.: Susan B. Anthony Coven No. 1, 1982); Ann and Julie Ann Forfreedom, eds., *Book of the Goddess* (Sacramento, Calif.: The Temple of the Goddess Within, 1980).

Books about different modern witchcraft traditions other than feminist by those who adhere to those traditions include Gerald B. Gardner, *Witchcraft Today* (London: Rider, 1954); Justine Glass, *Witchcraft, the Sixth Sense* (North Hollywood, Calif.: Wilshire, 1965); Pennathorne Hughes, *Witchcraft* (London: Longmans, Green and Company, 1952); Gareth Knight, *A History of White Magic* (London: Mowbrays, 1978); Leo Martello, *Witchcraft: The Old Religion* (Secaucus, N.J.: University Books, [1973]); Lady Sheba, *The Book of Shadows* (St. Paul, Minn.: Llewellyn, 1973); and Doreen Valiente, *An ABC of Witchcraft Past and Present* (New York: St. Martin's Press, 1973).

Background works about esoteric and mystical traditions include Dion Fortune, *The Esoteric Orders and Their Work* (St. Paul, Minn.: Llewellyn, 1971); idem, *The Mystical Qabalah* (1935; reprint, London: Ernest Benn, 1974); idem, *Avalon of the Heart* (London: Frederick Muller, 1934), published under the name of Violet Firth, and her novel, *Moon Magic, Being the Memoirs of a Mistress of That Art* (London: Aquarian Press, 1956); Christine Hartley, *The Western Mystery Tradition* (London: Aquarian Press, 1968); and Gershom Scholem, *Major Trends in Jewish Mysticism* (Jerusalem: Schocken, 1941).

Mircea Eliade's work is especially important to an understanding of relationships between culture and religion, particularly *Occultism, Witchcraft, and Cultural Fashions* (Chicago: University of Chicago Press, 1976); *Rites and Symbols of Initiation, The Mysteries of Birth and Rebirth*, trans. Willard R. Trask (1958; reprint, New York: Harper and Row, 1965); *The Sacred and the Profane: The Nature of Religion*, trans. Willard R. Trask (1957; reprint, New York: Harper and Row, 1959); *Shamanism, Archaic Techniques of Ecstasy*, trans. Willard R. Trask (1951; reprint, [Princeton, N.J.]: Princeton University Press, 1974).

Lesbian poet and writer Judy Grahn's work includes the following. Essays: *Another Mother Tongue: Gay Words, Gay Worlds* (Boston:

Beacon Press, 1984), and *The Highest Apple: Sappho and the Lesbian Poetic Tradition* (San Francisco: Spinster's, Ink, 1985). Novel: *Mundane's World* (Freedom, Calif.: Crossing Press, 1988). Poetry: *The Queen of Swords* (Boston: Beacon Press, 1988); *The Queen of Wands* (Freedom, Calif.: Crossing Press, 1982); and *The Work of a Common Woman: Collected Poetry* (Freedom, Calif.: Crossing Press 1981).

In addition to Paula Gunn Allen's work on Native American lesbianism already cited for chapter 1, an important article on Native American concepts of sexuality and gender is Evelyn Blackwood's "Sexuality and Gender in Certain Native American Tribes: The Case of Cross-Gender Females," in *Feminist Frontiers II: Rethinking Sex, Gender, and Society*, ed. Laurel Richardson and Verta Taylor (New York: Random House, 1989).

5. *From the Euro-American Mainstream*

Sonia Johnson's books are *From Housewife to Heretic* (Garden City, N.Y.: Doubleday, 1981); *Going Out of Our Minds: The Metaphysics of Liberation* (Freedom, Calif.: The Crossing Press, 1987); *The Ship That Sailed into the Living Room: Sex and Intimacy Reconsidered* (Albuquerque, N.M.: Wildfire Books, 1991); and *Wildfire: Igniting the She/Volution* (Albuquerque, N.M.: Wildfire Books, 1989). Sources connected to her running for the president of the National Organization for Women include her candidate information sheet and her opponent Judy Goldsmith's candidate information sheet, both from the National Organization for Women Conference, Indianapolis, Indiana, October 8–10, 1982.

Sources for her running for the president of the United States include an article with her running mate, Dick Walton, "Feminist and Progressive Perspectives Merge in the 1984 Citizens Party," *Citizens Voice*, Fall 1984, 5–6; a speech, "Independent Conscience . . . In a Christian Community?" given for the Citizens Party of Minnesota, Minneapolis, Minnesota, March 5, 1984; and the articles, "Why Women Should Support Me," interviewed by Barbara Beckwith, *Sojourner* (Cambridge, Mass.), April 1984, 10; and "War Is the Only Word for Women's Lives," *Sojourner*, June 1984, 11.

Articles about her bid for president are by Johnson Diaz, "Sonia Johnson Says She's Ready to Be 1st Woman President," *Minneapolis Star and Tribune*, March 16, 1984, sec. A, 14; Aron Kahn, "Citizens

Party Candidate Sonia Johnson Begins Bid," *St. Paul Pioneer Press & Dispatch*, August 12, 1984, sec. A, 1, 5; "Small Parties Also Seek Presidential Votes," *Minneapolis Star and Tribune*, November 5, 1984, sec. A, 3; and Richard Walton, "New and Different: A History of the Citizens Party," *Citizens Voice* [Indianapolis, Indiana], Fall 1984, 7.

Articles relating generally to her philosophy are "The Woman Who Talked Back to God," *Ms.*, November 1981, 51–54, 89–90, 110; "Message to a Gathering," *Woman of Power* 2 (Summer 1985): 16–19; "Sonia Johnson: Breaking Free," interview by Betsy Dalkind and Vanessa Cruz, *Sojourner*, January 1988, 16–17; and "Women, Desire and History," *Woman of Power* 16 (Spring 1990): 73–77. Joan Goessl's "Ex-Mormon Wants Own Community," *The Columbus Dispatch*, September 21, 1990, F3, discusses the turn that Johnson's vision has taken.

Responses to her philosophy and reviews of her work include Rosemary Curb, "Living as a Radical," review of *Going Out of Our Minds* in *The Women's Review of Books* 5, no. 1 (October 1987): 9–10; and "Letters to the Editor," *Sojourner*, August 1988, 5–6. The last are particularly critical and demonstrate the misgivings with which some feminists received the philosophy expressed in *Going Out of Our Minds.* Judith Galas, "Prophet in Her Own Land?" reviews *Wildfire: Igniting the She/Volution, New Directions for Women* 18, no. 6 (November–December 1989): 27, also negatively.

Materials that are helpful as background for American women's spirituality include Amanda Porterfield, *Feminine Spirituality in America, from Sarah Edwards to Martha Graham* (Philadelphia: Temple University Press, 1980); Georgia Elaine Fuller, "An Invitation to Feminist Spirituality: Some Theological Parameters" (Washington, D.C.: National Organization for Women, 1980); Janet Kalven and Mary Buckley, *Women's Spirit Bonding* (New York: Pilgrim, 1984); Nelle Morton, *The Journey Is Home* (Boston: Beacon Press, 1985); Rosalind Rosenberg, *Beyond Separate Spheres: Intellectual Roots of Modern Feminism* (New Haven: Yale University Press, 1982); Rosemary Radford Ruether, *New Woman/New Earth* (New York: Seabury Press, 1975); idem, *Sexism and God-Talk: Toward a Feminist Theology* (Boston: Beacon Press, 1983); idem and Rosemary Skinner Keller, eds., *Women and Religion in America*, vols. 1 and 2 (San Francisco: Harper and Row, 1981, 1983); Judith Weidman, ed., *Christian Feminism: Visions of a New Humanity* (San Francisco: Harper and Row, 1984).

Specific information about Mormon women can be found in Ladies of the Church of Jesus Christ of Latter-day Saints, *Mormon Women's Protest* (Salt Lake City: Deseret News, 1886); Louis J. Kern, *An Ordered Love: Sex Roles and Sexuality in Victorian Utopias—the Shakers, the Mormons, and the Oneida Community* (Chapel Hill: University of North Carolina Press, 1981); Marilyn Warenski, *Patriarches and Politics: The Plight of the Mormon Woman* (New York: McGraw-Hill, 1978); T.B.H. (Fanny) Stenhouse, *Tell It All: The Tyranny of Mormonism* (1874; reprint, n.p.: Centaur Press, 1971); and Anne Eliza Young, *Wife No. 19* (1876; reprint, New York: Arno, 1972). The last two are interesting in that they show some of the controversy surrounding polygamy in the late 1800s; these two books served as powerful antipolygamy propaganda. Particularly important to this study is Maureen Ursenbach Beecher and Lavina Fielding Anderson, eds., *Sisters in Spirit: Mormon Women in Historical and Cultural Perspective* (Urbana: University of Illinois Press, 1987).

General background material on Mormonism important to this study includes Leonard J. Arrington and Davis Bitton, *The Mormon Experience: A History of the Latter-day Saints* (New York: Alfred A. Knopf, 1979); Klaus J. Hansen, *Mormonism and the American Experience* (Chicago: University of Chicago Press, 1981); Stanley Hirshon, *The Lion of the Lord: A Biography of Brigham Young* (New York: Alfred A. Knopf, 1969); Mark P. Leone, *Roots of Modern Mormonism* (Cambridge, Mass.: Harvard University Press, 1979); Thomas F. O'Dea, *The Mormons* (University of Chicago Press, 1957); Jan Shipps, *Mormonism: The Story of a New Religious Tradition* (Urbana: University of Illinois Press, 1985); Eliza Snow Smith, *Biography and Family Record of Lorenzo Snow* (Salt Lake City: Deseret News, 1884); and Samuel W. Taylor, *The Kingdom or Nothing: The Life of John Taylor, Militant Mormon* (New York: Macmillan, 1976).

General background resources relating to women and politics include Sandra Baxter and Majorie Lansing, *Women and Politics: The Visible Majority*, rev. ed. (Ann Arbor: University of Michigan Press, 1983); Allison L. Noble, "Hysteria in Historical Perspective," in *Waving the Star Spangled Cross: Fundamentalism and the New Right*, ed. Georgia Elaine Fuller (Washington, D.C.: National Organization for Women, 1982); and Judith Hicks Stiehm, ed., *Women's Views of the Political World of Men* (Dobbs Ferry, N.Y.: Transnational, 1982), especially Drude Dahlerup, "Overcoming the Barriers: An Approach to the Study of How Women's Issues Are Kept from the Political Agenda."

Mary Daly's books include *Beyond God the Father: Toward a Philosophy of Women's Liberation* (Boston: Beacon Press, 1973); *The Church and the Second Sex* (Boston: Beacon Press, 1968; reprint, 1975, with the *Feminist Postchristian Introduction* and in 1985 with a *New Archaic Afterwards; Gyn/Ecology: The Metaethics of Radical Feminism* (Boston: Beacon Press, 1978); *Pure Lust: Elemental Feminist Philosophy* (Boston: Beacon Press, 1984); and *Websters' First New Intergalactic Wickedary of the English Language*, "in cahoots with" Jane Caputi (Boston: Beacon Press, 1987).

Daly's published articles include "Abortion and Sexual Caste," *Commonweal*, February 4, 1972, 415–19; "After the Death of God the Father," *Commonweal*, March 12, 1971, 7–11; "The Courage to Leave: A Response to John Cobb's Theology," in *John Cobb's Theology in Process*, ed. David Ray Griffin and Thomas J. J. Altizer (Philadelphia: The Westminster Press, 1977): 84–98; "The Courage to See: Religious Implications of the New Sisterhood," *Christian Century*, September 22, 1971, 1108–11; "An Exchange of Views: 'Underground Theology,'" with Aquinas M. Ferrara, *Commonweal*, August 9, 1968, 531–34; "The Forgotten Sex: A Built-In Bias," *Commonweal*, January 15, 1965, 508–11; "Gyn/Ecology: Spinning New Time/Space," in *The Politics of Women's Spirituality*, ed. Charlene Spretnak (New York: Anchor/Doubleday, 1982), 207–12; "Michael Novak and Christopher Derrick: A Study in Contrasts," review of Michael Novak's *A Time to Build* and Christopher Derrick's *Trimming the Ark* in *Commonweal*, September 6, 1968, 601; "Post-Christian Theology: Some Connections Between Idolatry and Methodolatry, Between Deicide and Methodicide" in *Women and Religion*, comp. Joan Arnold Romero (Tallahassee, Fla.: American Academy of Religion, Florida State University, 1973), 33–38.

Other articles include "Questions & Answers: Mary Daly on the Church," *Commonweal*, November 14, 1969, 215; "Return of the Protestant Principle," *Commonweal*, June 6, 1969, 338–41; "Sisterhood as Cosmic Covenant," in *The Politics of Women's Spirituality*, 351–61; "Short Essay on Hearing and on the Qualitative Leap of Radical Feminism," *Horizons* 2 (Spring 1975): 120–24; "Spiraling into the Nineties," *Woman of Power* 17 (Summer 1990): 6–12; "The Spiritual Revolution: Women's Liberation as Theological Re-education," *Andover Newton*

Quarterly, March 1972; "Theology after the Demise of God the Father: A Call for the Castration of Sexist Religion," in *Sexist Religion and Women in the Church: No More Silence,* ed. Alice Hageman (New York: Association Press, 1974), 125–42; "The Women's Movement: An Exodus Community," *Religious Education,* September–October 1972, 327–35; and selections from "The Women's Movement: An Exodus Community," published in *Women and Religion: A Feminist Sourcebook of Christian Thought,* ed. Elizabeth Clark and Herbert Richardson (New York: Harper and Row, 1977), 265–71.

Critiques of Daly's work include Christine Garside Allen, "Self-Creation and Loss of Self: Mary Daly and St. Teresa of Avila," *Studies in Religion* 6, no. 1 (Summer 1976–77): 67–72; and Michael Berenbaum, "Women, Blacks, and Jews: Theologians of Survival," *Religion in Life* 45 (Spring 1976): 106–18, which explores similarities between the thought of Mary Daly and some Jewish and black theologians. Audre Lorde's famous "An Open Letter to Mary Daly," in *This Bridge Called My Back: Writings by Radical Women of Color,* ed. Cherrie Moraga and Gloria Anzaldua (Watertown, Mass.: Persephone Press, 1981): 94–97, was in response to *Gyn/Ecology.*

Burton Cooper's "Metaphysics, Christology and Sexism: An Essay in Philosophical Theology," *Religious Studies* 16 (June 1980): 179–93, critiques ideas in Daly's *Beyond God the Father.* Julie Gowen's "Ought We to Abandon a Traditional Christian World-View?" *Studies in Religion* 8, no. 1 (Winter 1979): 83–92, argues with Daly's ideas in *Beyond God the Father,* as does Robert Kress's "God the Mother," in *Whither Womankind: The Humanity of Women* (St. Meinrad, Ind.: Abbey Press, 1975), 265–89, and Carl Raschke's, "The Death of God the Father," *ILIFF Review* 35 (Spring 1978): 55–56.

Karen Rubin's "Repartee," *Ohio Journal of Religious Studies* 4 (October 1976): 96–103, uses Daly's *Beyond God the Father* to begin a critique of Judaism. David Shield's "Christ: A Male Feminist View," *Encounter* 45, no. 3 (Summer 1984): 221–32, argues for a "relationship Christology" while accepting most of Daly's critique of Christianity. Mary Ann Stenger's "A Critical Analysis of the Influence of Paul Tillich on Mary Daly's Feminist Theology," *Encounter* 43 (Summer 1982): 219–38, suggests that Daly has made the feminist movement idolatrous, while Marjorie Suchocki's "The Challenge of Mary Daly," *Encounter* 41 (Autumn 1980): 307–17, attempts to reconcile Daly's vision of the transcending journey with Christianity. Another response to *Beyond God the Father* is Paul K. K. Tong's "The Sex of God: A Critique of Mary Daly's Transcendental Theology for Women's Liberation," in *God, Sex and the Social Project: The Glassboro Papers on Religion and Human Sexuality*, ed. James H. Grace (New York: Edwin Mellen Press, 1978), 39–49.

Discussions of Daly's place in feminist theology include Wanda Warren Berry, "Images of Sin and Salvation in Feminist Theology," Anglican Theological Review 60 (January 1978): 25–54; Elizabeth Clark and Herbert Richardson, "Radical Feminism, Radical Religion: Mary Daly," in their *Women and Religion* (New York: Harper and Row, 1977), 259–65; Anne Carr, "Is a Christian Feminist Theology Possible?" *Theological Studies* 43 (June 1982): 279–97; Sarah L. Darter, "Response" to G. McLeod Bryan's "Does Feminist Theology Liberate?" *Foundations* 19 (January–March 1976): 50–52; Mary Rose D'Angelo, "Remembering Her: Feminist Readings of the Christian Tradition," *Toronto Journal of Theology* 2, no. 1 (Spring 1998): 118–26.

Daly's place in feminist theology is also evaluated in Joan Chamberlain Englesman, "Patterns in Christian Feminism: A Bibliographic Essay," *Drew Gateway* 56, no. 1 (1985): 1–15; Deane W. Ferm, "Feminist Theology in America," *Scottish Journal of Theology* 34, no. 2 (1981): 157–78; Rita M. Gross, "Reflections on Mary Daly's *Gyn/Ecology*," *Anima* 7, no. 1 (Fall 1980): 47–51; Catharina Halkes, "The Themes of Protest in Feminist Theology Against God the Father," in *God as Father?* ed. Johannes-Baptist Metz and Edward Schillebeeckx (New York: Seabury Press, 1981), 103–109.

Other explorations of Daly's work include Beverly Wildung Harrison, "The Power of Anger in the Work of Love: Christian Ethics for Women and Other Strangers," *Union Seminary Quarterly Review* 36 (Suppl., 1981): 41–57; Susannah Herschel, "Current Issues in Jewish Feminist Theology," *Christian Jewish Relations* 19, no. 2 (1986): 23–32; Carter Heyward, "Ruether and Daly: Theologians Speaking and Sparking, Building and Burning," *Christianity and Crisis*, April 2, 1979, 66–72; Mary Spaulding Picchi, "Women Becoming Through Books and Bonding," *Journal of Women and Religion* 2, no. 1 (Spring 1982): 38–41; Ann-Janine Morey-Gaines, "Metaphor and Radical Feminism: Some Cautionary Comments on Mary Daly's *Gyn/Ecology*," *Soundings* 65 (Fall 1982): 340–51; June O'Connor, "Liberation Theologies and the

Women's Movement: Points of Comparison and Contrast," *Horizons* 2 (Spring 1975): 103–24; Renate Rieger, "Half of Heaven Belongs to Women, and They Must Win It for Themselves: An Attempt at a Feminist Theological Stock-Taking in the Federal Republic of Germany," *Journal of Feminist Studies in Religion* 1, no. 1 (Spring 1985): 133–44; Polly Ashton Smith, "Contrasts in Language Theory and Feminist Interpretation," *Union Seminary Quarterly Review* 35, nos. 1–2 (Fall–Winter 1979–80): 89–98; and Susan B. Thistlethwaite, "God and Her Survival in a Nuclear Age," *Journal of Feminist Studies in Religion* 4, no. 1 (Spring 1988): 73–88.

Selected reviews of Daly's work include Elizabeth R. Hatcher, "Daly's 'Hag-ography,' " review of *Gyn/Ecology* in *National Catholic Reporter*, April 27, 1979, 36; Coral Lansbury, review of *Websters' First New Intergalactic Wickedary of the English Language* in *The New York Times Book Review*, January 17, 1988, 9; Judith Long Laws, review of *Beyond God the Father* and George H. Tavard's *Woman in Christian Tradition* in *Sociological Analysis* 36 (Spring 1975): 82–84; Sara Maitland, "A New Psyche," review of *Pure Lust* in *New Statesman*, January 18, 1985, 28; Margaret R. Miles, "Mary Daly: Creation Recrafted," review of *Pure Lust* in *Christianity and Crisis*, November 26, 1984, 447–50; Rebecca Porper, review of *Gyn/Ecology* in *Union Seminary Quarterly Review* 35, nos. 1–2 (Fall–Winter 1979–80): 126–28; Francine Quaglio, review of *Gyn/Ecology*, *ILIFF Review* 37 (Winter 1980): 53–54; and Brita and Krister Stendahl and Nelle Morton, review of *Beyond God the Father* in *Drew Gateway* 44 (Winter–Spring 1974): 153–56.

Information on Daly's academic career can be found in her autobiographical introduction to *The Church and the Second Sex*, 5–14, and Michael Malec, "Incident at Boston College: Phasing Out Mary Daly," *Commonweal*, April 4, 1969, 61–62. Her troubles with Boston College continue: she was denied promotion to full professor in 1989.

6. *Conclusion*

Feminist material pertinent to this study about ethics or moral development in women, most of which does not consider lesbian concerns, includes Mary Field Belenksy and others, *Women's Ways of Knowing: The Development of Self, Voice, and Mind* (New York: Basic

Books, 1986); Nancy Chodorow, *The Reproduction of Mothering: Psychoanalysis and the Sociology of Gender* (Berkeley: University of California Press, 1978); Dorothy Dinnerstein, *The Mermaid and the Minotaur: Sexual Arrangements and Human Malaise* (New York: Harper and Row, 1976); Carol Gilligan, *In a Different Voice: Psychological Theory and Women's Development* (Cambridge, Mass.: Harvard University Press, 1982); Alison M. Jaggar and Susan R. Bordo, eds., *Gender/Body/Knowledge: Feminist Reconstructions of Being and Knowing* (New Brunswick, N.J.: Rutgers University Press, 1989); Nel Noddings, *Caring: A Feminine Approach to Ethics and Moral Development* (Berkeley: University of California Press, 1984); and Sara Ruddick, *Maternal Thinking: Toward a Politics of Peace* (New York: Ballantine, 1989).

Gilligan's work in particular inspired an outpouring of criticism and stimulated a good deal of work in the field. For instance, a good number of the papers presented at the 1988 "Explorations in Feminist Ethics: Theory and Practice" conference held in Duluth, Minnesota, were reactions or contained reactions to Gilligan's work. She has since revised her work or extended it in *Making Connections: The Relational Worlds of Adolescent Girls at Emma Willard School*, ed. Gilligan, Nona Lyons, and Trudy Hanmer (Cambridge, Mass.: Harvard University Press, 1990). Other work relating to Gilligan includes Jenefer Robinson and Stephanie Ross, "Women, Morality, and Fiction," *Hypatia* 5, no. 2 (Summer 1990): 76–90, in which some of Gilligan's ideas are applied to the study of fiction.

In turn, Nel Noddings's work, containing ideas similar to Gilligan's but going even further, also has inspired much criticism and debate. For instance, *Hypatia: A Journal of Feminist Philosophy* 5, no. 1 (Spring 1990): 101–26, carries a review symposium. Sara Ruddick's *Maternal Thinking* is reviewed in Jean Rumsey, "Constructing Maternal Thinking," *Hypatia* 5, no. 3 (Fall 1990): 125–31.

Recently, works exploring lesbian ethics, morality, and philosophy have emerged. These include Jeffner Allen, *Lesbian Philosophy: Explorations* (Palo Alto, Calif.: Institute of Lesbian Studies, 1986); Jeffner Allen, ed., *Lesbian Philosophies and Cultures* (Albany, N.Y.: State University of New York Press, 1990); Sarah Lucia Hoagland, *Lesbian Ethics: Toward New Value* (Palo Alto, Calif.: Institute of Lesbian Studies, 1988); Sarah Lucia Hoagland and Julia Penelope, eds., *For Lesbians Only: A Separatist Anthology* (London: Onlywomen Press, 1988).

Some reviews and responses to Hoagland's *Lesbian Ethics* include a review symposium in *Hypatia* 5, no. 3 (Fall 1990): 132–52; Alice Ginsberg, "Is There a Lesbian Ethic?" *New Directions for Women*, January–February 1990, 24; and Lorraine Ironplow, *NWSA Journal* 2, no. 1 (Winter 1990): 142–44.

Index